Ellis Yarnall

Wordsworth and the Coleridges

With other memories, literary and political

Ellis Yarnall

Wordsworth and the Coleridges
With other memories, literary and political

ISBN/EAN: 9783337068684

Printed in Europe, USA, Canada, Australia, Japan

Cover: Foto ©Suzi / pixelio.de

More available books at **www.hansebooks.com**

WORDSWORTH

AND

THE COLERIDGES

WITH OTHER MEMORIES
LITERARY AND POLITICAL

BY

ELLIS YARNALL

New York
THE MACMILLAN COMPANY
LONDON: MACMILLAN & CO., Ltd.
1899

All rights reserved

COPYRIGHT, 1899,
BY THE MACMILLAN COMPANY.

Norwood Press
J. S. Cushing & Co. — Berwick & Smith
Norwood Mass. U.S.A.

PREFACE

I owe the suggestion of this volume to my friend, Professor Albert H. Smyth. I am indebted to him also for kind and efficient help in preparing it for publication.

Professor Smyth's wide knowledge of English literature and his keen desire to further the love of it in others make his influence in Philadelphia akin to that of the late Professor Henry Reed.

The first of the following papers was written mainly in 1889. I have made slight changes in it since.

The paper, "A Visit to Wordsworth," was in part published by Dr. Christopher Wordsworth (afterward Bishop of Lincoln), in 1851, in his life of the poet; passages were omitted by him because of their reference to persons then living; there is no reason now why my record should not appear as a whole.

I rejoice to be able to say something in regard to Sir John Taylor Coleridge, — better known as Mr. Justice Coleridge, — the friend at once of Dr. Arnold and of Mr. Keble. Nothing in the way of memoir of this eminent man has ever appeared in this country, nor has any adequate life been written in England. Dr. Arnold's letters to him form a very important part of Stanley's "Life of Arnold." Judge Coleridge's letters to Arnold unhappily were not preserved; a like fate attended his letters to our great lawyer, Horace Binney. Judge Coleridge told me he had preserved all Mr. Binney's letters. Both Dr. Arnold and Mr. Binney, I believe, thought it their duty to direct that the letters they had received should be destroyed. In these two cases, at least, the loss to literature and to recent history has been serious.

In publishing what I can recall of William Edward Forster, I cannot but be impressed by the thought that what was his supreme desire as a statesman seems now at last to be fulfilled, — the essential union of England and America, — a union not of a treaty or of diplomatic arrangement, but the declaration, as by a common instinct, of two great peoples that their interests are one, and that in their standing together lies the chief hope for the peace and advancement of the world. Englishmen of far-reaching view have at different times expressed a wish for this union. As early as 1808 Bishop Watson, — Bishop of Llandaff, — a man of much weight of character and of high intelligence, declared it to be his strong desire that England should enter "as speedily as possible into an alliance, cordial, sincere, offensive and defensive, with America." I may note also that in 1804 Bishop Watson expressed it as his belief that America was destined to become the greatest naval power on the globe.

I have referred in my final paper to Mr. Bright's deep interest in America, his strong belief in our future, and his earnest wish for a cordial union of all English-speaking men.

My thanks are due to the publishers of *Lippincott's Magazine* for permission to reprint the articles "Walks and Visits in Wordsworth's Country" and "Charles Kingsley: a Reminiscence."

ELLIS YARNALL.

MAY PLACE, HAVERFORD, PA.,
    March, 1899.

CONTENTS

	PAGE
OCCASIONAL RECOLLECTIONS DURING SEVENTY YEARS	1
A VISIT TO WORDSWORTH, 1849	31
WALKS AND VISITS IN WORDSWORTH'S COUNTRY	53
SARA COLERIDGE AND HER BROTHERS, HARTLEY AND DERWENT COLERIDGE	103
SIR JOHN TAYLOR COLERIDGE AND LORD COLERIDGE (LORD CHIEF JUSTICE OF ENGLAND)	143
CHARLES KINGSLEY: A REMINISCENCE	181
OXFORD, AND THE AUTHOR OF "THE CHRISTIAN YEAR"	197
THE OXFORD COMMEMORATION, 1860	223
THE RIGHT HONOURABLE WILLIAM EDWARD FORSTER	239
ENGLAND AND THE HOUSE OF COMMONS IN THE CLOSING DAYS OF THE AMERICAN CIVIL WAR	279

GIGANTIC daughter of the West,
    We drink to thee across the flood;
We know thee most, we love thee best,
    For art thou not of British blood?
Should war's mad blast again be blown,
    Permit not thou the tyrant powers
To fight thy mother here alone,
    But let thy broadsides roar with ours.
        Hands all round!
        God the tyrants' cause confound!
To our great kinsmen of the West, my friends,
And the great name of England round and round.

TENNYSON (1852).

OCCASIONAL RECOLLECTIONS
DURING SEVENTY YEARS

OCCASIONAL RECOLLECTIONS
DURING SEVENTY YEARS

IT occurs to me to send my thoughts back over a portion of the great space of life that I have travelled, and to bring up in succession matters that were of interest to me in a period, let us say, of sixty, or even seventy, years.

The coming of Lafayette to America in 1824, what an event that was for young and old! For days and weeks there had been excitement and preparation here in Philadelphia. A triumphal arch in front of the State House, medals and badges for sale in the streets, rows of lamps and candles in all windows for the appointed illumination, — all this was enough to arouse a child's wonder. At last, the eagerly expected moment came, and there, in an open carriage, drawn by six cream-coloured horses, sat the hero — the Nation's guest. I gazed on him with a boy's amazement and delight. In pomp like this he went over all the land — a great and rejoicing nation offering him everywhere of their best. He had come to us in the fervour of his youth, and now, after fifty years, he was here to look on the land and the people whose independence he had helped to win. There were three millions at his first coming; he found them ten millions, and there seemed no limit to the promise of their future. It is good to think of that visit, and of the gratitude expressed in every conceivable way by an entire people.

There is a curious historical parallel in Lafayette's two returns from America: five years after his first return, on the closing of the War of the Revolution, he took a leading part in the great French Revolution; so, five years after his return from his visit to us of 1824–5, he was the chief actor in the Revolution of 1830, which drove Charles X. from the throne.

A vivid recollection which comes back to me of 1827 is the battle of Navarino. I wonder how many people know of that great victory. Even as a boy I shared in the transports of joy with which the news of it was received. The combined fleets of England, France, and Russia attacked the Turkish fleet in the Bay of Navarino and destroyed it utterly. It was clear at once, to the whole world, that this meant the independence of Greece. For five years the hearts of men in England and America had been wrung by tidings of the bloody deeds of the Turks. At last the great powers had intervened. But there was disquietude in England at the weakening of the power of Turkey, lessening her ability to make head against Russia. A single word in the King's speech in the opening of Parliament, the Duke of Wellington being then Prime Minister, was in men's mouths for years: the great battle was spoken of as an untoward occurrence. On the other hand, Lord John Russell spoke of it as a glorious victory, and as honest a victory as had been won since the beginning of the world. The Turks die hard, and though they have lost wide lands and millions of subjects in the past fifty years, they are still a great power.

The years from 1829 to 1833 were years of vast and sweeping change both in England and France. I remember, as if it were yesterday, the news of Catholic Emancipation, and the passing of the first Reform Bill, the tidings of the beginning of the Ministry of Earl Grey with Brougham made Lord Chancellor and raised to the peerage.

But in America there were great political struggles to occupy the mind. With 1829 John Quincy Adams's four years of rule came to an end, and our political system took a great plunge downwards under the Presidency of Andrew Jackson. Midway in that eight years' rule there was a progress of General Jackson through the Northern cities: he rode on horseback — probably the last President who so traversed our streets. An imposing figure truly! with his shock of grey hair, and his resolute look, and his natural grace of bearing, and his easy command of his horse, as with hat in hand he acknowledged the cheers of the people and bowed to the ladies who filled the windows on either side. The popularity of Jackson was retained to the last; in his daring and his strength of will he well represented the South. As his administration closed in 1837, the predominance of the South seemed assured to all time. But an agitation had begun at the North which was to keep the subject of slavery constantly before the people. The speeches and writings of the antislavery leaders infuriated the South, and made them the more resolute to secure for their bad system increased protection from the National Government. Few in number though the Abolitionists were, their leaders were of such ability and earnestness that they powerfully affected opinion. It chanced that I had abundant opportunity of listening to the talk of these leaders from the beginning of the movement. Under the roof of my Aunt Lucretia Mott, I met Benjamin Lundy, who might be called the American Clarkson; Harriet Martineau, who appeared here just as the agitation began; George Thompson the English Abolitionist; Gerrit Smith, the great landed proprietor of New York, who, from being a munificent supporter of the scheme of African colonization, had passed over to the antislavery camp; Wendell Phillips; the poet Whittier; and, last and greatest, William Lloyd Garrison. Lucretia Mott, the chief female figure of the movement, was a powerful help to it by the charm of her personal presence, her refinement, the deep earnestness of her manner, and what one might call her intellectual spirituality.

In Mrs. Mott's house I met Dr. Channing, whose writings against slavery were of earlier date than that of the beginning of the movement. I recall his grave, thoughtful face and the old-time dignity of his bearing. My first meeting with Emerson was at the same house. Frederika Bremer I met there, too, and

I recall her speaking of the devotion to Emerson which she had found to be the feeling of the Boston circle. A lady, herself of high accomplishments, had said: "If he but mentions my name, I feel ennobled." Emerson was not of the movement, though he was in sympathy with it. He was so gracious in manner, and so gentle in his ways, and so kind of heart, that I could perfectly understand how strong was his hold upon all who were about him.

I was a looker-on, as it were, while the antislavery agitation was under full headway, for I never was convinced that the mode of attack of which Garrison was the chief champion was wise. The years went on, and the condition of the slaves grew worse. The Fugitive Slave Law of 1850, which denied the right of trial by jury to a man seized in a Northern State and claimed as a slave, greatly strengthened antislavery feeling. There was case after case under this law in Philadelphia, in Boston, and elsewhere, which almost led to riot.

At the time of which I write I had come to know Charles Sumner, who was for some months in Philadelphia for medical treatment, after the assault made upon him in the Senate chamber by Brooks, of South Carolina. Other years went by, and in the spring of 1860 I was arranging to go to Europe, and having occasion to write to Mr. Sumner, I asked him his opinion upon the political situation, or, what he thought was at hand: it was the year for a Presidential nomination. He replied that he was confident that whoever was nominated by the Republicans at Chicago would be elected; that he felt equally sure the Gulf or Cotton States would not acquiesce in the result, but would raise the black flag, and attempt to set up a separate government — that he, for one, would not lift a finger to retain them. I reminded him of this letter two years afterwards when we were in the full tide of war. I was sitting with him in his own apartment at Washington. He said he had been of opinion that we ought to let the Slave States go, until the actual breaking out of war — that Judge Chase was of the same opinion, and had come to him — "here in this room" — and asked him to go to New York and make a speech advocating this policy of acquiescence, or rather, surrender. Suddenly, however, war was begun by the South. "I went at once to Mr. Lincoln," said Mr. Sumner, "and told him I was with him now, heart and soul; that under the war power the right had come to him to emancipate the slaves."

It will be remembered that Horace Greeley openly advocated letting the Slave States go. "Erring sisters depart in peace," were his words. I have always been of the opinion that with him and with Judge Chase there was a passionate longing for the Presidency — that each thought his chance would be good for a nomination as Chief Magistrate of "the United States of the North."

The summer of 1860 I passed in England. The rain of all that season was incessant, and the wheat harvest was ruined. There was one result of these torrents which I, as an American, little foresaw. A great market was given to our Northern and Western States for their breadstuffs during the year that followed, when a war had begun which was to strain our resources to the utmost. But in that midsummer season of 1860 one's thoughts in England were occupied with the details of Garibaldi's brilliant descent upon Sicily: of the melting away of all opposition; of his crossing to Italy; of his entry in triumph into Naples, the entire population hailing him with transports of joy as their deliverer.

I interrupt my survey, so to call it, of events, to refer to Garibaldi's coming to England in 1862. The wildest excitement was caused by his presence in London. The Government feared an outbreak should he proceed to Birmingham as was his plan. At their suggestion Garibaldi's host, the Duke of Sutherland, offered the hero his yacht, which was then at Portsmouth, if he would like to proceed at once to the Mediterranean, to his island home. Garibaldi was beginning to be weary of the adulation and turmoil, and so fell in with the Duke's suggestion, and the Government was relieved of their anxiety. Various were the conjectures as to the cause of the sudden flight. *Punch* said he had been pestered out of his life by applications for his autograph, and had given away the contents of two hair mattresses in reply to requests for locks of his hair. I add, what has just now a certain significance, that Archbishop Trench notes in his journal of this date (1862) a saying then current in London. The Dowager Duchess of Sutherland had seemed greatly drawn to Garibaldi: "Why should not Garibaldi marry the Duchess?" said some one. The instant reply was, "Garibaldi has a wife already." "Oh," said Lord Palmerston, "that doesn't matter — Gladstone will explain her away."

To return to my proper narrative. News came to England of the nomination of Lincoln at Chicago. Who was Abraham Lincoln? was on all sides the inquiry. I could tell my friends little about him. But it was plain that a stormy season was at hand. I returned to America in October and found intense excitement prevailing. I obtained at once a volume of 250 pages, containing a full report of speeches of Lincoln and Douglas during the contest in Illinois of 1858. Douglas's term of service as senator was expiring, and if he failed to secure its renewal, his chance for the Presidential nomination of 1860 would be gone. He was a man of great ability, but unscrupulous as a politician, and of a coarse mind. Charles Sumner, who had had bitter passages with him in the Senate, spoke of him once in a letter to me in terms of strong dislike. His restless energy, and his skill as a demagogue, had given him extraordinary success. But there had arisen in his own State a rival who, besides gifts of mind, had the strength of high moral purpose. The volume of which I have spoken was the record of the long debate between these two men

— the United States senatorship being the prize for which each was striving. I read it with extreme care, and saw that, throughout, Mr. Lincoln had clearly the advantage. In a letter to England for publication in *The Guardian*, of the date of October, 1860, I said: "Mr. Lincoln is a man of vigorous understanding: his utterances are marked by so much originality as to stamp him as a man of genius." This favourable judgment as to Mr. Lincoln, expressed before he had become President, was more and more my conviction as the weeks and months went on. December, January, and February, were months of intense agitation. All minds were stirred. I talked with men of wisdom and experience wherever I had opportunity. Horace Binney, then eighty years of age, said to me, referring to a plan of settlement known as the Crittenden Compromise, that he for one would never agree to it, let the consequences of refusal be what they would. He said he was old, and he might have added, as the Duke of Wellington once said of himself, his "life had been passed in honour." He said he would not at the end of it take upon his conscience the sin of slavery. The Crittenden Compromise would have put this weight on the consciences of the people of all the land.

One State after another declared itself out of the Union, and neither the Government at Washington nor any State Government except Massachusetts, was making any preparation to bring back these "erring sisters." Mr. Russell, as correspondent of the *London*

Times, wrote, as the result of his intercourse in New York with leading men, that there would be no war. "Compromise, concession," was the burden of the talk he heard. Even men of high patriotic spirit feared the Union was gone. The late Morton McMichael, a man for whom I felt warm regard, and in whose judgment I had great confidence, said to me in February, 1860, that no one could see the press of the country (he was editor of the leading newspaper of Philadelphia) as he saw it, without feeling that the Union could not be preserved. All we could do, he said, was to seek to lessen the difficulties which would follow separation. On the other hand, the then Bishop of Pennsylvania, Bishop Bowman, said people might talk as they liked about the success of the secession movement, but no one could see the interior of Pennsylvania, as he saw it, without being convinced that the body of the people would never consent to the dismemberment of the country.

At the end of February came the progress of Abraham Lincoln from Springfield, Illinois, to Washington. From city to city he went by a zigzag course, welcomed everywhere by countless multitudes. His reception in Philadelphia, though wanting in show or accessories of every kind, was very impressive. As I saw approaching, along the wide street, the dense mass of men, with horses' heads and plumes rising among them, and by and by the slowly moving concourse drew near, it was impossible not to share in the excitement that all felt at the thought that a man chosen from among thirty millions was moving onward to a work of awful perplexity, solemnity, and peril. There was prodigious interest in the sight of one on whom so heavy a responsibility had fallen. Even in the distance I thought I discerned a light in his eye showing him to be a man of mark.

I may not say much of the uprising of the people which followed the attack upon Fort Sumter, nor of the four awful years of war. It was an amazing error on the part of the South — their beginning the war; the Government at Washington would have had great difficulty in beginning it — there was doubt whether a majority of the people would support them in such beginning. It was the attempt to victual Fort Sumter which drew the fire of the South, and made them the aggressors.

About a month before Bull Run I spent a few days in Washington, and had the honour of an interview with the President. I was received by him in the large audience chamber on the second floor of the White House; he sat at a table, at the end of the room, with one of the windows at his right looking down on the gardens. His manner was courteous, his look open and resolute, and at the same time gentle. His eyes were deep-set and of a certain fullness and lustre, and his features were expressive. He was composed and cheerful; there was a serenity about him, indeed, which seemed surprising, considering the heavy responsibility which was upon him.

He talked quietly of the contest which was just beginning: said the South had the advantage that the fighting would be on their own ground. I remember thinking he overrated the Union feeling of the South. He spoke a good deal of the attitude of England toward us, and, what was thought, the too early recognition of the South as belligerents. This had caused great, perhaps undue, excitement at the North. He said he had never been in England, but he thought the state of things there was this: The aristocracy, who had hitherto had control of the Government, might be unfriendly to us, regarding us as a menace to their system — "One of their lords has just said 'the bubble has burst'" (this, I think, was a remark of Sir John Burgoyne in the House of Commons) — and the cotton spinners of Manchester, either from cupidity, or from a natural wish to obtain cotton, so as to give employment to their hands, might wish the South to succeed; but he believed the body of the people — the middle and the lower classes — still had their old feeling in regard to slavery. This last remark showed the confidence felt by Mr. Lincoln in the steadfastness of England as a whole, and also his conviction that they knew slavery to be the real cause of the quarrel, and that the fate of the system was bound up in its issue. The President was certainly right as to the feeling of the majority of the English people. I was told in Liverpool, just before the war closed, by men whose sympathies had been strongly with the North, that nowhere in England had the

Southern sympathizers dared to call a public meeting in support of the Confederate cause.

I was deeply impressed by this interview. Although the struggle which was to decide so much had scarcely begun, I felt that I was in the presence of a true leader of men. I knew the humble life from which Abraham Lincoln had come, and yet he seemed to me a man of heroic mould, and one who was to do great deeds. I went away from him with a rejoicing heart, feeling that, in the hour of our deepest need, a man of clear mind and singleness of purpose — indeed of the noblest impulses — would be our supreme chief and leader.

A month from the time of this interview came the catastrophe of Bull Run. Well do I remember hours passed in the office of Morton McMichael, as the details came in of the terrible disaster. I recall the pale faces, the gloom, almost despondency, written on every countenance. "It is not, all is lost but honour," said Mr. Henry Carey, "for honour has been lost as well." Commodore, afterwards Admiral, Dupont came in: he alone was serene; his look was almost cheerful. "Gentlemen," he said, "this is war!"

The country rallied quickly, however, from this disaster, and there can be no doubt that the prolonging of the war, due to the defeat, led to the more effectual making an end of slavery, and thus to a lasting peace. I need say no more of the war and of our American matters.

One incident of the year 1838 caused a thrill of emotion on this continent, and I remember as if it was yesterday my own feeling — the arrival at New York of a steamship from England, the steamer *Sirius*. A tremendous event this truly! as drawing the New World nearer to the Old. Deep was the impression that was made. The going abroad became a vision of delight to old and young. I remember hearing Emerson say, some forty years ago, with a certain sarcasm: "The object of education in the United States seems to be to fit persons to travel in Europe." There was admonition in his question which followed, "Who are these Americans who are passing their time in Paris and elsewhere who seem so little missed in their own country?"

My first voyage to England was in 1849. I have always considered that we in America are Englishmen over again, and so, when I landed in England, I still felt myself, in a certain sense, at home. I say this, although every ancestor of mine for two hundred years was born in America. A deep interest in English literature and in English politics had animated me always, true though, I consider, was my love for my own country, and keen my desire for its advancement. I venture to quote, as some justification for the feeling which has always animated me, the words of Mr. Phelps, our late Minister to England, at his leave-taking in London, 1889. "You are not sending me away," he said to the distinguished company he was addressing, "you are not sending me away empty-handed or alone. I go freighted and laden with happy memories, inexhaustible and unalloyed, of England, its warm-hearted people, and their measureless kindness. Spirits more than twain will cross with me, messengers of your good-will. Happy the nation that can thus speed its parting guest! Fortunate the guest who has found his welcome almost an adoption, and whose farewell leaves half his heart behind." I put with this passage, so felicitous in expression, an extract from a letter from Lord Coleridge to myself, written immediately after the Phelps dinner.

"We sent away Mr. Phelps in a perfect gale of good wishes. I like him very much, and truly grieve at his departure. I have known a good many American Ministers, and some of them very remarkable, almost great men, but I never knew one so *delightful* in all ways, learned, accomplished, amiable, a most charming companion to spend a week with, and yet a most prudent and dignified Minister; he is one of the very best men in all ways you have ever sent us. We became real friends, and it would be a sorrow to me to think that I should never see him again."

Lord Coleridge adds, in reference to a remark of mine, for which I naturally take shame,—

"I am surprised that he was, as you tell me, somewhat unknown in America. I can only say it reminds me of Lord Brougham's famous sarcastic dedication to Lord Wellesley in which, after celebrating Lord Wellesley himself, he adds (to the effect, I forget the words) the rare felicity of England — so rich in men of genius and capacity for affairs — that she can *spare* from her councils such men as he."

I saw in London, at my visit of 1849, the Duke of Wellington. I stood, at about five in the afternoon, at the entrance of the House of Lords. Some one

c

who was near gave me one famous name after another as Peers, temporal and spiritual, went in. A great debate was to take place on a motion of Lord Brougham's. Soon a carriage drew up, and there was the cry, "The Duke, the Duke!" The Duke of Wellington was handed out. I can never forget the strangely softened, the benignant expression of the aged face which I had now the happiness to look upon. He acknowledged slightly the deferential bearing of all who stood by, as he passed from his carriage to the Peers' entrance of the House of Lords. His meek look was what first struck me — a mild serenity — the happiest result of advanced age. His hair was white, but his complexion was clear and delicate. He was in full evening dress, knee breeches and black silk stockings, blue coat and white waistcoat, a broad ribbon across his breast — the ribbon of the Garter.

I was present afterwards at the debate, and watched from my seat in the gallery the Duke as he sat close to Lord Brougham, listening with his hand to his ear, to the words of that great orator. He remained, I think, during the whole of the speech, which lasted two and a half hours. As I listened I hardly perceived the passage of time. I am not sure whether it was then, or on another occasion, that Lord Brougham said, looking directly at the Duke, "For, my Lords, there are few men who, like my noble friend, have been equally great in council and in the field."

With my own impression of Wellington given above, it was a delight to me to read Carlyle's account of him as he saw him in June, 1850, a year after the date of my seeing him; it was at a ball at Lady Ashburton's. He says:—

"By far the most interesting figure present was the old Duke of Wellington, who appeared between twelve and one, and slowly glided through the rooms — truly a beautiful old man: I had never known till now how beautiful: and what an expression of graceful simplicity, veracity, and nobleness there is about the old hero, when you see him close at hand! His very size had hitherto deceived me. He is a shortish, slightish figure, about five feet eight, of good breadth, however, and all muscle or bone. His legs I think the short part of him, for certainly on horseback I have always taken him to be tall. Eyes beautiful light blue, full of mild valour, with infinitely more faculty and geniality than I had fancied before. The face wholly gentle, wise, valiant, and venerable. The voice too, as I again heard, is aquiline, clear, perfectly equable, uncracked that is — and perhaps almost musical, but essentially tenor, almost treble voice. Eighty-two, I understand. He glided slowly along, slightly saluting this and that other, clear, clean, fresh as this June morning itself, till the silver buckle of his stock vanished into the door of the next room. Except Dr. Chalmers I have not for many years seen so beautiful an old man."

It is good to connect great men with each other, so I add a description of Wellington of the date of 1826, twenty-five years earlier than that of Carlyle's mention of him. I quote from Eckermann's "Conversations with Goethe." Eckermann says:—

"If you ever look at his face, all the portraits are naught. One needs only see him once never to forget him, such an impression does he make. His eyes are of the serenest brilliancy; one feels the effect of his glance; his mouth speaks even when it is closed; he looks a man who has had many thoughts, and has lived through the greatest deeds, and whom nothing more can disturb. He seemed to me as hard and tempered as a Damascus blade. By his appearance he is far advanced in the fifties; is upright, slim and not very tall or stout. There was something uncommonly cordial in his salutation, as he passed through the crowd, and with a very slight bow touched his hat with his finger. Goethe listened to my description with visible interest. 'You have seen one hero more,' said he, 'and that is saying something.' Napoleon was mentioned. Goethe said of him, 'What a compendium of the world.'"

Lord John Russell was Prime Minister in that year of my first visit to England, 1849. I heard him in the House of Commons, — a man of halting, hesitating speech, but whose words, all the same, were well chosen and weighty. I had the good fortune, also, to hear Sir Robert Peel, an orator of infinite grace. The debate was on the Encumbered Estates Bill, the second of the great measures for the relief of Ireland passed by the British Parliament. The Catholic Emancipation Bill of 1829 was the first. Mr. Napier, member for Dublin University, followed Sir Robert Peel. One sentence of his speech comes back to me. Speaking of Ireland, he said, " Sir, I am sure there is no member of this House who does not feel deep sympathy with that unhappy country in its present misery." It was the year following the great famine.

I have spoken of the debate in the House of Lords in which Lord Brougham made his great speech; he moved a resolution of censure of the Government for not withholding assent to the action of the Canadian Parliament by which the rebels of 1838 were to be remunerated for their losses, chiefly in the burning of houses, barns, etc. Lord Derby, "the Rupert of debate," spoke with great fire and energy in support of Brougham's motion. Lord Lyndhurst had spoken on the same side, saying, at the end, that it was perhaps the last time he should trouble their Lordships. Lord Campbell, speaking for the Government, rather jeered at this remark of Lyndhurst. Lord Derby denounced Campbell for his sneering reference to the speech of the venerable man. (As it happened, however, Lord Lyndhurst spoke at intervals for fifteen years afterward.)

Lord Brougham's motion prevailed by a good majority, but the House of Commons refused to follow the Lords. Earl Grey was then the Colonial Secretary: it was his wisdom that inspired Lord Russell's Government in their refusal to withdraw from Canada the self-rule they had but just conferred.

It scarcely befits the gravity of my record, but it may perhaps help to the understanding of what the going to Europe was fifty years ago, if I mention the following incident. I was walking, soon after my first return, in a street in Philadelphia with Dr. Allibone, of Dictionary fame. There were cases of merchandise or other obstruction, and we had to go single file. "After you," said my friend; "you have been to Europe."

I have told in papers which follow of many of my

personal experiences in visits to England, subsequent to that of 1849. It occurs to me to say here what I can of a man of whom comparatively little is known except as he appears in his writings. John Stuart Mill never took part in what would be called society; he seemed to live only for intellectual cultivation, and for setting forward in the world what he thought would further the real improvement of men. There is a noble passage in a speech made by him in the House of Commons which I give here as a key to the essential features of his character, and as a preface to what I have to say as to my personal sight of him.

"I beg very strongly indeed to press upon the House the duty of taking these things into serious consideration, in the name of that dutiful concern for posterity which has been very strong in every nation that ever did anything great, and which has never left the minds of any such nation until, as in the case of the Romans under the Empire, it was already falling into decrepitude and ceasing to be a nation. . . . Whatever has been done for mankind by the idea of posterity — whatever has been done for mankind by philanthropic concern for posterity — by a conscientious sense of duty for posterity — even by the less pure but still noble ambition of being remembered and honoured by them, — all this we owe to posterity, and all this it is our duty, to the best of our limited ability, to repay. All the great deeds of the founders of nations, and of those second founders of nations, the great reformers; — all that has been done for us by the authors of those laws and institutions to which free countries are indebted for their freedom, and well-governed countries for their good government, — all the heroic lives which have been led and the deaths which have been died in defence of liberty and law against despotism and tyranny, from Marathon and Salamis down to Leipsic and Waterloo — all those traditions of wisdom and of virtue which are enshrined in the history and literature of the past, — all the schools and universities by which the culture of a former time has been brought down to us, and all that culture itself — all that we owe to the great masters of human thought, to the great masters of human emotion — all this is ours, because those who preceded us have taken thought for posterity."

It is well known that for many years — perhaps twenty — Mr. Mill lived in the closest intellectual companionship with Mrs. John Taylor; their thoughts and speculations, he says, were completely in common. She was united, Mill also says, to one for whom he had "the sincerest respect, and she the strongest affection. Her incomparable worth," he declares, "had made her friendship the greatest source to him both of happiness and of improvement" during many years in which they "never expected to be in any closer relation to each other." Mr. Taylor's premature death in July, 1849, was followed in April, 1851, by Mr. Mill's marriage to Mrs. Taylor; their partnership of "thought, feeling, and writing, which had long existed, became a partnership of their entire existence."

It is proper to say that the Carlyles, and Mrs. Grote and the Austins and Sir Henry Taylor, with whom Mill had intimate companionship, seem hardly to have had a share in his friendship with Mrs. Taylor: he was not the man to make explanations to them, or to crave their forbearing judgment. Mr.

Carlyle speaks of her, in his caustic way, in one of his letters, as Mrs. Platonica Taylor.

Mr. Taylor, as I have said, died in July, 1849. It was in June of that year that Mr. Herbert Taylor, the eldest son of Mr. and Mrs. Taylor, with whom I had become acquainted upon a visit he had made to Philadelphia some months before, said to me when I was with him in London, "I cannot ask you to our house for my father is dying." In 1851, my friend Herbert Taylor was again in Philadelphia. He gave me a paper on the "Enfranchisement of Women," which he said was from the pen of his mother: he added, "my mother has become Mrs. Mill." He told me then of the long friendship there had been between his mother and Mr. Mill, for whom he seemed to have nothing but respect and regard. The following year, 1852, I was in London and received an invitation to dine with Mr. and Mrs. Mill at their home, Blackheath, near Greenwich. What I have written above will show that I had no knowledge of Mrs. Mill but what had been told me by her son. Seven years were to pass before Mill gave to the world his estimate of her mind and character in his dedication of his book on Liberty. Some of his words are as follows:—

"To the beloved and deplored memory of her who was the inspirer and in part the author of all that is best in my writings — the friend and wife whose exalted sense of truth and right was my strongest incitement, and whose approbation was my chief reward, I dedicate this volume. . . . Were I but capable of interpreting to the world one-half the great thoughts and noble feelings which are buried in her grave, I should be the medium of a greater benefit to it than is ever likely to arise from anything that I can write unprompted and unassisted by her all but unrivalled wisdom."

My visit to Mr. and Mrs. Mill was in the second year of their marriage: the record in my journal is mainly this:—

" Mr. Mill is of dignified appearance, about forty-five years of age, somewhat bald, complexion delicate, of a grave but sweet courtesy. He has a nervous twitching of the eyelids, which perhaps leads to his raising his hand now and again to his brow. There is something almost of timidity in his manner, which surprises one, considering his great place in the world as a writer. He is especially courteous in giving careful heed to what is said to him. You feel him to be a man of good heart, and of entire simplicity. I was struck with his deferential attention to remarks of his wife from her end of the table. Mrs. Mill looks to be in very weak health, having a curvature of the spine. Mr. Mill took her out to dinner, I think because of her enfeebled condition. I took out Mrs. Taylor, an old lady, I presume Mrs. Mill's mother-in-law of her previous marriage. Her two sons and her daughter, Miss Helen Taylor, made up the party. My seat was at Mrs. Mill's right. Her face is thin and pale, but her eyes are of a peculiar lustre, and they seem to dilate when she speaks in an animated way, and her soul looks out of them. A woman of keen intellect there can be no doubt whatever—marvellously in fellowship with her husband in all his thought. When she looks fully at you and becomes interested in her subject, she seems to put you under her spell. I recalled my feeling when with Mrs. Henry Nelson Coleridge; it seemed strange to me that these two women, each so gifted, living at the same time in London, should have known nothing of each other.

"There was talk of the English Universities and of English scholarship — Mr. Mill spoke disparagingly of both — said they were not to compare with the German. Mrs. Mill was careful to impress upon me that her husband was competent to give this opinion, being himself of excellent classical learning. Mr. Mill spoke of our American slavery, in answer to a remark of mine, with strong condemnation; he would not admit that any defence for it could be made. Kossuth, who has lately been here, as also in America, he expressed sympathy with — as to his faults which people spoke of, it was but another way of saying he was an Hungarian. 'Puseyism' was spoken of. Mr. Mill said it was the 'romance of Church of Englandism.' Of Dr. Pusey both Mr. and Mrs. Mill spoke as a true and a very earnest man, for whom they felt sincere respect."

I have little other record of conversation on this, to me, most interesting occasion. The feeling that chiefly remains with me, after the great lapse of years, is my sense of the intellectual companionship of Mr. Mill and his wife. He had at that time written nothing concerning her:[1] it seemed plain to me that here was a mind which was on a level with his own.

John Stuart Mill became a Member of Parliament in 1865. He consented to stand for Westminster only on the condition that no money whatever was to be contributed by himself toward the expenses of the election. I remember standing with William Edward Forster and Matthew Arnold in Forster's drawing-room on the evening of the day the announcement was made that Mill was to stand. Forster made the

---

[1] Herbert Taylor told me that some of the copies of Mill's "Political Economy" were dedicated to Mrs. Taylor, not the whole issue.

prediction that he would not succeed in the House. His first speech was, it is true, a failure, but on every subsequent occasion he was listened to with the greatest interest. Mill stood again in 1868, but was defeated by W. H. Smith, a man of great wealth and influence.

In 1849, I went by steamer from London to Rotterdam, so that my first sight of the continent was Holland, with its canals, and its windmills, and its quaint costumes, and customs, some of which are no longer the delight of travellers. Ascending the Rhine, I entered the Grand Duchy of Baden, and at the town of Carlsruhe my further progress on the east bank of the river was stopped by military operations. An insurrection against the rule of the Grand Duke had only been put down by the coming of fifteen thousand Prussian troops, with the Prince of Prussia at their head, afterward the Emperor William. The remaining insurgents were shut up in the walled town of Rastadt, fifteen miles distant, and the Baden troops with the Prussians were laying siege to it. With much difficulty my companion and I obtained permission to go down in a military train to look on at the siege. I enjoyed hugely the excitement of it all, and the novel feeling of being near to actual warfare. I mention this because of the following curious circumstance. A month or two ago (1889), at a Civil Service Reform dinner in Philadelphia, my seat chanced to be next to Mr. Carl Schurz, whom I had never met before. After some preliminaries of talk, I said to him, " You, I believe, were of the force which was shut up in Rastadt exactly forty years ago, when the Prussians and the Baden troops laid siege to the town." He answered quickly, "I was," and seemed much surprised. I told him I was present on one of the days of the siege as a looker-on. I spoke of a little old church in the village of Mugglesturm close to Rastadt, the spire of which we had ascended to look across to the walled town. He said he knew the church well; they "had a fight there at a sortie on June 30." My visit was on July 4. Mr. Schurz, as I knew, then a very young man, was one of the leaders of the insurrection, and would doubtless have been shot if he had been captured. The place, I think, held out for six weeks. "How did you get away?" I asked. He said, "Through the sewer;" he and two companions; they were for three days without food.

Little did I think that of the military leaders, shut up in that small town, was one who was to fight, in one of the decisive battles of the world, on the soil of my own State, Pennsylvania. General Schurz commanded a division at Gettysburg.

I will not indulge in any raptures in regard to my first sight of Switzerland, though the day of one's first glimpse of a snow mountain is one to date from. I may refer to my journey from Geneva to Paris, when my Swiss tour was over, because the mode of travel is entirely of the past. I went by malle-poste, limited to two passengers. Railway there was none in that part of France. At three in the afternoon we left Geneva in a sort of open barouche, with four horses, — my Geneva fellow-traveller and I. We had each a cold chicken and a bottle of wine; and my companion had some macaroons which, he said, were a *specialité* of Geneva. I remember their perfection to this day! The postilion cracked his whip portentously, and the guard, from his high seat behind, blew his horn. Off we went at high speed. In ascending the glorious slopes of the Jura we went at a fast trot, but for the rest of the way, wherever the ground would permit, at full gallop. So we sped along, night and day, through the poplar valleys of France, by Dijon, and by many a village of white-walled houses — making the journey of some 330 miles at an average speed of ten or eleven miles an hour. I remember the irresistible appeal of a beggar at Dijon — it was that we would not refuse him, we who were travelling so joyfully!

It was in the grey of the morning that I had my first sight of Paris. Our entry was in the quarter of the Place de la Bastille — something truly to awaken memory! — on and on, through the then silent streets to the beautiful Rue de Rivoli and to the Hotel Meurice. The windows of the room assigned me opened upon the leads. I stepped out and there before me was the fair garden of the Tuileries; in the distance were the towers of Notre Dame and the dome of the Invalides, to the right was the Obelisk, and far away the Arc de Triomphe — to the left the stately palace of the Tuileries, glorious renaissance work — now, alas! every stone of it gone.

To many who read, the mention of these names will bring back happy memories. I found the great buildings daubed with the words "Liberté, Egalité, Fraternité." It was the first year of the Republic under the presidency of Louis Napoleon. I had the strongest sense that there was no stability in the then state of things — that there would be no continuance of constitutional government under the then Chief Magistrate. "You don't suppose he is only to be President for three years," Lucien Murat, then a member of the Assemblée Nationale, said to me. In two years came the *coup d'état*, and then the miserable personal rule of Louis Napoleon began, of which the end was not to be for twenty years. When I next saw Paris in 1852, Murat, formerly of Bordentown, New Jersey, had become his Imperial Highness, the Prince Lucien Murat. Most true was the after remark of Gambetta, "the Bonapartists were not a party, but a horde."

A VISIT TO WORDSWORTH, 1849

A VISIT TO WORDSWORTH

It was about noon on the eighteenth of August, 1849, that I started with my friends from their house near Bowness to drive to Ambleside. Our route was along the shore of Lake Windermere. My friends congratulated me on the clearness of the atmosphere and the bright skies. Sunlight is all important in bringing out the full beauty of the Lake Region, and in this respect I was very fortunate. I had been already deeply moved by the tranquil beauty of Windermere, for as I came out of the cottage, Elleray, formerly Professor Wilson's, where I had passed the night, there it lay in all its grandeur, — its clear waters, its green islands, and its girdle of solemn mountains. It was quite dark when I was conducted to this cottage the night before, so that I saw the lake for the first time in the light of early morning. The first impression was confirmed by every new prospect as we drove along. The vale seemed a very paradise for its sweet seclusion. I had been told that, after Switzerland, I should find little to attract me in this region, but such was not the case. Nothing can be more lovely than these lakes and mountains, the latter thickly wooded and rising directly from the water's edge. The foliage is of the darkest green, giving to the lake in which it is reflected the same sombre hue.

It was half past one when we reached Ambleside, when I left Mr. and Mrs. B—— and walked on alone to Rydal Mount. At two o'clock I was at the wicket gate opening into Wordsworth's grounds. I walked along the gravel pathway leading through shrubbery to the open space in front of the long two-story cottage, the poet's dwelling. The view from it is its chief charm. Rydalmere, with its islands, and the mountains beyond it, are all in sight. I had but a hasty enjoyment of all this beauty; nor could I notice carefully the flowers which were around. It was evident that the greatest attention had been paid to the grounds, for the flowerbeds were tastefully arranged, and the gravel walks were in complete order.

My letter of introduction was from my friend, Professor Henry Reed, Wordsworth's chief American disciple. I was shown to the drawing-room. It was with a curious emotion that I felt myself in the house of the great poet and awaiting his coming. It was a long apartment, the ceiling low, with two windows at one end looking out on the lawn and shrubbery. Many engravings were on the walls. The famous Madonna of Raphael, known as that of the Dresden gallery, hung directly over the fireplace. Inman's portrait of the poet, Professor Reed's gift to Mrs. Wordsworth, had a conspicuous place. I could have waited patiently a long time indulging the thoughts which the place called up. In a few minutes, however, I heard steps in the entry, the door was opened, and Wordsworth came in; it could be no other — a tall figure, a little bent with age, his hair thin and grey, and his face deeply wrinkled. The expression of his countenance was sad, mournful I might say; he seemed one on whom sorrow pressed heavily. He gave me his hand and welcomed me cordially, though without smiling. Leading the way, he conducted me at once to the dining room. I could not but notice that his step was feeble. At the head of the table sat Mrs. Wordsworth, and their three grandchildren made up the party. It was a quaint apartment, not ceiled, the rafters dark with age being visible; having a large old-fashioned fireplace with a high mantelpiece.

Wordsworth asked after Mr. George Ticknor of Boston, who had visited him a few months before, and for whom he expressed much regard. Some other questions led me to speak of the progress we were making in America in the extension of our territory; the settlement of California, which was then going forward, the eager rush of population to the Pacific coast — all this involving the rapid spread of our English speech. Wordsworth at this looked up, and I noticed a fixing of his eye as if on some remote object. He said that considering this extension of our language, it behoved those who wrote to see to it that what they put forth was on the side of virtue. This remark, although thrown out at the moment, was made in a serious, thoughtful way, and I was much impressed by it. I could not but reflect that to him a deep sense of responsibility had ever been present; to purify and elevate had been the purpose of all his writings.

Some inquiries having been made as to my travels, "What are they doing in France?" was a question that followed. I said every one felt there was no stability in the existing government; a speedy change was looked for; all was uncertainty. Referring to the revolution of the previous year, Wordsworth remarked that Louis Philippe and Guizot had shown a sad want of courage, but for this the result might have been very different. Lamartine he spoke of very slightingly, "a poor writer of verses, not having the least claim to be considered a statesman."

Queen Victoria was mentioned; her visit to Ireland which had just been made; the courage she had shown. "That is a virtue," said he, "which she has to a remarkable degree."

Mrs. Wordsworth invited me to take wine with her; and this reminds me that I have said nothing about her. She seemed most refined and simple mannered, about the same age as her husband, slender, her face much furrowed, features small; she was dressed in black. I could see that she was still mistress of her household, presiding with dignity and natural grace. Dinner being over, she rose, saying they followed the American fashion of not sitting long at the table, and led the way to the drawing-room. She took a seat on one side of the bright fire, and Wordsworth on the other. He seemed now fully in the vein for conversation, although the sadness of his manner still continued. I knew the cause of this: it was grief for the loss of his daughter, Mrs. Quillinan.

Inman's portrait of him I alluded to as being very familiar to me, the copy which hung in the room calling it to mind: this led him to speak of the one painted by Pickersgill for St. John's College, Cambridge. "I was a member of that college," he said, "and the Fellows and students did me the honour to ask me to sit, and allowed me to choose the artist. I wrote to Mr. Rogers on the subject, and he recommended Pickersgill, who came down soon afterwards, and the picture was painted here." He believed he had sat twenty-three times. My impression is he was in doubt whether Inman's or Pickersgill's portrait was the better one. I think it was this mention of honours which had been paid to him which seemed to bring to mind the University degrees he had received. Oxford and Durham had made him D.C.L. Cambridge would have done the same had he not declined. Mrs. Wordsworth smiled as he said this, though without looking up from her knitting, as if he was speaking too much of his own dignities. But there was perfect simplicity and naturalness in his way of saying this.

Trinity College, Cambridge, was mentioned, which was founded by Henry VIII. Of that king he spoke in terms of the strongest abhorrence. I wish I could recall his exact words; the concluding sentence was,

"I loathe his very memory." I alluded to Holbein's portrait of Henry which I had lately seen at Oxford — at the Bodleian Library. "Yes, there he is," he said, "his hand grasping the dagger." The subject which came up next was the Chancellorship of Cambridge. Prince Albert's election he much regretted. The Earl of Powis, he thought, ought to have been chosen, one who had served the Church faithfully, and was an eminent member of the University. Prince Albert, he considered, had no claim whatever: had he (Wordsworth) still retained his connection with the University, he should have gone up to give his vote against him. The Heads of Houses and others had allowed themselves to be influenced by a wish to please the Queen; which was not a worthy motive in a case like this. He spoke strongly, saying, at the same time, that he was not unmindful of the position he held as Poet Laureate. He said Prince Albert's German education, his training at Bonn, was in itself a disqualification. He was supposed to entertain opinions opposed to classical study as pursued at the English Universities, and to have intimated a wish for extensive changes. This Wordsworth deprecated strongly: he spoke with great animation of the importance of the study of the classics — Greek especially. "Where," said he, "would one look for a greater orator than Demosthenes, or finer dramatic poetry, next to Shakespeare, than that of Æschylus and Sophocles, not to speak of Euripides?" Herodotus he thought "the most interesting and instructive book next to the Bible, which had ever been written." Modern discoveries had only tended to confirm the general truth of his narrative. In this, and perhaps other things that Wordsworth said, there was something of the extravagance which might be allowed in talk to make one's meaning clear.

Continuing to speak of Cambridge, he considered the rule an unfortunate one which obliged those holding Fellowships to resign them at the end of seven years unless they took Holy Orders. Many men, he said, began the study of law when this period was over, but finding their academic life had unfitted them for this profession, leading them as it did to the open world, they returned to the University, and took Orders as though they could not help themselves. Archdeacon Hare was one of these, and Bishop Thirlwall (the Bishop of St. David's). Of the former he had a high opinion, although he did not agree with him as to some of his judgments — his extreme admiration for Luther, for instance. Bishop Thirlwall, he said, he did not altogether like, his manner was disagreeable to him — he had a "sneering way of talking." Mrs. Wordsworth reminded her husband, in her quiet way, that he was now a bishop. "Well, I hope he has improved, then. I speak of my own intercourse with him some years ago." Moreover, Mr. Thirlwall had proposed, while he was a Fellow at Cambridge, that the attendance of the students at the Daily Service should no longer be strictly required. "This my brother, who was Master of Trinity, and whose will was law at the University, strongly opposed."

France was our next subject, and one which seemed very near his heart. He had been much in that country at the outbreak of the Revolution and afterward during its wildest excesses. He was at Orleans at the time of the September massacres in Paris. Addressing Mrs. Wordsworth, he said: "I wonder how I came to stay there so long, and at a period so exciting." He had known many of the abbé's and other ecclesiastics, and thought highly of them as a class: they were earnest, faithful men: being unmarried, he must say they were the better able to fulfil their sacred duties; they were married to their flocks. In the towns there seemed, he admitted, very little religion; but in the country there had always been a great deal. "I should like to spend another month in France," he said, "before I close my eyes."

Seeing Manning's Sermons on the book-shelves, I alluded to them, and mentioned that I had heard the Archdeacon in London a short time before. Mrs. Wordsworth took interest in my account and joined almost for the first time in conversation. The sermons were evidently well known to her and much valued. Wordsworth said to her, calling her "Mary," "Did I buy that copy?" "No," said she; "it was a present." "From the Archdeacon?" he inquired. "No; a present to me from Miss Fenwick." There was tenderness in the tones of his voice when speaking with his wife.

"Peace settles where the intellect is meek," is a familiar line from one of the beautiful poems which Wordsworth addressed to her, and this seemed peculiarly the temper of her spirit — peace — the holy calmness of a heart to which Love had been "an unerring light."

I cannot forbear to quote here that beautiful passage near the end of "The Prelude," in which he speaks for the first time of his wife. After apostrophizing his sister, "Child of my parents; Sister of my soul," and dwelling on what she had been to him from his boyhood up, he adds: —

> "Thereafter came
> One whom with thee friendship had early paired;
> She came, no more a phantom to adorn
> A moment, but an inmate of the heart,
> And yet a spirit, there for me enshrined
> To penetrate the lofty and the low;
> Even as one essence of pervading light
> Shines, in the brightest of ten thousand stars
> And the meek worm that feeds her lonely lamp
> Couched in the dewy grass."

I have been led away from my narrative, but I wished to note how much I felt drawn to Mrs. Wordsworth, as I saw her thus for the first time. She was then in her eightieth year. Little could I foresee that again, and yet again, I was to be under her roof, and partake of her gracious hospitality. As the years went on, and I knew her better, I could feel how true the words were that she had been "like the Poet's Guardian Angel for near fifty years."

After an hour or two had passed I rose to go. Wordsworth, without rising himself, begged me to sit down again: they had no engagements; at this season they gave themselves up to visitors. For eight months of the year they saw only their immediate neighbours. "Pray sit down again, if you like." I could not resist this. Mrs. Wordsworth added they had visitors constantly, and from various quarters — more Americans by far than all other foreigners put together.

I ventured to remark to Wordsworth that I had observed from a note, in the last-published volume of his poems, that he looked with favour on what is known as the Oxford movement in the English Church, the results of which were everywhere visible. I asked him whether late events had led him to alter his judgment. He replied deliberately that his opinion was unchanged. "I foresaw," said he, "that the movement was for good, and such I conceive it has been beyond all question." Continuing to speak of the English Church, he said there ought to be an increase in the number of Bishops, — they ought to be five times as many; the duties in Parliament of the present bench were important, and took up much of their time. The clergy having no representatives in the House of Commons, the presence of the Bishops in the House of Lords was the more necessary.

It is of course impossible to give the whole of what was said, or to do justice to the conversation by what I am able to recall of it. I may note that Wordsworth's manner throughout was animated, and that his words were felicitous to such degree as to enchain attention. There was sustained vigour, and a mode of expression denoting habitual thoughtfulness.

I rose a second time to go. Wordsworth told me I was to say to his friends in America that he and his wife were well, that they had had a great grief of late in the loss of their only daughter. He added, "I suppose we shall never get over it." Two years had then passed since the death of Mrs. Quillinan. I recalled that the poet had himself condemned "long and persevering grief" for "objects of our love removed from this unstable world," reminding one so sorrowing of that state:—

> "Of pure, imperishable blessedness
> Which reason promises, and Holy Writ
> Ensures to all believers."

But, as if foreseeing his own case, he has added in words of touching power:—

> "And if there be whose tender frames have drooped
> Even to the dust, apparently, through weight
> Of anguish unrelieved, and lack of power
> An agonizing sorrow to transmute,
> Deem not that proof is here of hope withheld
> When wanted most: a confidence impaired
> So pitiably that, having ceased to see
> With bodily eyes, they are borne down by love
> Of what is lost, and perish through regret."

I could see most clearly that it was the weakness of his bodily frame which took away his power of tranquil endurance. Bowed down by the weight of years, he had not strength to bear this further burden, — grief for the child who had always been the object of his tenderest love; the one, too, who had been, more than either of his other children, the companion of his mind.

I turned to take leave of his granddaughter, who had remained in the room. He said in his simple way, "That is the child of our eldest son." I mention this because his manner in telling me was kind and gentle; there seemed affection in the tones of his voice. He walked out into the entry with me, and then asked me to go again into the dining room to look at an old oak cabinet richly and curiously carved. It bore a Latin inscription stating that it was made three hundred years ago for William Wordsworth, "who was the son of," etc., giving the ancestors of the said William for many generations, and ending, "On whose souls may God have mercy." This Wordsworth repeated twice in an emphatic way, as if taking comfort in the religious spirit of his ancestor while adopting for himself the solemn ejaculation.

I asked to see the cast from Chantrey's bust of him, which he at once showed me; also a crayon sketch by Haydon, and one by Margaret Gillies.

We went out together upon the lawn and stood for a while to enjoy the views; Wordsworth pulled aside the shrubbery or hedge in places, that I might see to better advantage. He accompanied me to the gate, and then said, if I had a few minutes longer to spare, he would like to show me the waterfall which was close by, — the lower fall of Rydal. I gladly assented, and he led the way across the grounds of Lady Fleming — which were opposite to his own — to a small summer house. The moment we opened the door, the waterfall was before us, the summer house being so placed as to occupy the exact spot from which it was to be seen, the rocks and shrubbery around closing it in on every side. The effect was magical. The view from the rustic house, the rocky basin into which the water fell, and the deep shade in which the whole was enveloped made it a lovely scene. Wordsworth seemed to have much pleasure in exhibiting this beautiful retreat; it is described in one of his earlier poems, "The Evening Walk."

As we returned he walked very slowly, occasionally stopping when he said anything of importance; and again I noticed that looking into remote space of which I have already spoken. His eyes, though not glistening, had yet in them the fire which betokened the greatness of his genius. This no painter could represent, and this it was that gave his countenance its high intellectual expression. His features were not good; indeed but for this keen grey eye with its wondrous light his face could hardly have been called pleasing; but this atoned for all. His step I have already said was feeble, tottering; there was, too, this peculiarity that he walked with so uneven a gait as to encroach on my side of the path. One hand was generally thrust into his half-unbuttoned waistcoat. His dress was a black frock coat, grey trousers, a black waistcoat, and cravat of black silk carelessly tied; his appearance, in fact, was somewhat rough, but not slovenly; his clothes were not old fashioned, nor did he dress as an old man in any peculiar way.

The few minutes I was to devote to the Falls became a walk and further talk of three-quarters of an hour. One of the questions Wordsworth asked me at this time was, "What age do men reach in America?" He wished to know whether the average of life was longer with us than in England. He spoke of Mr. Everett, whom he had seen and of whom he thought highly. Webster he had also met; his dark complexion and his eye gave him somehow the look of our North American Indians.

I mentioned Henry Taylor's name to him. He said he knew him well, that he was a very estimable man, and of remarkable abilities. He added that he was without the advantage of a classical education, and this Wordsworth considered a great loss. He had acted lately with much propriety and forbearance in declining promotion which was offered him in the Colonial Office where he had long been engaged; he was content with the lower station, although his salary would have been almost doubled had he accepted the higher. With the former he had more leisure for literary work and for his family; this, in short, was more to him than money.

Of Hartley Coleridge he spoke with much affection: he was beloved by all who knew him, notwithstanding his wayward and careless life. "There is a single line," he added, "in one of his father's poems which I consider explains the after-life of the son. He is speaking of his own confinement in London, and then says: —

"'But thou, my child, shalt wander like a breeze.'"

Of Southey he said that he had had the misfortune to outlive his faculties; his mind, he thought, had been weakened by long watching by the sick bed of his wife, who had lingered for many years in a very distressing state.

The last subject he touched on was the international copyright question — the absence of protection in our country to the works of foreign authors. He said mildly that he thought it would be better for us if some acknowledgment, however small, was made. The fame of his own writings, as far as pecuniary advantage was concerned, he had long regarded with indifference; happily he had now an income more than sufficient for all his wants.

I happened to have in my pocket a small volume of selections from his poems made some years before by Professor Reed. I produced it and asked him if he had ever seen it. He replied he had not. He took it with evident interest, turned to the title-page, which he read, with its motto. He began the preface then, in the same way. But here I must record a trifling incident, which may yet be worth noting. We were standing together in the road when a man accosted us, asking charity, — a beggar of the better class. Wordsworth, scarcely looking off the book, thrust his hand into his pockets, as if instinctively acknowledging the man's right to beg by this prompt action. He seemed to find nothing, however; and he said, in a sort of soliloquy, "I have given to four or five already to-day," as if to account for his being then unprovided. Wordsworth, as he turned over one leaf after another, said, "But I shall weary you." "By no means," said I; for I could have been content to stand there for hours to hear, as I did, the Poet read from time to time, with fitting emphasis, the choice passages which Professor Reed had quoted in the preface, and the biographical sketch which followed. Most impressive was it to hear from the lips of the venerable man such words as these: "His has been a life devoted to the cultivation of the poet's art for its best and most lasting uses, a self-dedication as complete as the world has ever witnessed." A further remark, that he had "outlived many of his contemporaries among the poets," he read with affecting simplicity, his manner being that of one who looked backward to the past with tranquillity, and forward with sure hope. It was clear that he felt that his life was drawing rapidly to a close.

He made but little comment on Professor Reed's

notice of him. Occasionally he would say, as he came to a particular fact, "That's quite correct," or after reading a quotation from his own works, he would add, "That's from my writings." These quotations he read in a way that much impressed me; it seemed almost as if he was awed by the greatness of his own power, the gifts with which he had been endowed.[1] It was a solemn time to me, this part of my interview; and I felt it to be indeed a crowning happiness to stand, as I did, by his side on that bright summer day, and listen to his voice. I thought of his long life; that he was one who had felt himself from early youth a dedicated spirit,—

> "singled out
> For holy services,"—

one who had listened to the teachings of Nature, and communed with his own heart in the seclusion of these beautiful vales and mountains until his thoughts were ready to be uttered for the good of his fellowmen. And there had come back to him in all the later years of his life offerings of love and gratitude and admiration from perhaps as great a multitude as had ever before paid their homage to a living writer.

[1] Mr. Lowell ("Among my Books") does me the honour to quote this sentence. He says finely, to somewhat the same effect: "'The fact that what is precious in Wordsworth's poetry was a gift rather than an achievement should always be borne in mind in taking the measure of his power," and further, "Wordsworth's better utterances have the bare sincerity, the absolute abstraction from time and place, the immunity from decay, that belong to the grand simplicities of the Bible. They seem not more his own than ours and every man's, the word of the unalterable mind."

Still holding the little book in his hand, he said, "I will write my name in it if you like." I produced my pencil gladly, and he wrote with a trembling hand: "William Wordsworth, Rydal, August 18th, 1849." "You can mend it," he said. I am glad to note this little act of kindness.

He walked with me as far as the main road to Ambleside. As we passed the little church built by Lady Fleming, there were persons, tourists evidently, talking with the sexton at the door. Their inquiries, I fancied, were about Wordsworth, perhaps as to the hour of service the next day (Sunday), with the hope of seeing him there. One of them caught sight of the venerable man at the moment, and at once seemed to perceive who it was, for she motioned to the others to look, and they watched him with earnest gaze. He stopped when we reached the main road, saying his strength was not sufficient for a further walk. Giving me his hand, he desired again to be remembered to his friends in America, and wished me a safe return to my own home, and so we parted. I went on my way happy in the recollection of this to me memorable interview. My mind was in a tumult of excitement, for I felt that I had been in the familiar presence of one of the noblest of our race. The sense of Wordsworth's intellectual greatness had been with me during the whole interview. I may speak, too, of the strong perception of his moral elevation which I had at the same time. He seemed to me a man living as in the presence of God by habitual recollection. A strange feeling almost of awe had impressed me while I was thus with him.

Believing as I do that his memory will be had in honour in all coming time, I am indeed thankful that I was permitted to have the intercourse with him of which I have now sought to tell. I owed this great happiness to my dear friend, Professor Henry Reed. I was in a manner his representative as I drew near to the great and gracious presence. The kindness with which I was received was the acknowledgment which the poet was prompt to make of a devotion as absolute and unwearied as any of which literary history affords us an example. Professor Reed was, during all his mature years, the instant and unwearied upholder of Wordsworth's poetry. He had the profoundest sense of its value, and he accepted almost as a divine call the duty of bringing its holy and elevating influences home to the hearts of his countrymen. Wordsworth was quick to discern that here across the sea was one whose heart and mind were kindred to his own. The letters to Professor Reed which Dr. Wordsworth's "Memoirs" contain would seem to have been the most important that Wordsworth wrote. Alas! that it was not granted to this true-hearted man to see face to face the great poet toward whom he felt such utter loyalty of heart.

WALKS AND VISITS IN WORDSWORTH'S COUNTRY

WALKS AND VISITS IN WORDS-WORTH'S COUNTRY

August 11, 1855.— In company with my friend, the Rev. Derwent Coleridge, I called to-day at Rydal Mount. I had great interest in entering again the grounds and the house which six years ago I visited with such eager expectation. Everything remains as it was in the poet's lifetime — the books and the pictures and the furniture. Wordsworth's chair stands in its accustomed place by the drawing-room fireside. Mrs. Wordsworth seems also unchanged. Her manners are simple and unpretending, but she received me very cordially. As was natural, almost the first inquiries were after Mrs. Henry Reed and her children. She spoke with much feeling of Professor Reed and Miss Bronson, who scarcely a year ago perished in the *Arctic*. They left Rydal Mount for Liverpool to embark, and it was little more than a week after their parting from this dear venerable lady that the waves closed over them. Mrs. Wordsworth is almost eighty-five, and is as clear in mind as ever. You forget her great age in talking with her. And what tenderness there is in the tones of her voice, and what truthful simplicity in her words! We did not remain very long. I accepted her invitation to drink tea the next evening in company with Mr. Coleridge. As we drove away, we passed the spot where Wordsworth gave me his hand in parting six years ago, and but six months before his death. Later in the day, Mr. Coleridge and I took a walk along the Brathay to Skelwith Force and back, a round of six miles. The valley through which we went was familiar ground to Mr. Coleridge, he and his brother Hartley, — "My poor brother Hartley!" as Mr. Coleridge says when he speaks of him, — having spent five or six years there in their schoolboy days. We went to the cottage where they had lived, and the well-remembered rooms brought up to my friend a crowd of recollections of forty years ago. He talked much of those early days as we walked together along that sweet valley. We reached the Force, which is a pretty waterfall, and returned on the other side of the valley. It rained occasionally, but one gets used to this in England.

August 12, *Sunday.* — I went to the new Ambleside church this morning. It is one of Gilbert Scott's works, but not altogether pleasing. I sat with Dr. John Davy, brother of Sir Humphry. We were close to the memorial window for which Dr. Davy had applied, through Professor Reed, for American contributions. When the service was over, I remained to study this window. Its appropriate inscription is: —

> "Gulielmi Wordsworth Amatores et Amici,
> partim Angli, partim Anglo-Americani."

Other smaller windows are near by, commemorating members of the Wordsworth family, so that the corner becomes a Wordsworth chapel. One window remains without inscription.

At two o'clock I started for my walk to Grasmere, five miles distant, where I had agreed to meet Mr. Coleridge. My way at first was along the Rothay by the lovely road at the base of Loughrigg, which mountain seems to embrace as with an encircling arm one side of the Ambleside valley. There was deep shade here and there, and for a part of the way there was the shadow of the mountain itself. I passed Fox How, where there are only servants at present. Other pretty houses, with lovely shade about them, I also passed, and the sweep of the road gave me a perpetually changing view. Then I crossed a bridge, and soon found myself in the Vale of Rydal. Skirting the small Rydalmere, I next entered the sweet Grasmere Vale. In the distance was the church which was my destination, the square tower being a striking object in the view. It was a day of wonderful brightness, and the green of the mountain sheep-pastures and the purple of the slate rock, which is seen here and there, made a lovely contrast in the sunlight.

The church, which I reached at length, is the one commemorated by Wordsworth in the "Excursion":—

> "Not raised in nice proportions was the pile,
> But large and massy, for duration built,

> With pillars crowded, and the roof upheld
> By naked rafters intricately crossed,
> Like leafless under-boughs 'mid some thick grove."

The interior is interesting. The pavement is of blue flagstones worn and uneven. The pillars support two rows of low stone arches, one above the other, and on these rest the beams and other framework, black with age, which uphold the roof. The pillars are square and are of separate stones, and all has the look of rude strength, the rough work of very ancient days. The congregation was large. Mr. Coleridge preached. When the service was over I waited a while to look at the tablet to Wordsworth, which is on the wall directly over the pew he occupied for many years. The inscription is a translation from the Latin of the dedication to him of Mr. Keble's "Lectures on Poetry," and is as follows: —

> "To the memory of
> WILLIAM WORDSWORTH,
> A true philosopher and poet,
> Who by the special gift and calling of
> Almighty God,
> Whether he discoursed on man or Nature,
> Failed not to lift the heart
> to holy things,
> Tired not of maintaining the cause
> of the poor and simple,
> And so in perilous times was raised up
> to be a chief minister,
> Not only of noblest poesy,
> but of high and sacred truth."

Mr. Coleridge and I now started for the walk we had arranged to take together. It was to be a vigorous climb, and then a descent and a circuit of the vales of Rydal and Grasmere; and we had two hours for it. We took a narrow road leading up the mountain on the west side of Grasmere Lake: coming down a little, we ascended once more to look down on Rydal Water. The views were very lovely, and the mountain-air was exhilarating. These lakes, with their dark mountain settings, are like mirrors in their black transparency. Rydal Water is dotted with islands, each with its few trees, everything seeming in miniature. We went to a house which is the highest human habitation in England, save one on the top of Kirkstone Pass. The people occupying it knew Mr. Coleridge well: they showed me, at his request, the kitchen with its pavement of flagstones, and the opening between the rafters which served for the chimney — a curious specimen of Westmoreland cottage-life.

We reached at length Rydal Mount, which was our destination, and found there Miss Edith Coleridge, daughter of Sara Coleridge; William Wordsworth, a grandson of the poet; and Mr. Carter, Wordsworth's secretary for forty years. Young Wordsworth has his grandfather's face: he seems thoughtful, and, though silent, his manner is prepossessing. He is about twenty years of age, and is an undergraduate of Balliol College, Oxford.

Mr. Coleridge left us soon after tea, having to return to Grasmere. I walked out on the terrace with Mr. Carter, and enjoyed the fine view it commands of the valley of the Rothay, with Lake Windermere in the distance. It is a double terrace, with flower-beds interspersed, rich in bloom and fragrance. On either hand there is shrubbery of luxuriant growth, and one wall of the house is ivy-grown. All speaks of loving and tender care. Much of the work of raising the terraces was done, I believe, by Wordsworth's own hands. There are seats here and there on which one would be tempted to spend many an hour watching the changing lights on the distant hillsides and the fair valleys. Mr. Carter pointed out to me the valley down which "the Wanderer" and his party came to the "churchyard among the mountains" (the Grasmere church). He showed me also the stone with its inscription —

> "In these fair vales hath many a tree
>   At Wordsworth's suit been spared,
> And from the builder's hand this stone,
>   For some rude beauty of its own,
>   Was rescued by the bard:
> So let it rest, and time will come
>   When here the tender-hearted
> May heave a gentle sigh for him
>   As one of the departed."

Mr. Carter was most helpful to the poet during the long years of his association with him. One could fancy that he appreciated from the first the dignity of the service he was thus rendering. Mrs. Wordsworth has only a lease of Rydal Mount: at her death it must pass to strangers, for neither of her sons will be able to live there. I have omitted to say that she is rapidly losing her sight, but she has scarcely any other infirmity of age.

August 13.— Early this morning I started for an excursion which had been planned for me by Mr. Coleridge. I went by coach from Ambleside, ascending the Kirkstone Pass. I was outside, and could enjoy at first, as I looked back, the sweet morning view of Lake Windermere with its islands and its fair green hillsides. But soon the sharp ascent of the road brought us between steep mountain-declivities, shutting out all view except their desolate grey slopes. There were but scanty patches of grass here and there: all else was stony and barren. I walked in advance of the coach, enjoying the silence and the solitude, and the grand slopes of the naked mountains on either hand. Up and up we went, until at last the summit of the pass is reached. There stands the old stone house said to be the highest inhabited house in England — a rude enough dwelling, and at present an alehouse. Beginning now our descent toward Patterdale, we had from the summit of the pass a view of the little lake of Brotherswater, and soon our road was along the margin of this fair high-lying tarn. The mountains stand quite around the lake, leaving only space for the road. From the foot of the pass a drive of a few miles brought us to Patterdale, and there my coach-journey ended. I climbed to a stone-quarry on the hillside opposite, and thence had a view of the valley through which I had just passed, and of the lake of Ullswater stretching off to the right. Returning to the inn at Patterdale, I engaged a boat to take me to Lyulph's Tower, distant five or six miles. A young man with drawing-materials and pack slung over his shoulder was about to leave the inn. I asked him to take a seat with me, and we were soon side by side in the open boat on the beautiful lake. From the level of the water the mountains rising on either hand appeared in their full dignity. The lake is quite shut in by these steep and lofty hills. For a while the clouds were threatening, but we dreaded wind more than rain, for these lakes are often lashed by sudden storms. We landed and climbed to Lyulph's Tower, and there below, in its fair loveliness, lay the sweet Ullswater, this upper reach of it being of quite wonderful beauty. Thence we made our way to Aira Force, a mile distant — a dashing waterfall in a narrow gorge. Its height is about eighty feet. The "woody glen" and the "torrent hoarse," as Wordsworth describes it, are appropriate words.

A mile farther we found a road and a little inn. We asked for luncheon, but in the principal room, to which we were shown, two travelling tailors were at work. It seemed pleasanter to be in the open air, so we had our table under the trees outside. My companion proved to be a clergyman: he was fresh from Oxford, and had just taken orders. We had fallen at once into intimacy, but we had immediately to part company. My way was onward to Keswick, a walk of eleven miles. I ascended first a long hill, and then my route wound along or around the side of a mountain. Above and below me was bare heath or mountain-moor: there were no trees whatever. For near two hours I saw no house or sign of cultivation, nor did I meet a human being. The wind blew strongly in my face, but my blood coursed through all my veins, and I had ever before me a wide sweeping view. I descended at length into the fair valley through which the Greta flows, and about two hours more of steady walking brought me to Keswick. My stopping-place, however, was at the inn at Portinscale on the banks of Derwentwater, a mile out of Keswick, where I had agreed to meet Mr. Coleridge. I dined, and was resting after my long walk, when I heard his voice in the hall inquiring for me. With him were three other gentlemen, one of them the friend with whom he was staying, who asked me to return with them and drink tea at his house. One of the four was Dr. Carlyle, a brother of the Chelsea philosopher, himself a man of letters, the prose translator of Dante. I soon found myself in a pretty drawing-room looking out on Derwentwater. Mr. Leitch was our host. We had a great deal of animated talk at the teatable, and later in the long twilight Mr. Coleridge read to us the " Ancient Mariner " and " Genevieve," his father's matchless poems. He reads extremely well. We sat by one of the large windows, and the lake stretching before us and the mountains beyond seemed to put one in the mood for the poetry.

August 14.— I went to Mr. Leitch's to breakfast this morning, meeting nearly the same party, and had another hour of pleasant talk. Then Dr. Carlyle, Mr. Coleridge, Mr. Leitch, and I rowed across the lake. Landing near the town, Mr. Coleridge and I took leave of the others and went up into Keswick, and so out to Greta Hall, the former residence of Southey, now occupied by strangers. It has a lovely situation on a knoll, Skiddaw looking down upon it, and other mountains standing around and in the distance, and the Greta flowing, or rather winding, by; for it is a stream which has many twists and turnings. We called at the house, and Mr. Coleridge sent in his name, telling the servant he had a friend with him, an American, to whom he would like to show some of the rooms, adding, " I was born here." There was a little delay, for the occupant of the house was a bachelor and his hours were late. So we looked first at the grounds, and my friend, as we walked slowly along under the trees and looked down on the Greta, seemed to be carried altogether back to his childhood. On that spot it was that his brother Hartley used to tell to him and to their sister Sara, as well as to Southey's children, stories literally without end — one narration in particular in its ceaseless flow going on year after year. " Here, too," said my friend, pointing to a small house near by, " was the residence of the Bhow Begum." Need I add that this reference was to that strange book, "The Doctor"?

We were now summoned to the house, and though

we saw no one except the civil housekeeper who accompanied us, all was thrown open to us. My friend at every room had some explanation to make: "This was the dining-room;" "here was Mr. Southey's seat;" "here sat my mother." One room was called Paul, for some one had said its furniture was taken wrongly from another room — robbing Peter to pay Paul. Upstairs was the library, the room of all others sacred, for there had passed so much of the thirty years of Southey's life of unwearied labour. The very walls seemed to speak of that honourable industry. I looked from the windows on those glories of lake and mountain which had been the poet's solace and delight, and recalled his own description of the view in "The Vision of Judgment": —

"Mountain and lake and vale; the hills that calm and majestic
Lifted their heads in the silent sky."

Near the library was the room in which he died after years of mental darkness. In the same room Mrs. Southey had been released from life after a still longer period of mental decay.

Leaving Greta Hall with all its interesting associations, we returned to the road. Near the gateway were some cottages. "An old fiddler used to live here," said Mr. Coleridge. Then inquiring of some men at work near by, he learned to his surprise that he was still there. "But it is more than forty years since I knew him: he used to teach me to play on the violin." "He is still there," the men repeated; and

F

we entered the cottage. An old man rose from his seat near the fire as Mr. Coleridge asked for him by name. "Do you remember me?" said my friend. "You gave me lessons on the violin more than forty years ago, until my uncle Southey interfered and said I should play no longer: he feared it would make me idle." "I remember you perfectly," said the old man. "You would have done very well if you had kept on." Then followed mutual inquiries. The wife of the old man sat by his side crippled with rheumatism, from which he himself also suffered. "But she bears it very patiently, sir," said he. There seemed Christian submission in the old people — a tranquil waiting for the end.

Our next visit was to Miss Katherine Southey, who lives in a beautiful cottage close at the foot of Skiddaw. Three little children, Robert, Edith, and Bertha Southey, grandchildren of the poet, came out to meet us. Miss Southey greeted her cousin warmly. She is of cheerful, agreeable manners. We talked of Greta Hall, and the cousins called up their old recollections. Mr. Coleridge went upstairs to see the aged Mrs. Lovell, his aunt, the last of her generation, so to say — sister of Mrs. Coleridge and Mrs. Southey. It was one of Southey's good deeds that he cared for this lady from the beginning of her early widowhood as long as his own life lasted. She was, I believe, one of his household and family for more than forty years; and since his death his children have continued the same dutiful offices. (As I copy these notes, now long after the date of my visit, I may add that Mrs. Lovell died in 1862, aged ninety-one.)

Miss Southey showed me some of the manuscripts of her father — very minute, but exquisitely neat and clear. When the cousins took leave of each other, Miss Southey's eyes were filled with tears. We now took to our boat again, and started for the Falls of Lodore at the other end of Derwentwater. We stopped at Marshall's Island, so called from the owner, who has made it a summer residence of marvellous beauty, though the extent of it is but five acres. Trees of every variety adorn the grounds. The house is in the centre, of stately proportions: the drawing-room in the second story opens upon a balcony commanding a view which is beyond measure enchanting. Books in profusion lay upon the table, and pictures and drawings were upon the walls, all telling of refinement as well as of abundance of this world's goods. Returning to our boat, my friend and I took the oars. Our next stopping-place was at St. Herbert's Island — a hermitage a thousand or more years ago. A few remains of what may have been an oratory are still to be seen. St. Herbert was the friend of the good St. Cuthbert, whose especial shrine and memorial is Durham Cathedral. Once a year, according to Bede, he left his cell to visit St. Cuthbert and "receive from him the food of eternal life." And in Wordsworth's verse is embalmed the tradition that, pacing on the shore of this small island, St. Herbert prayed that he and his friend might die in the same moment; "nor in vain so prayed he:"—

"Those holy men both died in the same hour."

At length we reached Lodore. Here our real work was to begin. We climbed to the top of the hill down which the stream falls over rocks piled upon rocks, forming a succession of cascades. It was a ladder-like ascent of no little difficulty. After admiring the view of the rocky chasm and the falls, we turned to enjoy the prospect which opened before us from Ladderbrow, as it is called. Derwentwater lay stretched before us, and Skiddaw rose in its giant majesty in the distance. The view is a celebrated one. We then entered the wood, crossed a beck or small stream, losing our way once, and at length reached an upland valley — Watendlath — very retired and secluded, with its small hamlet, and near by a tarn — "A little lake, and yet uplifted high among the mountains." The day was cloudy, but there was not much mist. Climbing another ridge, we found ourselves looking down upon Borrowdale and the little village of Rosthwaite, one of the loveliest views I ever beheld. Sunlight was upon the vale while we stood in the shadow. We were looking up Borrowdale to the Sty-head Pass. As we descended into the valley we could enjoy the view of it every step of the way. At Rosthwaite we had luncheon. It was half past three. We had still a mountain to climb; and as there was something of danger, for we might lose our way should the mist increase, we took a guide, a man well known to Mr. Coleridge — one of the dalesmen of Borrowdale. We started at a vigorous pace, and, following the course of a stony brook, ascended the steep mountain-side. It was very sharp work, for it was an absolutely continuous ascent, and there was no pathway whatever. There was no sign of human habitation. On either hand were only the stony mountain slopes. It seemed a long and weary way, but at the end of two hours of steady climbing we reached the summit. A cold mist here enveloped us. We hastened on, our guide accompanying us a short distance over the moor as we began our descent: he saw us clear of the mist and safely on our way. When we had reached an eminence from which we could look down into Far Easdale, our route was clear to us, and we turned and waved our adieus to our friendly guide. We were already a long way off from him, and he was resting where we had left him, waiting to see that we took the right course. Descending rapidly, we went on and on through the desolate and lonely valley of Far Easdale — a vale within a vale, for it opens into Easdale. Hereabouts it was that George and Sarah Green lost their way and perished on a winter's night, as the story is recorded in Wordsworth's verse and De Quincey's exquisite prose. So dreary is the solitude that scarcely a sheep-track is to be found in the valley. All around there is nothing but a bare and stony heath.

We hastened on, for Mr. Coleridge knew there would be anxiety in regard to us, as evening was drawing on. Another ascent being accomplished, we looked down into Easdale, surrounded by its mountain-girdle. The sun was setting, and as we were drawing near our destination I almost forgot my fatigue. At length we reached Mr. Coleridge's cottage at the entrance to the Vale of Grasmere. Mrs. Coleridge came out to meet us, and expressed much relief at seeing us. She knew the perils of a long walk over these lonely mountains.

I found an invitation for me from Mrs. Fletcher, a venerable lady of eighty-five, who had been a friend of Jeffrey, and one of the literary circle of Edinburgh of sixty years and more ago. After refreshing ourselves, my friend and I sallied forth. Lancrigg is the name of Mrs. Fletcher's beautiful cottage. We found a brilliant company assembled. Mrs. Fletcher welcomed me with sweet but stately courtesy. "I am always glad to see Americans," she said; "my father used to drink General Washington's health every day of his life." Her look was radiant as she said this: there was light in her eyes and colour in her cheeks, and altogether her appearance was most striking. I never saw a more beautiful old age. I talked with her son, Mr. Angus Fletcher, a sculptor of some distinction. A bust of Wordsworth and one of Joanna Baillie, works of his, were in the drawing-room. He told me of his having lately been to see Tennyson, who is on Coniston Water in this neighbourhood, in a house lent him by Mr. Marshall of Marshall's Island. Mr. Fletcher said he asked Tennyson to read some of his poetry to him. "No," was the reply; "I will do no such thing. You only want to take me off with the blue-stockings about here." But they got on well together in their after-talk, and Tennyson, softening a little, said he *would* read him something. "Nothing of my own, however; I will not give you that triumph. I will read you something from Milton." "Oh, very well," said Mr. Fletcher; "I consider that quite as good poetry."

The evening over, a drive of six miles brought me to the friends with whom I was staying at Rothay Bank, near Ambleside.

August 15. — Dined to-day at Rydal Mount — the one o'clock dinner which is always the hour there — with Mrs. Wordsworth, young William Wordsworth, and Mr. Carter. Six years almost to a day since I last sat in that quaint room in the familiar presence of the great poet himself. It is a low room without a ceiling — the rafters showing. A great number of small prints in black frames are on the walls, chiefly portraits. There are portraits of the royal family also, but these are in gilt frames; they were the gift of the Queen to Wordsworth. I was glad to see again the bust of Wordsworth by Chantrey, and also the old oak cabinet or armoire with its interesting Latin inscription, both of which the great poet showed to me as among his choice possessions. James, who has lived there for thirty years, waited at the table. Mrs. Wordsworth asked me to take wine with her, — the courtesy of the old days, — the single glass of port which she drinks daily. It was the last day of her eighty-fourth year.

The library, which adjoins the drawing-room, is smaller in size, and the collection of books is not large. I noticed that many were presentation copies: in one of them, a folio volume describing the Skerryvore Rock Lighthouse — was the following inscription (the author of the book was the architect of the lighthouse): "To William Wordsworth, a humble token of admiration for his character as a man and his genius as a poet, and in grateful remembrance of the peace and consolation derived from the companionship of his writings during the author's solitude on the Skerryvore Rock."[1]

John, the loquacious but intelligent coachman of the friend at whose house I am staying, told me of his waiting at dinner at Rydal Mount a good many years ago: his then master was one of the guests. Miss Martineau, Hartley Coleridge, and F. W. Faber were present. Mr. Faber had then charge of the little church at Rydal. There was a rush and flow of talk, as one could well imagine — such a chatter, John said, as he had never heard — but the instant Wordsworth spoke all were attention. John himself was awed by the great man's talk, and described well its power. He told me also of a slight incident in regard to Wordsworth's last hours. Very shortly before his death it was thought he might be more

---

[1] The architect was Alan Stevenson, uncle of Robert Louis Stevenson.

comfortable if he were shaved. Accordingly, he was raised in the bed, and his faithful servant was about to minister to him in this way when Wordsworth said in his serious, calm voice, "James, let me die easy." I may note here something which has been told me in regard to poor Hartley Coleridge's last days. During his illness a little child, the daughter of an artist who lived near him, quite an infant, used to be brought to him, and he would sit for hours holding it in his arms and looking down upon it with mournful tenderness.

Sunday, August 19.— Walked to the Rydal church this morning. Just as I reached the porch, I saw Mrs. Wordsworth with her arm extended feeling for the door. I went forward to assist her; she turned her kind face toward me, not knowing who it was. I told my name. "Oh," said she, "I am glad to see you. You will take a seat with us, of course." William, her grandson, was now close behind us. We went to the pew, the nearest to the chancel on the left, and I sat in what had doubtless been Wordsworth's seat. The prayer-book I took up had on the fly-leaf, "Dorothy Wordsworth to William Wordsworth, Jr., 1819." The service over, Mrs. Wordsworth said to me, "You will dine with us, of course." She took my arm, and as we went out of the church I was struck with the looks of affectionate reverence in the faces of those we passed. As we walked along she said in her kind way, "I should have been glad if you had taken up your abode with us while here, but you expected to leave Ambleside immediately when I last saw you." The Misses Quillinan, the step-daughters of the late Dora Quillinan, who was Dora Wordsworth, were the guests beside myself to-day. In the drawing-room after dinner it was interesting to me to look at the portrait of the elder Miss Quillinan (Jemima), taken when a child six years old, and to recall the lines addressed to her, or rather suggested by the picture:—

> "Beguiled into forgetfulness of care,
> Due to the day's unfinished task, of pen
> Or book regardless, and of that fair scene
> In Nature's prodigality displayed
> Before my window, oftentimes and long
> I gaze upon a portrait whose mild gleam
> Of beauty never ceases to enrich
> The common light."

The sonnet, too, beginning—

> "Rotha, my spiritual child! this head was grey
> When at the sacred font for thee I stood,
> Pledged till thou reach the verge of womanhood,
> And shalt become thy own sufficient stay"—

came naturally to my mind as I talked with the younger sister. These ladies are intelligent and refined, and of very pleasing manners: their mother was a daughter of Sir Egerton Brydges. They live at a pretty cottage underneath Loughrigg, not far from Fox How.

We went to church again at half past three: I walked with Mrs. Wordsworth. She spoke of herself — said she was rapidly growing blind: in the last week she had perceived a great change. One would get used to the deprivation, she supposed, however. Her life had been a happy one, she added: she had very much to be thankful for. Her manner in church, I may mention, is most reverent, her head bowed and her hands clasped. As I returned from church with her, a tourist accosted me: Could I tell him which was Mr. Wordsworth's house? I pointed it out to him. "We have many such inquiries," Mrs. Wordsworth said.

I had now to make my final adieus to the dear venerable lady. (I little thought I should ever see her again.) Her serene and tranquil old age, I said to myself, would be a remembrance to me for life. She wished me a good voyage and a safe return to my friends.

William Wordsworth kindly went with me for a mountain-climb. We ascended Loughrigg, from which we looked down on three lakes, Windermere, Rydal, and Grasmere — a last view of all this beauty. How lovely were the evening lights on mountain and valley!

Rothay Bank, Ambleside, August 7, 1857. — Again, after a two years' absence, I find myself in this sweet region. With my kind host, Mr. C——, I went this morning to call on Mrs. Arnold at Fox How. We found six or eight persons in the drawing-room. It was my first meeting with Mrs. Arnold: she came forward to receive us, welcomed me cordially, and presented me to her three daughters, Mrs. Twining, Mrs. Cropper, and Miss Frances Arnold. I was fresh from Wharfeside, the home of her eldest daughter, Mrs. Forster. We talked about that home of such peculiar intellectual brightness, and I told of the happy days I had passed there. Mrs. Arnold's manners are gentle and winning. She asked me what evening I could spend with them, and Sunday was agreed upon. Fox How I was most glad to see with the stream of life flowing on in it: when I was last here the family were away. Mr. Penrose, a brother of Mrs. Arnold, a clergyman of Lincolnshire, Mrs. Penrose, and Dr. and Mrs. Perry of Bonn were the others in the room. Dr. Arnold's portrait was on the wall, also prints of Mr. Justice Coleridge, of Archbishop Whately, of Wordsworth, and of Julius Hare. The views from the windows had their own peculiar beauty, half hidden though the landscape was to-day in rolling mist.

August 8. — Walked to-day along the beautiful road under Loughrigg, that huge winding mountain, past Fox How and many other lovely country homes. Went then into the Vale of Rydal and skirted this beautiful lake, watched the reflections in the water, and gazed on the noble hills which surround the vale. I continued on: Grasmere came in sight — a large lake with a view in the distance of the square white tower of the church under whose shadow Wordsworth lies. I passed the cottage in which Hartley Coleridge lived and in which he died. At length I reached the head of the lake, and then the church which was my destination. Once more I stood at the grave of Wordsworth, that sacred spot which, as I believe, many generations will visit, and whence a voice, we may hope, will ever speak to men of the beauty of this fair earth and the higher glory of which it is the shadow. The great poet lies by the side of his daughter, Dora Quillinan; next to her lies Dorothy Wordsworth, his sister; then Edward Quillinan and his first wife; and there is space left for Mrs. Wordsworth. Sarah Hutchinson, Mrs. Wordsworth's sister, also lies here: on the stone which marks her grave is the following:—

"Near the graves of two young children,
removed from a family to which through life she was devoted,
Here lies the body
of
SARAH HUTCHINSON
the beloved sister and faithful friend
of mourners who have caused this stone to be erected
with an earnest wish that their own remains
may be laid by her side, and a humble hope
that through Christ they may together
be made partakers of the same Blessed Resurrection."

Here follow the dates of her birth and death, and then—

"In fulfilment of the wish above expressed here repose
the remains of
WILLIAM WORDSWORTH,
DOROTHY WORDSWORTH."

[Space being left for Mary Wordsworth.] A little farther on are the graves of the two young children alluded to in the foregoing. On the tombstone of one is this inscription:—

> "Six months to six years added he remained
> Upon this sinful earth, by sin unstained.
> O Blessed Lord, whose mercy then removed
> A child whom every eye that looked on loved!
> Support us, make us calmly to resign
> What we possessed, but now is wholly Thine."

I lingered near an hour around these graves, and then retraced my steps along the water-side and beneath the shade of the solemn hills. I passed Town End, once the residence of Wordsworth, and halfway between Grasmere and Rydal I climbed the old road to the Wishing Gate, from which there is a beautiful view of Grasmere. Looking down on this fair and peaceful scene, I did not wonder that what Wordsworth calls "the superstitions of the heart" had invested the place with a magic power. It seemed natural, too, to think that only what was best and purest in each soul would be touched by the spell.

> "The local Genius ne'er befriends
> Desires whose course in folly ends,
> Whose just reward is shame."

Continuing my walk, I reached the Vale of Rydal, and then turned by the pretty shady ascending road leading to Rydal Mount. I entered by the small gateway the fair terraced garden so rich in bloom and fragrance. I saw once more the old greeting, *Salve!*

as I stood on the threshold. James, the old servant, welcomed me and conducted me to the drawing-room. I found Mrs. Wordsworth seated in her old place by the fireside. Her greeting was simple and cordial, but only by my voice could she know me, for I saw at once that she was quite blind. Her grandson William was with her. She was cheerful and bright, and talked of the events of the day in the sweet quiet manner peculiar to her, and with clear intelligence, and yet she was within a few days of being eighty-seven. She was mindful, too, of the duties of hospitality, for finding I had walked about eight miles she insisted on ordering some luncheon for me. I had a good deal of talk with young Wordsworth. His resemblance to his grandfather has become quite remarkable. He has the same dreamy eyes and the same forehead. But there seemed a benediction in the very presence of Mrs. Wordsworth, so much did her countenance express peace and purity, so gentle and so sweetly gracious was her bearing.

August 9, *Sunday.* — I went this afternoon to the little Rydal church, and I sat in Mrs. Wordsworth's pew. No one was there but young Wordsworth. Mrs. Arnold's pew is directly opposite, both being at the end of the church nearest to the chancel. Mrs. Arnold and her three daughters were present. The old clerk from his desk near the pulpit said at the end of the service, " Let us sing to the praise and glory of God the 'undredth psalm — the 'undredth psalm," and then with feeble step walked down the aisle to take his place as leader of the choir. The preacher was a stranger, and the sermon was an appeal for missions. He seemed a good and earnest man, but his manner was odd, and some things he said were odd too. The woman of Samaria was the text: "You remember that when Dr. —— of the Scotch Church was in the Holy Land he visited the well, and as he sat there he took out his Bible to read the chapter, and he let it fall into the well, and it was not recovered for a long time afterward: the well was deep." But still stranger was what followed. Speaking of our Lord's humility: " We do not hear of His going about except on foot, never in any vehicle. Once only do we hear of His riding on an ass, and that was a borrowed one." There was a quaintness in this that was worthy of the old days, and certainly there was nothing of irreverence in the preacher's manner. John Mason Neale, I remember, quotes somewhere the following equally quaint utterance from a Middle-Age writer: —

> " Be Thou, O Lord, the Rider,
> And we the little ass,
> That to the Holy City
> Together we may pass."

After the service I walked up to Rydal Mount with Mrs. Arnold. Mrs. Wordsworth was in the drawing-room. It was an interesting sight to see the two ladies talking with each other — on the one side reverence and respect, on the other strong regard, and on both manifest affection. I thought, would the poet and the teacher have been what they were to the world but for the help and example which each had at hand in his household life?

At half past six I went to Fox How, where I was to drink tea. We were a large party at the table: we did not remain long, however, for we were to ascend Loughrigg to see the sun set. We had a lovely climb in the long summer twilight. We wandered on to a jutting rock, and from thence we saw the sun go down in glory behind the mountains, leaving a splendour of crimson in the light clouds for long afterward. Below us was Loughrigg Tarn, which Wordsworth has somewhere commemorated. Mrs. Twining told us of a walk with the poet she recalled, though she was very young at the time, which occasioned the poem: her father too was with them. A row of pines ascending a mountain on the opposite side of the valley was pointed out as " Fan's Funeral " — " A joke against me," said Miss Arnold. It seemed that in childhood she had somehow got the impression that it was a troop of mourners following a bier — perhaps some one had said, " How like a funeral !" — and many times afterward, in visiting the spot, the child still supposed it was a funeral, and wondered it should be so long stationary.

As we came down the mountain, Miss Arnold spoke of her recollection of the day of Wordsworth's death. She and one of her young friends were almost alone at Fox How. They knew that the end was at hand, and their minds were filled with the thought of it. They climbed one of the hills looking down on

Rydal Mount, their hearts bowed with a solemnity of feeling — burning, one might almost say, within them as they thought of the moment that approached. Suddenly as they looked they saw that the windows of the house were being closed, and they knew thus of the faring forth of the great soul. It was almost as if they themselves had witnessed his departure. I could well understand how the solemn Nature around would have a grave and awful look to them as they pondered in their young hearts that ending and that beginning. I spoke of Wordsworth's own lines on hearing that " the dissolution of Mr. Fox was hourly expected ": —

> " A power is passing from the earth
> To breathless Nature's dark abyss;
> But when the great and good depart,
> What is it more than this —

> " That man, who is from God sent forth,
> Doth yet again to God return?
> Such ebb and flow must ever be:
> Then wherefore should we mourn?"

At Fox How we assembled again in the pleasant drawing-room: books were brought out, and passages referred to which had been suggested in our walk. At length the bell was rung for prayers, and the servants came in: Mr. Penrose officiated. One could not but think how often Dr. Arnold's voice had been heard there saying the same office. Some refreshment was brought in. I remained but a few minutes longer. Mrs. Arnold asked me to dine with them on Wednesday.

August 10. — My kind host has arranged an excursion of about three days, that I may see a part of this Lake District which is seldom visited. We started from his gate at ten o'clock by coach for Broughton, by way of Coniston Water — a beautiful drive, the weather delightful and all very promising. At Broughton we had a glimpse of the valley of the Duddon. Thence we went by rail along the seacoast as far as Ravenglass, a lonely fishing village. Here we hired a car for Strand's near Wast Water, a distance of seven or eight miles. We stopped, however, a mile from Ravenglass, at Muncaster Castle, " the seat of the ancient family of the Penningtons." The guidebooks say that Henry VI. was entertained here on his flight after the battle of Hexham, and that when he left Muncaster he gave to Sir John Pennington an enamelled glass vase. The glass has been carefully preserved in the castle, the tradition being that the family would never want a male heir while it remained unbroken. We drove through the park by a winding road, which brought us to the castle. The chief thing here is what is known as the terrace, cut on a hillside, and commanding a view which is said to be the finest in Cumberland. All around are noble trees and beautiful shrubbery and gay flowers, so that one could hardly think the great sea so near. Indeed, it had seemed like enchantment, the turning in from the bleak coast to all this rich foliage and summer beauty. Very lovely are the grounds, because so unartificial. Nature has been the great beautifier.

After we left the terrace we came to a little church quite embosomed in the trees — as secluded a nook as one could imagine: it is in the castle grounds, but is the church of the neighbourhood.

We continued our drive. Alas! the promise of the morning was not fulfilled. Clouds had gathered, and at length the rain began. At Strand's we found rooms in a very small inn, and concluded to stay there quietly for the night. So we had our tea-dinner, and composed ourselves to such indoor occupation as was possible. Books there were few of — some volumes of Swift's works, two volumes of poems — Liverpool poets of fifty years ago who had not achieved fame. However, with the aid of these notes, which had fallen in arrear, and with occasional talk, the hours were beguiled.

August 11. — Still rainy and lowering. We breakfasted and waited, hoping for fair-weather signs. The rain did for a while cease, and I drove alone to Wast Water, two miles distant. This lake of black waters, with the bare mountains rising round it, showed well under the sombre sky. The mountains were capped with mist, so I could only imagine their height, but the whole length of the lake lay stretched out before me. In desolate savage beauty this surpasses all the other lakes of the region. It is said to look its best on gloomy days: its dark colour is perhaps due to the great depth of the water.

Returning to the inn, I found my friends all ready for our start for Seathwaite, eight miles distant. We had still to keep to the one-horse car, the only vehicle to be had in these out-of-the-way places. At Seathwaite we obtained an open carriage for the rest of the journey, eighteen miles. We passed through Egremont, and saw the ruins of the castle — through Ennerdale, and stopped to look at the churchyard, the scene of Wordsworth's beautiful pastoral "The Brothers." At Scale Hill, which was our destination, we had again good weather, and it was a lovely view with which our journey for the day closed. My friends' carriage was awaiting us at the hotel, and the coachman had brought us our letters. He left Rothay Bank this morning, and came by way of Keswick, a drive of thirty miles. We dined, and then, as the clouds had broken away and the sun was about setting, we went out to enjoy the evening. We climbed the hill, from which a beautiful view of Crummock Water opened before us. John the coachman came up afterward, bringing his bugle, on which he plays very well. He soon set for us "the wild echoes flying," and all the vale below was filled with the sound. We then wandered away to the edge of the lake and watched the play of the evening light on the tranquil waters.

August 12. — We started at half past six this morning to drive to Keswick to breakfast, twelve miles. The weather was beautiful, and all the fair vales and hills were in their full loveliness in the morning light. As we drew near Keswick we saw from a hill Derwentwater and Bassenthwaite Lake, and the town in the centre of the valley, which lay below us. We passed the church where Southey lies, and then crossed the Greta and drove by Greta Hall, and so into Keswick. Here we breakfasted, and our horses had a two hours' rest, and we then started again for Ambleside, seventeen miles. We ascended first the long hill from which there is the noble view of the Vale of Keswick and of its lakes, and of Skiddaw and the other mountains — a view which twice before I have had the happiness to see. When I last looked down on it, it was under a cloudy sky: now there was the full beauty of sunlight. But every foot of the way between Keswick and Ambleside has its charm: Southey calls it the most beautiful drive in the world. Why should I attempt to describe it? I may note the wonderful reflections in the lakes of Grasmere and Rydal, especially the latter. There was no ripple to disturb the glassy transparency. The islands, the sloping shores, the hedges, and the grazing sheep, all were doubled, and no water-line was to be seen. I suppose the mountains around protect the lake from currents of wind, and give a blackness to it which makes it so excellent a mirror.

At a little after one, my friends set me down at the entrance to Fox How. I was to dine there to meet Thomas Arnold and William Wordsworth, and we were to have a walk together in the afternoon. But Arnold had been suddenly called to Dublin, and had just started. Wordsworth, however, was there, and with him Mr. Henry Crabb Robinson, who had just come to spend a few days at Rydal Mount — an old man of eighty-three, but fresh and gay and wonderfully fluent in discourse. He was a great friend of Wordsworth's, and was twice his companion in travelling on the Continent. Southey, Coleridge, and Lamb he knew well also. I was presented to him, and reminded him that five years ago I had the honour to breakfast with him in London — a fact which, I grieve to record, he seemed quite to have forgotten.

Dinner was soon announced, and the large table was again well filled. Mr. Robinson took the talk pretty much. He sat on Mrs. Arnold's right, and I was directly opposite. Perhaps it was having me in full view that led him to speak so much of the Americans he had known in the last forty years. He told us of his chance meeting with young Goddard of Boston in Switzerland in 1820, when he and Wordsworth were travelling together, and how that meeting had caused poor Goddard's death. Wishing to be in Wordsworth's company, he had asked Mr. Robinson's permission to join them in the ascent of the Rigi. He altered by so doing his course of travel, and a day or two afterward, in crossing the Lake of Zug in an open boat with a companion, a storm came on, the boat was upset, and he was drowned; his companion escaped by swimming to shore. We recalled Wordsworth's elegiac stanzas on the occasion, and I ventured to add, as a conclusion to the story, that when

Professor Reed was getting together the American contribution to the Wordsworth memorial window, a letter came from Mrs. Goddard, the mother of the young man who near forty years before had perished, desiring to take part in the commemoration, and referring to the imperishable monument to her son which the great poet had reared. She was then eighty-five, and had lived to give this token of her gratitude.

Mr. Robinson had a great deal to say about the Rev. James Richmond, an American, a man of genius, but famous chiefly for his eccentricity. But I need make no further note of his discourse. He diverged perpetually, and sometimes did not come back to the main track of his story. I was half sorry that my presence should be the occasion of his talking so much about my countrymen. I should have preferred a subject which would have been of more interest to the others who were present. But it was idle to attempt to direct the current of his speech. Equally futile was Mrs. Arnold's effort to retain possession of the joint which was placed before her, and which she was about to carve. Mr. Robinson insisted with peremptory courtesy on relieving her, and as he brandished the great knife, continuing the while his animated talk, there was naturally a less skilful performance of the duty which was then of immediate urgency. Glances were exchanged by Mrs. Arnold with some of her guests, in part of apology and in part of amusement at the spectacle. And, sooth to say, the fair tablecloth suffered from Mr. Robinson's double mind.

I remained most of the afternoon at Fox How, walking about the grounds or sitting under the shade of trees near the house, talking with one or other of the ladies. Seldom have I passed pleasanter hours. In the evening I was again with Mrs. Arnold and her daughters on a visit at one of the neighbouring houses. Nine o'clock came, and with it the *Times*, which was eagerly opened. The news from India is just now of absorbing interest. [It will be remembered that this was the year of the Sepoy Rebellion.] I should mention that Mrs. Arnold read us this afternoon letters from her son William, author of "Oakfield," from the Punjaub. Under date of February last he speaks of a Mohammedan secret organization, having its centre at Delhi, and ramifications everywhere, which he thinks means evil. He is the more of this opinion because his Persian secretary, whom he thinks very ill of, belongs to it. Writing under date of June 15, he says the Bengal Sepoy no longer exists, and that the civilization of fifty years has gone in a day. The laying of the Atlantic cable is another matter of great interest just now. All England is watching its progress. Despatches from the ship come almost hourly as it steams westward.

August 16. — My last Sunday in England. I went by the beautiful Fox How road to Rydal to church, and sat in Mrs. Wordsworth's pew. She and Mr. Crabb Robinson and William Wordsworth were there.

Mrs. Wordsworth to-day enters her eighty-eighth year. I sat by her side as I did two years ago, in this same pew, the Sunday before I sailed. Her meek countenance, her reverent look, I saw once more — the face of one to whom the angels seemed already ministering. Service being over, I shook hands with her, and received a kind invitation to dine at Rydal Mount. Leaning on Mr. Robinson's arm, she went out, Wordsworth and I following. Mrs. Arnold and her daughters stopped to make their congratulations on her birthday, as others did, following her afterward with loving looks. We ascended the steep hill, Mr. Robinson talking, as usual, a great deal.

Once more I was at Rydal Mount; there were the books, the pictures, the old chairs. I went upstairs with Wordsworth to his room; it is the one that Dorothy Wordsworth, the poet's sister, occupied so long — the room in which she died. The house is very old, the passages narrow, the ceilings low, yet there is an air of comfort everywhere. At dinner Mr. Robinson was the talker, as he always is. He told us of his intercourse with Goethe. He said he never mentioned Wordsworth's name to Goethe, fearing that he would either say he had never read his poetry or that he did not like it. He said Southey was only a collector of other men's thoughts: Wordsworth gave forth his own. Wordsworth was like the spider, spinning his thread from his own substance; Southey the bee, gathering wherever he could. Mrs. Wordsworth did not join us at table till the dessert came in. Then her one glass of port having been poured out for her, she took it in her hand and turning her face toward me, said, "I wish you your health, and a prosperous voyage and a safe return to your friends!"

The interval after dinner was short. I received, if I may so say, Mrs. Wordsworth's final blessing and went my way, thankful it had been given me to draw near to one so pure, to a nature so nobly simple. Not only her children, but all who have come in contact with her, will rise up to call her blessed. Surely, thrice blessed was the poet with such a wife; and indeed he himself with wonderful fulness has declared she was almost as the presence of God to him: —

> "That sigh of thine, not meant for human ear,
> Tells that these words thy humbleness offend;
> Yet bear me up — else faltering in the rear
> Of a steep march: support me to the end.
>
> "Peace settles where the intellect is meek,
> And Love is dutiful in thought and deed;
> Through thee communion with that love I seek;
> The faith Heaven strengthens where *he* moulds the creed."

My last evening in this sweet region was spent at Fox How. With Mr. Thomas Arnold and Miss Arnold I once more in the long twilight climbed Loughrigg Fell. There stretching out before us was range after range of grey mountains, with Skiddaw in the distance — a solemn and peaceful view, and to me a leave-taking of one of the loveliest regions of the earth.

Hotel, Windermere Station, July 4, 1873. — Again,

after sixteen years' interval, I am on the threshold of this lovely region. I have been walking in the twilight hours through bowery lanes, hoping to reach the lake; but I took a wrong direction, and only when it was time to return did I get from a high part of the road a glimpse of the fair waters. I passed many gateways, with broad gravelled drives leading from them, doubtless to beautiful homes, for all this neighbourhood is occupied by lovely dwellings, more or less secluded and embowered in all luxuriant greenery. It was between nine and ten o'clock when I got back to the solitude of the hotel. There were people there, no one of whom I knew. I can stand being alone with Nature; but the constrained silence of the coffee-room of an English inn is a trifle depressing.

July 5.— I started early in a fly for the ferry at Bowness, then crossed the lake in almost a toy steamer to the Nab promontory, and thence took my way on foot by a quickly ascending road toward Hawkshead. From the summit of the ridge I looked back upon Lake Windermere, with its wooded promontories and its islands and its encircling mountains. The morning was beautiful, and the whole scene was in its rich summer loveliness. I had forgotten how fair and glorious were these Westmoreland lakes and mountains. Farther on I came to Esthwaite Water, a lake a mile and a half in length, and soon afterward I entered the Vale of Hawkshead. The old church, on a rocky eminence, is the chief object as you approach the town. At the base of the hill on which it stands is the grammar school at which Wordsworth received his first lessons, as he tells us in "The Prelude." I found carpenters at work in the old school-room, and one of them told me he had himself been a scholar there, and he showed me the desk at which Wordsworth sat. The schoolhouse, the church, and the streets of the town had all a quaint and antique look. I could fancy there had been little change since Wordsworth and his brother Christopher, afterward master of Trinity College, Cambridge, were scholars here, near a hundred years ago. It had been the chief object of my pilgrimage — the sight of this schoolhouse. Coniston was my further destination. A coach was standing at the door of an inn, which I found was just starting for this place, so I climbed to an outside seat, and found as my sole companion a good-natured man who at once entered into talk with me. He seemed a well-to-do man, and as he told me soon whence he had come and whither he was going, I naturally imparted to him what had been the object of my pilgrimage to Hawkshead. He seemed to find it hard to account to himself for my enthusiasm; still, the only inquiry he made of me in endeavouring to enlighten himself was a singular one. "Was he a rich man?" he asked me, referring to Wordsworth. I was obliged to admit that he was not. Then we talked of the races at Newcastle, and on this subject my companion had greatly the advantage of me.

We descended upon Coniston Water by a long

steep hill. The hotel known as the Waterhead Inn is beautiful as to architecture, and there were about it flower-beds with geraniums in glorious bloom — such splendour of colour as I never saw before. I went out in a boat on the lake, and enjoyed for a while the view of the hills around. Then rain came on, and I had to row quickly back, and my remaining hours were spent at the inn. But the spacious coffee-room commanded such a delightful view that there was little hardship in remaining indoors. At about five in the afternoon I started on the coach for Ambleside. I was on top, by the coachman, a civil fellow who knew every foot of the way. Three young ladies sat on the still higher seat behind. They were of severe propriety of manner, but they were refined, and talked with a careful modulation of voice which is peculiarly English. The afternoon was dull, but it did not rain. The road was perpetually either up hill or down, and the views every step of the way were lovely. We went through Yewdale, and stopped within a few minutes' walk of Skelwith Force, a waterfall reminding one of a single portion of Trenton Falls. Time was allowed us to see this, and then we climbed to our high seats again, the young ladies having the help of a ladder, and drove along the banks of the Brathay, passing as I drew near Ambleside the gateway of the pretty house which had been a home to me in two former visits. Alas! the dispensers of that gracious hospitality, my kind host and hostess, have both been removed by death. At the Salutation Inn,

Ambleside, I received the welcome answer that I could have a room: the travelling season has begun, and as I had not written in advance, I had my fears.

July 6. — It rained last night when I went to bed, but the day broke gloriously, and this wonderful, this enchanting region seemed to have a new and fresh charm. A young Canadian joined me in my walk to the Rydal church just under Rydal Mount. There was the little church just as I had last seen it, only that it had been greatly improved as to the exterior architecture. Inside it was but little changed: the old high-backed pews remained. There in her accustomed place, in the large square pew near the chancel, sat Mrs. Arnold, and by her Miss Frances Arnold, both fronting the small congregation. I looked at the pew on the other side and missed the sweet and aged face of Mrs. Wordsworth. But the whole church seemed a memorial of her. My meeting with Mrs. Arnold and Miss Arnold was very pleasant and cordial when the service was over; they asked me to dine with them, and introduced me to the dean of Durham, who was with them. Mrs. Arnold and the dean drove. Miss Arnold said she would walk, so she and her nephew (a son of Thomas Arnold, looking wonderfully like his uncle, Matthew Arnold) and I went by that most lovely road which winds underneath Loughrigg. The walk and the talk were delightful to me; the day was of rare splendour, and there was the unspeakable beauty of the valley and of the mountains around.

At Fox How, Mrs. Arnold and the dean were in the garden; the dear old lady (she is now eighty-two) came forward and made the kindest inquiries about those I had left at home, and was in every way most gentle and gracious. And then we walked into the house, and into the drawing-room, and it seemed like a bit of enchantment, the view from the window looking back over the way we had come — the solemn mountains shutting all the beauty in, as it were, giving a framework and a setting to it. We sat and talked, and there was such a sense of kindly feeling as to make the hospitality I was enjoying doubly grateful. The ladies went away for a moment, and I could look at the books and the pictures. Everything spoke of culture and of thought. Much seemed to have been added to the room since I last saw it. A fine drawing in water-colour, a portrait of Mrs. Arnold, hung over the fireplace — a recent picture. On the table I saw two thick volumes — the memoir and letters of Sara Coleridge. I had not known that the book was out: it seemed strange that I should see it for the first time at Fox How.

Our talk at dinner was very pleasant. The dean of Durham is Dr. Lake; he was, as Miss Arnold informed me, Dr. Arnold's favourite pupil. The fact of his being a dean was proof of his learning and high reputation; for in latter times these appointments are only given on the ground of distinguished merit. He said Emerson dined with him some months ago when at Durham; that he spoke of having seen a good deal of Carlyle when in London; that he, Carlyle, was out of health and depressed. The loss of his wife preyed on him; he was unable to sleep, and the chief comfort he found in his sleepless hours was in saying over and over again the Lord's Prayer. Emerson's daughter was travelling with him, but being unwell, she could not go to dine at the dean's. At the table something from Keble was quoted, but neither Emerson nor the dean could get it right. "Oh, I'll ask my daughter," said Emerson. Emerson went with the dean to the cathedral service, and seemed greatly impressed by it. We talked of the Hare book, "Memorials of a Quiet Life." Miss Arnold had known well both Augustus and Maria Hare, as well as Julius and Esther Hare; indeed, it was probably at Fox How that the engagement of Julius Hare to Esther Maurice took place. The writer of the "Memorials" was well known to them at Fox How — a man of some eccentricity of character. Miss Arnold said she had within a few days talked about the book with Miss Martineau, who denounced it on some fantastic ground or other. Miss Arnold said it was not pleasant to her to hear this adverse criticism — "But you know one cannot tell a lady of great age, through a trumpet, that you utterly object to what she is saying." The dean spoke of Professor Jowett with admiration, though he could not wholly agree with him. Of Maurice the dean spoke with great respect; he said Hutton, the editor of the *Spectator*, was the chief representative of his opinions. Mr. Forster, too, might be mentioned as a leading man on whom the teaching of Maurice had had a strong influence. Mrs. Arnold took part with much animation in all the talk; she seemed perfectly bright in mind. I was delighted to see her cheerfulness and serenity, and to feel that her closing days had so much of joy in them.

As I climbed Loughrigg late in the afternoon I thought of the long thirty years of Mrs. Arnold's widowhood, and of how much had been given to cheer its loneliness, — the loving dutifulness of her children, her home in this beautiful region, around which must cling, for her, such vivid and tender associations, the ever recurring evidences of the fruitfulness of her husband's teaching. All this must have brought peace to her in the slowly passing years. I thought of Wordsworth, too, when, my view widening with each step, I at last reached a height from which I could look down on Rydal Water as well as Windermere. I wondered whether this grand Nature had made the man, or whether his genius had invested it with something of the charm which it has now for all beholders. I stood among grey mossy rocks; sheep were browsing on the grassy spaces between; below me lay the whole Ambleside Valley, with the church in the centre. A very Sabbath stillness seemed on all the hills and in the vale beneath. I said to myself, "Surely to any man such sights as these must give elevation of mind: how much more to a poet!" I could understand the good that must have come to Wordsworth, wandering as he did over these hills, with the thought ever present to him that Nature was to be his teacher, and that it was to be his work to interpret her to men.

Late in the afternoon I called on the Misses Quillinan (Jemima and Rotha, commemorated by Wordsworth), and had pleasant talk with them over the past. They told me that my friend of former visits, William Wordsworth, the poet's grandson, was now at home from India on a visit; he has been head of a college at Poonah for twelve years. I shall hope to see him when I reach Cockermouth. The ladies told me that the old Wishing Gate had been removed, and a new gate put in its place; they showed me a bar of the old gate, and I sought to make trial once more of its mystic power. The Misses Quillinan, as being the step-daughters of Dora Quillinan, are the nearest, and indeed the only, representatives of Wordsworth remaining here in the neighbourhood of Rydal Mount.

July 7.— I left Ambleside to-day for Keswick. I was on the outside of the coach, and had a full view of the slopes of the hills, the green of the pastures, fretted here and there by crags; and I saw the sweet lakes once more, Rydal and Grasmere, and farther on there were numerous flocks of sheep coming down the mountains, probably for the shearing. Dogs were guiding them and keeping them together with wonderful and unerring instinct. And then we passed Thirlmere, which is the highest of the English lakes. Here the view had become wild and desolate, the hillsides bare and rocky. We descended from this high valley into a fair smiling country once more. The coach stopped at the entrance to St. John's Vale, and I determined to walk to Keswick by that route. It is a narrow, winding valley, shut in by deep hills, with a stream flowing through it. On either side of the water there is thick wood, but with open spaces here and there, and farmhouses. The rocks which overhang the vale at about the centre have the look of a fortress. I entered the vale of the Greta, and then descended the long Saddleback, and made my way at length to the Portinscale Hotel; there I rested after my three hours' walk, and in the evening went on by rail to the neighbourhood of Cockermouth, where I was to spend a few days at the house of some friends.

Of this visit I need make but little record. I saw at Cockermouth the square and respectable mansion, quite the most considerable house in the town, in which Wordsworth was born April 7, 1770. The house has undergone but little change, it is said, since that date. I met William Wordsworth, too, as I had hoped I should. He and his wife were staying with his father, the Rev. John Wordsworth, vicar of Cockermouth. He was bearded and bronzed and otherwise changed, as a man well might be after twelve years in India. His wife showed more of the ill effect of the climate; her appearance was extremely delicate.

I may note one interesting incident which Mr. Wordsworth told me. He had been on a visit to Professor Jowett at Oxford, and was there on a Saturday, the day on which Jowett gathers about him people of distinction. "On this occasion," said Wordsworth, "I was to hand out to dinner a particular lady, but her name was not mentioned to me, or at least I did not catch it. She, however, was told that I was a grandson of Wordsworth. 'Oh,' said she, 'I began to read Wordsworth when I was fifteen, and have gone on ever since with continually increasing pleasure;' and then her talk flowed on with such strength and power, and showed such elevation of mind and such grasp and mastery of all learning, that I was certain she could be no other than Mrs. Lewes. So I asked her if she was not the author of "Middlemarch," and she said she was. In the drawing-room afterward she showed herself on the same level with Greek scholars and men of science, with whom she talked, filling with wonder all who listened."

Mr. Wordsworth spoke of his important position at Poonah, giving him direction of the education both of Hindoos and Europeans. I could not doubt his fitness for the work he had undertaken; but I remembered what I thought was the promise of sixteen years ago, and I fancied that whatever India might have gained, England had lost a man of letters — perhaps a poet. He was the last of my friends of the Lake District with whom I had intercourse in that visit of 1873. It chanced that he accompanied me on my journey from Cockermouth to Carlisle, and there, on the threshold as it were of the region, we parted — he for the East when his brief furlough should be over, I for the West. I felt always that I had much in common with him; but now, with half the globe between us, and the changes which the flowing years might bring, the chance was small of our ever meeting again.

SARA COLERIDGE AND HER BROTHERS, HARTLEY AND DERWENT COLERIDGE

SARA COLERIDGE AND HER BROTHERS, HARTLEY AND DERWENT COLERIDGE.

My introduction to the son and the daughter of Samuel Taylor Coleridge was by a letter from Professor Henry Reed. With the kindness of heart peculiar to him, he came to me the evening before I left Philadelphia, to tell me he had just received a long and very interesting letter from Mrs. Henry Nelson Coleridge, — the poet's daughter Sara (she had married her cousin), — that she had written in a manner so open and friendly that he felt quite justified in giving me a note of introduction to her — here it was.

I had known her, in a way, because of other remarkable letters from her, which Professor Reed had allowed me to see; I had especially been brought into association with her from the pleasure with which I had read her notes to her father's "Biographia Literaria." Marvels of learning and wisdom these notes seemed to be; but what especially had charmed me was the criticism they contained, supplementing her father's, of the poetry of Wordsworth. Henry Nelson Coleridge, a man of high accomplishment, had begun the editing of the "Biographia Literaria," but, after his early death, it was left to his widow to complete the commentary and to publish. A distinct gain to literature are her additions and criticisms; her soul speaks out to one as she aims to interpret her father to the world. One cannot but think what would have been the joy and comfort of Coleridge had he known what his daughter was to do for his fame.

It was with something of the ardour of youth that I called on Mrs. Coleridge in London in June of 1849. I was now to have my first meeting in England with one of the band of writers to whom I had been indebted for many happy hours. My love of literature had been great from boyhood, and my feeling for Wordsworth's poetry was almost a passion. The lady I was soon to see was the one in all England who best represented Wordsworth, her mind being in part the creation of his own.

I see her now as she entered her pretty drawing-room, her face pale, her complexion almost transparent, her eyes large and of a peculiar lustre. I could well understand that she had been beautiful in youth. She received me with gentle cordiality. I felt sure that her feeling for my introducer could not but be warm, so like-minded was he in his interest in literature, and so at one with her in his estimate of her father's writings, and his deep sense of the value to the world of the poetry of Wordsworth. I was received, as I have said, with much kindness, and was an eager listener to Mrs. Coleridge's pleasant and animated talk on the subjects of the day. The Oxford Tract writers, Newman and others, were much in the minds of men at the time. Manning, still in the English Church, had published sermons in the manner of Newman, but much more rhetorical. Mrs. Coleridge spoke of him as a "much weaker Newman." Dr. Pusey she had been greatly impressed by as a preacher. But she could not give her assent to the theories of the Tract writers, as a whole, regarding them as essentially at variance with the teaching of the English Church. At that time men of the highest grasp were delivering themselves on questions of theology. Sara Coleridge had inherited a deep interest in these questions. Her talk impressed me much; for I felt how rich was her mental endowment, how high and pure her thought. Aubrey de Vere, in speaking of her, has dwelt on "the radiant spirituality of her intellectual and imaginative being," and no words can better describe the charm of her personal presence. Yet there was, as I talked with her, a look almost of languor in her eyes, an undefined something showing that her health might be frail. The hand of death was probably even then on her, known only to herself. I learned afterward that she gave no sign to those nearest to her of her dread anticipation.

I was able to see Mrs. Coleridge again after my return from the Continent. I was with her for an hour and a half. She talked with peculiar animation; there was the glow of genius in her face — a radiant expression that put one under a spell. She expressed regret that I was not to remain in London to take part in their Winter Society. I said to myself, what joy would be greater!

The cholera was at that time a subject of dread in London because of its ravages in Paris of two months before, the deaths there having been nine hundred a day for many days.

I may note here an incident, personal to myself, of the cholera visitation in Paris of June, 1849. I was in London at the time, and met, one morning, at a house at which I had my lodgings, a gentleman who had arrived from Paris the night before. I was present as he told the lady of the house that he had left Paris suddenly because he had been obliged to close his establishment — his men would not remain. "I had no fear myself," he said, "my father died in my arms; I kissed him when he died." He spoke with strong emotion, and I remember the tears which were in the eyes of the lady to whom he talked. He seemed a man of cultivation and refinement; I did not learn his name. Six weeks afterward I was in Paris, and was asked by an American friend to go with him to meet M. Henri Gerente, the leading maker of stained glass in Paris. My friend wished to give him an order for a window for the church of St. James the Less, Philadelphia. M. Gerente was of high reputation; he had just done important work at Ely Cathedral; and the Government of Louis Philippe had given over to him the restoration of the Sainte Chapelle, especially the renewal of the great windows of that glorious gem of thirteenth century Gothic. It was at the Sainte Chapelle we were to meet him. We found him there. Behold, it was the gentleman with whom I had had my early morning meeting in London! He drew rapidly for us the design he proposed for the St. James the Less window — a series of medallions in which the figures would be very small, and thus a jewel-like radiance secured. We instantly approved. The east window at St. James the Less — as glorious a piece of colour as there is in America — stands, I trust, for all time, to sustain our judgment.

After some study of the lovely Sainte Chapelle, under M. Gerente's guidance, he drove with us to Notre-Dame, where very important work was going on — the rebuilding of the South Transept; Viollet-le-Duc had charge of this, the most eminent architect of France, perhaps of Europe. We were fortunate in finding him there. M. Gerente presented us to him, a man tall and of striking presence. When my friend and I drove away, we left M. Gerente standing on the pavement in front of the great western towers; he waved his hand to us; I see him now as he smiled in bidding us adieu. A fortnight afterward he died of cholera. Though I did not then know of it, it was about the time of my visit to Mrs. Coleridge.

I note here a passage from a letter of Mrs. Coleridge to Professor Reed, of some months later, referring to my visit. I make the extract, partly because of the message of kindness it contains, and partly because it is in itself somewhat singular.

"I think I have not written to you since I saw your friend Mr. Yarnall. Will you give my kind remembrances to him, and say that I look back to our last conversation with much interest, and that both my brother and I should feel much pleasure in seeing him again if he ever revisited England. He was here at a fearful time, when the mysterious visitation of cholera, and its sudden destruction of human life, kept me in a perpetual tremor. I thought with concern that he was about to go back into the cholera atmosphere of highest intensity; but he appeared calm and strong in spirit, and, in the midst of pity for him, I felt envy, after a sort, of his firmness and tranquillity."

I cannot recall the slightest feeling of anxiety on my own part. Yet the fact remains that not long after I left London the visitation came, and the deaths were for a time over two thousand a day. I went northward, after leaving London, and, from some chance of travel, I was in the town of South Shields, near Newcastle on Tyne, on a certain day in August. I said to myself, as I walked in the narrow streets, "What a place this would be for cholera to find victims!" A year later I read in the official record of the ravages of the disease in England that the place of greatest mortality in proportion to population was this town of South Shields, and that the day on which the deaths rose to the greatest number was the day on which I chanced to walk through its streets.

During the three years that passed before my next visit to England, I had some correspondence with Mrs. Coleridge. Once I wrote while on a journey to the Northwest. My letter was of some length, telling of the new country I was seeing, and speaking also of matters of literature in which I had then interest. There came at once a reply, fourteen pages — the large letter sheet of those days, closely written. Its arrival is a vivid remembrance to me. I read it again and again, struck always with its wisdom, its felicity of expression, its keen and subtle criticism on literary matters. It lies before me now in its faded pages, and I find as I go over it that my judgment in regard to it is the same as at my first reading. I had told, in my letter, of the tragic death of a young man of excellent promise to whom I was strongly bound. Referring to this she speaks of such deaths as "an evidence that here we have no abiding city — that the best estate of frail mortals, so frail as earthly beings, so strong in the heavenly part of their constitution, is when they feel themselves to be strangers and pilgrims here below. What a depth," she says, " of consolation there is in some of those expressions in the eleventh chapter of the Hebrews! How they articulate the voices of immortality within us, and countervail the melancholy oracle of Lucretius with their calm and confident assurances!"

I give this as showing what was the supreme and animating feeling of the writer. Through all the intellectual brightness of the letter, and varied as are its contents, there is manifest her deep sense of religion. She speaks of her weakened health, says she cannot give a good account of herself; but there is no word of murmuring. At the end she says with what seems the prompting of a saint-like thought for another out of the depth of acquiescence in the hard trial allotted for herself, " May you long have health and strength to enjoy the infinite delights of literature, and the loveliness of this bright breathing world, which the poets teach us to admire, and the Gospel makes us hope to find again in that unseen world whither we are all going." Strange that now, after forty-eight years, I can record the fulfilment of this gracious desire for me.

I had but one other letter from her after this long one; it showed increasing bodily weakness, though the same kind thought for others. With the feeling I have for her memory I cannot deny myself the pleasure of noting here that she speaks of a letter of mine telling, among other things, of a winter visit to Niagara as having quite brightened her invalid room.

Carlyle's " Life of Sterling" she comments on, " Very beautiful and interesting as a biography, but very painful in its avowal of Pantheism." She resents Carlyle's reference to her father, says the chapter on him is a pure libel. She adds, " But my father's folly and sin in the eyes of the Pantheist is his firm adherence to Christianity, not only ideal, but historical, factual, and doctrinal." She will write again if *strength admits.* " If you do not hear again, you will understand that *strength has failed."* She speaks of her longing to see again her own native hills and streams—and then exclaims, " O that my remains, and those of my dear mother, could rest in that dear Keswick churchyard where my Uncle Southey's lie, with those hills around!"

I sailed for England four months after this letter was written, having the hope strong within me that some further personal intercourse might be granted me. Alas! it was not to be. I heard in Liverpool of the death of Mrs. Coleridge; it had occurred while I was at sea.

Sara Coleridge was, as to her mental part, almost the child of Southey. She grew up under his roof at Keswick, and drew in daily from the outpourings of his affluent mind. His fine library was open to her, and the example of his life of unwearied industry as a student and a writer was ever before her. The *In labore quies* of Southey's bookplate was the motto by which her own life was guided. And in all matters of conduct, and of high endeavour, he was her loving and unerring teacher. She said of him in emphatic words, that he was upon the whole the best man she had ever known. As to her intellectual part she was probably even more indebted to Wordsworth, whose impressive discourse she had constant opportunities of listening to at Rydal Mount, and at Greta Hall, and in rambles, in the company of the great poet, among the mountains. With Dora Wordsworth, her bosom friend, she grew up under the influence and in the companionship of men of the noblest gifts. She showed in all her after life the blessing which had come to her in heart and mind in the opportunity which had been granted her. It is said of her that in the serene and lofty regions of the spiritual province of human nature she walked hand in hand with her father; her interests were kindred with his own, but in her case there was no alloy of lower impulse to weaken her thought. Well does her own daughter say of her:—

"Possessing, as she did, a knowledge of theology rare in any woman (perhaps in any layman), she had received from heaven a still more excellent gift, even the ornament of a meek and quiet spirit."

But to dwell more particularly on the early years of Sara Coleridge in the house of Southey, one can readily imagine what the charm to him must have been of helping in the development of a mind so gifted as that of this fair young creature, who seemed to live only for intellectual effort and enjoyment. Under his guidance she had taught herself French, Italian, German, and Spanish; before she was five and twenty she had made herself acquainted with the leading Greek and Latin classics. There could have been little opportunity, in that far Cumberland region, for a young woman to obtain anything equivalent to college training. Had there been such opportunity, money would have been wanting, and Southey had never a year's income in advance. The charge of the three children of Samuel Taylor Coleridge,—Hartley, Derwent, and Sara,—and of their mother, was, in part at least, upon Southey; his reward came in their unceasing devotion and affection.

On my first visit to Mrs. Coleridge she referred with much feeling to the loss of her brother Hartley; he had died in January of that year. Tears filled her eyes as she spoke of him. Though she had been long separated from him, he was the object of her tenderest love. I may note here what I read when her letters were published. Speaking of the death of Hartley, she says: —

"Nothing has ever so shaken my hold upon earth. Our long separation made me dwell the more earnestly on thoughts of a reunion with him; and the whole of my early life is so connected with him, he was in my girlhood so deep a source of pride and pleasure, and at the same time the cause of such keen anguish and searching anxiety, that his departure brings my own before me more vividly, and with more of reality, than any other death ever has done."

Again she writes: —

"He was the most attaching of men; and if tributes of love and admiration, of deep regard, — in spite of his sad infirmity, which did himself such wrong, — could remove or neutralize sorrow, my cup would have lost its bitterness. Never was a man more loved in life or mourned in death."

The comfort and the joy which Sara Coleridge must have been in her girlhood to both her brothers can well be imagined. I remember at Heath's Court Mr. Justice Coleridge, father of the late Lord Coleridge, taking down from his shelves "An Account of the Abipones, an Equestrian People of Paraguay," in three volumes, octavo, from the Latin of Martin Dobrizhoffer. He told me that Hartley Coleridge had begun the translation, the money he was to receive for it from Murray being needed for his college expenses. He soon tired of the work, however, and his sister, then twenty years of age, undertook it, and brought it to completion — truly an extraordinary achievement. Her father said of it, " My dear daughter's translation of this book is unsurpassed for pure Mother-English by anything I have read for a long time." And Charles Lamb spoke of her as " the unobtrusive quiet soul, who digged her noiseless way so perseveringly through that rugged Paraguay mine. How she Dobrizhoffered it all out puzzles my slender latinity to conjecture."

But no words can be better than those of Aubrey de Vere to tell of the chief characteristics of this remarkable woman. He says : —

"With all her high literary powers she was utterly unlike the mass of those who are called literary persons. Few have possessed such learning; and when one calls to mind the arduous character of those studies, which seemed but a refreshment to her clear intellect, like a walk in mountain air, it seems a marvel how a woman's faculties could have grappled with those Greek philosophers and Greek Fathers, just as no doubt it seemed a marvel when her father, at the age of fourteen, 'woke the echoes' of that famous old cloister with declamations from Plato and Plotinus. But in the daughter as in the father, the real marvel was neither in the accumulated knowledge nor in the literary power; it was the spiritual mind.

"'The rapt-one of the Godlike forehead,
　The Heaven-eyed creature,'

was Wordsworth's description of Coleridge. Of her some one had said, Her father had looked down into her eyes, and left in them the light of his own.

" When Henry Taylor saw Sara Coleridge first, as she entered Southey's study at Keswick, she seemed to him, as he told me, a form of compacted light, not of flesh and blood, so radiant was her hair, so slender her form, so buoyant her step and heaven-like her eyes."

But beside the help which Sara Coleridge may have given her brothers, it fell to her to comfort and support her mother during that excellent lady's long years of trial. A single letter which the Memoir contains makes it clear that the mother's reliance, up to a late period of life, was upon the daughter for spiritual help and consolation. Mrs. Coleridge, the elder, though not without ability, was never the companion of her husband in intellectual things, nor could she reach the level of either of her gifted children. She was weak of nerves and of anxious temperament. Until her daughter's marriage at the age of twenty-seven, the two were never separated. The mother was in a fever of anxiety as to the daughter always, as to her health, and as to everything concerning her. Strange had been the trials in the life of the mother in the alienation of her husband, and his long separation from her; for the last twenty-five years of his life they had lived wholly apart.

With Samuel Taylor Coleridge genius was accompanied by eccentricity in largest measure. We must take a great man as he is given to us, and in regard to Coleridge we must follow his own rule as applied to art criticism, and not judge of him by his defects. Southey had upon him, in large degree, the stress and burden of his brother-in-law's shortcomings. He said of him, "Coleridge whenever he sees anything in the light of a duty is unable to perform it." In a further moment of irritation, he said, even as to his intellectual part, " Coleridge writes so that there are but ten men in England who can understand him, and I am not one of the ten." With Wordsworth and with his sister Dorothy, with Mrs. Wordsworth and her sister Sarah Hutchinson, Coleridge's companionship was of the closest. The Journals of Dorothy Wordsworth, now given to the world in full, are the record of this extraordinary fellowship. Sara Coleridge never failed in filial devotion to her father, although she was separated from him during almost her whole life.

I never saw Hartley Coleridge, but I seem almost to have known him, so much have I heard of him, and so vividly present does he seem to one in his writings, fragmentary though they are. Great as the failure of his life was, the impression he made on literature was extraordinary. Now, near fifty years after his death, his intellectual gifts and the charm of his personal character are constantly referred to. Aubrey de Vere, in Reminiscences just published, says of him, " He is said always to have lived an innocent life, though astray; and he might, perhaps, have been more easily changed into an angel than into a simple strong man." At my first visit to the Lake country, and at every later visit, I heard words of kindness spoken of him from gentlefolk and simple. He could never have had an enemy. Wordsworth himself spoke to me of him with tender regard. The great poet felt for him almost as a son, as did Mrs. Wordsworth; his death affected them deeply. "Let him lie by us," was Wordsworth's request, as arrangement was being made for his burial in the Grasmere churchyard. Hartley Coleridge's one weakness was intemperance. Probably until he went to Oxford the failing hardly showed itself. It is stated that he was of premature birth: perhaps to this fact his weakness of will was in some way due. The undergraduate life of Oxford of eighty years ago presented great temptations. His wonderful gifts of intellect, as well as his oddity of manner, made him a favourite guest at "wine parties." Says Alexander Dyce:—

"He knew that he was expected to talk, and talking was his delight. Leaning his head on one shoulder, turning up his dark bright eyes, and swinging backward and forward on his chair, he would hold forth by the hour (for no one wished to interrupt him) on whatever subject might have been started,—either of literature, politics, or religion,—with an originality of thought, a force of illustration, and a facility and beauty of expression which I question if any man then living, except his father, could have surpassed."

Hartley Coleridge's career at Oxford was distinguished, and he won a Fellowship at Oriel. At the close of his probationary year, he was judged to have forfeited this on the ground mainly of intemperance. Says Derwent Coleridge:—

"The stroke came upon his father with all the aggravations of surprise, as a peal of thunder out of a clear sky. I was with him at the time, and have never seen any human being, before or since, so deeply afflicted; not, as he said, by the temporal consequences of his son's misfortune, heavy as these were, but for the moral offence which it involved."

Thus did what promised to be a brilliant career come to an end. The thirty years that followed, though blameless but for the one infirmity, were years of little connected literary achievement.

"He lived" [as said James Spedding] "the life of a solitary student by the banks of Grasmere and Rydal; dependent, indeed, upon the help of his relations for what small provision he needed, but requiring no more than they could cheerfully supply. Everywhere he was a welcome guest to the high and low, the learned and the ignorant. Here his defects could do least injury to himself or others. His wanderings were but transient eclipses. The shadow past, he came forth as pure and bright as before. Once when some of his friends thought of asking him to visit them in the south of England, the project being mentioned to Wordsworth, he strongly disapproved of it, 'It is far better for him to remain where he is,' said he, 'where everybody knows him, and everybody loves and takes care of him.'"

It seems proper to note here words of Derwent Coleridge in loving extenuation of Hartley's failure and fall.

"My brother's life at school was so blameless, — he seemed and was not merely so simple, tender-hearted, and affectionate, but so truthful, dutiful, and thoughtful, — so religious if not devout, that if his after years had run in a happier course, the faults of his boyhood might well have been overlooked, and nothing seen but that which promised good. An eye sharpened for closer observation may, in the retrospect, descry the shadow of a coming cloud. A certain infirmity of will — the specific evil of his life — had already shown itself. His sensibility was intense, and he had not wherewithal to control it. He could not open a letter without trembling. He shrank from mental pain — he was beyond measure impatient of constraint. He was liable to paroxysms of rage, often the disguise of pity, self-accusation, or other painful emotion, — anger it could hardly be called, — during which he bit his arm or finger violently. It looked like an organic defect — a congenital imperfection. I do not offer this as a sufficient explanation. There are mysteries in our moral nature upon which we can only pause and doubt."

I cannot but note here a remarkable incident of his childhood as showing what one might almost fancy to be the forbearance of a dumb animal in regard to him. He came in one day with the mark of a horse's hoof on his pinafore, and it was found on inquiry that he had been pulling hairs out of a horse's tail; it was easy to imagine — indeed, it was his father's firm belief — that the animal had pushed him back with a gentle shove.

Little need be said of the poetry of Hartley Coleridge; it came near to excellence, and but for the catastrophe of his life might have reached the highest level. His sonnets are probably nearest to those of Wordsworth of all the moderns. His prose is vigorous and of easy flow; the best of it is to be found in his "Biographia Borealis, or Lives of Distinguished Northerns." I quote the following from the "Life of Lord Fairfax": —

"Fifty thousand subjects of one King stood face to face on Marston Moor. The numbers on each side were not far unequal, but never were two hosts, speaking one language, of more dissimilar aspects. The Cavaliers flushed with recent victory, identifying their quarrel with their honour and their love, their loose locks escaping beneath their plumed helmets, glittering in all the martial pride which makes the battle day like a pageant or a festival; and prancing forth with all the grace of gentle blood, as they would make a jest of death; while the spirit-rousing strains of the trumpets made their blood dance and their steeds prick up their ears. The Roundheads, arranged in thick dark masses, their steel caps and high crown hats drawn close over their brows, looking determination, expressing with furrowed foreheads and hard closed lips the inly-working rage which was blown up to furnace heat by the extempore effusions of their preachers, and found vent in the terrible denunciations of the Hebrew Psalms and Prophets. . . . The Royalists regarded their adversaries with that scorn which the gay and high-born always feel or affect for the precise and sour-mannered. The Soldiers of the Covenant looked on their enemies as the enemies of Israel, and considered themselves as the elect and chosen people — a creed which extinguished fear and remorse together. It would be hard to say whether there were more praying on one side or swearing on the other, or which, to a truly Christian ear, had been the most offensive."

One other extract I give from its being of interest as a condemnation, sixty years beforehand, of the Revised Version. The passage is in the "Life of Dr. Jno. Fothergill."

"We doubt whether any new translation, however learned, exact, or truly orthodox will ever appear to English Christians to be the real Bible. The language of the Authorized Version is the perfection of English, and it can never be written again, for the language of prose is one of the few things in which the English have really degenerated. Our tongue has lost its holiness."

I came to know the Rev. Derwent Coleridge through the introduction of his sister immediately after my first visit to her. I was very kindly received, in part from the warm feeling of both the brother and the sister for Henry Reed. Even by letter the sweet nature and refined mind of the American professor had become abundantly manifest, and their regard for him was as though he was of their own blood. Derwent Coleridge was then the Principal of St. Mark's College, Chelsea, a training school for youths who looked to become teachers, or who expected to prepare themselves for Holy Orders. I spent a delightful Sunday there. The chapel service was choral, Mr. Helmore, the chief authority on Plain Song, being the leader. It was the period when interest in choral music had just been awakened. Mr. Coleridge intoned the service and preached the sermon. Afterwards I walked with him in the college grounds — the flowers and shrubbery being in all their June freshness — and we had full and pleasant talk. I felt at once his intellectual brightness, and perceived how wide had been his range of reading and of study. His large dark eyes were fixed upon me as we talked, seeming to look me through. Very soon I perceived how kind he was of heart. At luncheon I first met Mrs. Derwent Coleridge — a beautiful woman of much dignity and grace of manner. In the drawing-room afterward, Mr. Coleridge placing his hands on either side of the head of his daughter Christabel, then about eight years old, said, "This is the best representative of S. T. C. I can show you." I saw the full eyes of the poet and something of the dreamy look of genius. Miss Christabel Coleridge, I must mention, grew up to be a writer of books, novels, and short stories of excellent merit.

I found myself drawing close to Derwent Coleridge; his affectionate nature was manifest to me from the first. The day which I passed with him so happily proved the beginning of a friendship to last until his death, at the end of nearly thirty years. For twenty-five years I had correspondence with him; he had the gift of letter writing common to his race. And in my frequent visits to England I saw him nearly always. I walked with him for days in the Lake country; I visited Rydal Mount with him after Wordsworth's death; and I made visits with him in Devonshire. Of our talk on that first day I remember that he spoke of the group of men who had been around him at Cambridge — Praed (of whom he was the biographer), Moultrie, also a poet (who lived to advanced age), Macaulay, Chauncey Hare Townshend, and Henry Nelson Coleridge. With all of these his intimacy had continued of the closest. He spoke with great respect of our Washington Allston, and repeated a remark of Allston's on his death-bed, concerning Samuel Taylor Coleridge, "He was the greatest man I ever knew, and more sinned against than sinning." I record this because of what I know to have been a saying of Wordsworth's, "I have known many remarkable men, but the most wonderful man I ever knew was Coleridge." I feel compelled to add, however, the following as a deliverance of Wordsworth's, in a moment, let us presume, of impatience, at a late period of Coleridge's life. Wordsworth with Rogers had spent an evening with Coleridge at Highgate. As the two poets walked away together — "I did not altogether understand the latter part of what Coleridge said," was the cautious remark of Rogers. "I did not understand any of it," was Wordsworth's hasty reply. "No more did I!" exclaimed Rogers, doubtless much relieved.

Three years from the date of my first visit to Derwent Coleridge I was again in England. I very soon made my way to him at Chelsea, and was warmly welcomed. He gave me the details of his sister's illness and of her then very recent death. Her disease was cancer. Two years before her medical attendant had become aware of its existence and saw how great was her danger. Hope for her, however, was cherished; but for the last few months the progress of the disease was rapid. She bore her sufferings with remarkable fortitude. There was everything they could desire as to her frame of mind; there was stoicism — rather religious resignation — which was remarkable. Her own words had been, in a letter written a few months before her death: "My great endeavour is not to foreshape the future in particulars, but knowing that my strength always has been equal to my day, when the day is come, to feel that it will be so on to the end, come what may, and that all things, except a reproaching conscience, are 'less dreadful' than they seem." She quoted then from the "White Doe of Rylstone,"—

> "Espouse thy doom at once, and cleave
> To fortitude without reprieve,"

adding, "Wordsworth was more to my opening mind in the way of religious consolation than all books put together except the Bible."

Mr. Coleridge continued, in regard to his sister. She had gone on with her literary labours to the last, and was able to complete the preface to a forthcoming edition of her father's poems in an admirable way. It was wonderful that one so much the victim of disease could have had such clearness of mind. My friend showed deep feeling as he spoke of his own love for his sister; she had been his companion in childhood; he had been her tutor, had taught her Latin; they had wandered together over the beautiful Cumberland region; he had carried her on his back over the streams. He turned his face from me, he could say no more. My talk with him had been in his study. He took me into the drawing-room to see Mrs. Coleridge and his niece, Miss Edith Coleridge, the daughter of Sara Coleridge, the tones of whose voice brought her mother vividly to my mind. I had a most pleasant interview with them all; their manner was natural, though grave; they seemed to look upon me as one who had a right to share with them their sorrow.

Mr. Coleridge accompanied me on my return to London, a walk of two and a half miles. We talked of poetry — Mrs. Browning's, Mr. Coleridge said, with all its beauty, was often imperfect, showed want of finish. Mr. Browning's, though very powerful, was rugged and rough; neither were likely to live, because of their defects. I may add here what I know to have been a remark of Tennyson's. "Browning would do well to add something of beauty to the great things he gives to the world." Mr. Coleridge spoke of the high art and finish of Tennyson's poetry and the splendour of it, spite of the evidence everywhere of great elaboration. His brother Hartley's poems he thought the perfection of spontaneity. As we walked on, he said to me, "You ought to see Mr. Rogers," — then, after reflecting a moment, he added, " I am going to breakfast with him to-morrow, and if you will call at twelve at his house, St. James's Place, I think I shall be able to introduce you to him. You must take your chance," he said, "for he is in extreme old age — eighty-eight — and may not be well enough to see you." I thanked him, and said I was quite willing to take the risk. He said Rogers was perhaps the only man in London who had seen Garrick act. He might have added that Rogers could have talked with Johnson, for at the age of fifteen he had knocked at Johnson's door, Bolt Court, but, his courage failing him, he ran away before it was opened. Mr. Coleridge spoke also of Mr. Henry Crabb Robinson as a notable person whom I ought to see — a link between the present generation and the past (I did see Mr. Robinson both at his house in London and some years afterward in the Lake Region). We stopped at Mr. Moxon's, to whom Mr. Coleridge introduced me, — the publisher of the modern poets, — himself, too, a poet. He owed his position in life to Mr. Rogers, who lent him money and enabled him to advance himself in the world.

I drove the next day to St. James's Place, according to appointment. Mr. Coleridge came to me at once and said he had prepared the way for me with Mr. Rogers, and that I must come in. I was ushered into the famous breakfast room, where I found the venerable man seated in a large armchair, dressed in black and wearing a black cap — his features fine, his look placid, but his face very pale. His pallor, indeed, was what first struck me. He welcomed me and said at once, "You knew my friend Mr. Wordsworth." Mr. Coleridge had told him this. I sat near him and we had a few minutes' talk. But the appearance of great age awes one almost as much as great reputation. Mrs. Derwent Coleridge and her niece, Miss Edith, were there, and another lady and Lord Glenelg. Mr. Coleridge took me round the long room to see the pictures, — Raphael and Rembrandt, Rubens and the Poussins and Claude, the famous Giotto, two heads taken from the burial of St. John — all most interesting. It was a brief pleasure. When I was taking leave of Mr.

Rogers, he held my hand, evidently wishing to say something. He rang for his attendant. "Edward," said he, "when can this gentleman breakfast with me?" "There is no day till Friday," said Edward. Then taking the book in which engagements were noted, Edward corrected himself. "Thursday there is, sir." "Put him down for Thursday," said Mr. Rogers. Then to me. "You'll breakfast with me on Thursday." I bowed my acknowledgments and took my leave.

A further instance of Mr. Coleridge's kindness in giving me sight of a man of distinction in letters was upon my visit to England in 1857, when he invited me to meet Macaulay. I had declined going to dinner as I knew the party had been made up some time before I reached London. I accepted for nine o'clock. When I reached Chelsea I found the ladies already in the drawing-room. Mrs. Coleridge told me to go at once to the dining room — the servant would announce me. Accordingly I was ushered in, was warmly received by Mr. Coleridge, who made room for me next to himself. On his left sat the great man. I looked with keen interest on the pale but handsome countenance. Age was beginning, prematurely, to give signs of its approach, though he was but fifty-seven; his hair was grey, his complexion pallid. But the flash of the eye, the rapid change of expression, the vivacity, the quick movement of the head — all showed a keenness of the mental faculties as yet unimpaired.

The talk at first was about Nollekens — some details

as to his parsimony Macaulay gave. Then he came to speak of art in general; he did not consider the faculty for it a high gift of mind. He told of Francis Grant, an eminent portrait painter to whom Sir George Cornewall Lewis had lately been sitting. The artist, knowing Lewis was an author, thought he ought to make acquaintance with his books that he might talk with him about them. Accordingly he read "The Monk." Lewis, in order to show him it was quite impossible he could have written the novel in question, said it appeared two years before he was born. All who know the author of the "Credibility of Early Roman History" would appreciate his appealing to dates to show he was not also the author of "The Monk." Music, Macaulay also maintained, was an art which it required no high mental power to master; he could conceive of a great musician and composer being a dull man. Mozart, the Raphael of music, he believed was not in other ways remarkable; he was a wonderful performer at six years old. "Now," said Macaulay, "we cannot conceive of any one being a great poet at the age of six — a Shakespeare, for instance." Some one said, "But we know very little about Mozart."

The talk somehow turned to Homer, whether or no the Homeric poems were the product of one mind. Macaulay maintained they were; it was inconceivable that there could have been at the Homeric period more than one poet equal to the production of the "Iliad" and the "Odyssey." He considered there had been six great poets, — Homer, Shakespeare,

Dante, Milton, Sophocles, and Æschylus. Appearing, as these had, at long intervals of time, could it be supposed that at the Homeric age there was more than one with a great endowment of "the vision and the faculty divine?" Then as to the "Iliad" and the "Odyssey" being both the production of Homer — the first being admitted to be, that the other was seemed to follow as a matter of course; it was the test of Paley over again — the finding the watch and the presumption from it of a maker; and in this case there was the watchmaker's shop close by. He urged, too, that Homer was the only great poet who did not, in narrating past events, use the present tense — speak of them as happening at the moment. He quoted a long passage from "Paradise Lost," to show how Milton would fall into the present tense having begun in the past. The fact that, throughout the many thousand lines of Homer, no instance of the sort could be found, seemed to make it clear that but one person produced them. Other quotations Macaulay made from Burns and from old ballads — all showing his wonderful memory. The full flow of the great man's talk was sometimes checked by the wish of others at the table to be heard. Among the persons present were Blore, the architect of Abbotsford (a friend of Sir Walter Scott's), Mr. Helmore, the writer on Plain Song, and Mr. Herbert Coleridge, son of Sara Coleridge, a young man of brilliant promise. The year after his mother's death he had won a double First Class at Oxford. Macaulay and he had the discussion about Homer chiefly to themselves.

Macaulay declined returning to the drawing-room; his carriage was in waiting; he was afraid to make the exertion of going again upstairs. A shortness of breath troubled him. I will add, it was in the following year he was made a peer; and in the year afterward, 1859, he died. A saying of his, perhaps at the dinner table, reported by Mr. Coleridge, was that what troubled us most in life were trifles — insignificant things. "If a hundred megatheriums were let loose on the world, in twenty-four hours they would all be in museums."

I put with this slight record of a meeting with Macaulay the following note of Hawthorne's sight of the same remarkable man in 1856, a year previous to my interview. At a breakfast given by Monckton Milnes, Hawthorne, who had taken in Mrs. Browning, says he had been too much engaged in talk with her to attend much to what was going on elsewhere: —

"But," he adds, "all through breakfast I had been more and more impressed by the aspect of one of the guests sitting next to Milnes. He was a man of large presence, grey haired, but scarcely as yet aged; and his face had a remarkable intelligence, not vivid nor sparkling, but conjoined with great quietude, and if it gleamed or brightened at one time more than another, it was like the sheen over a broad surface at sea. There was a somewhat careless self-possession, large and broad enough to be called dignity; and the more I looked at him, the more I knew that he was a distinguished personage and wondered who. He might have been a Minister of State; only there is not one of them who has any right to such a face and presence. At last — I do not know how the conviction came — but I became aware that it was Macaulay, and began to see some slight resemblances to his portraits. As soon as I knew him I began to listen to his conversation, but he did not talk a great deal — contrary to his usual custom; for I am told he is apt to engross all the talk to himself. Mr. Ticknor and Mr. Palfrey were among his auditors and interlocutors, and as the conversation seemed to turn much on American subjects, he could not well have assumed to talk them down. I am glad to have seen him — a face fit for a scholar, a man of the world, a cultivated intelligence."

Derwent Coleridge had something of his father's power of continuous and most impressive discourse on questions of high import. I listened again and again to deliverances which were revelations to me, as by a sudden flash, of the departed eloquence. I would fain have made record at once of what seemed to me expressions of subtle and ingenious thought. Alas! the effort was beyond me.

I remember Mrs. Derwent Coleridge's telling me of her recollections of her father-in-law in her early married life. She listened with great wonder, she said, to the flow of his discourse; there was no hesitation or pause — on and on it went. The bedroom candles would be brought in and placed on a table near the door of the drawing-room. Coleridge would move slowly across the room, continuing his discourse the while, continuing it as he went through the hall to the staircase, continuing it as he slowly mounted the stairs, until his voice was lost in the distance. Mrs. Coleridge said also that it was her wish and that of Mr. Coleridge, soon after their marriage, that their father should come to live with them. This was proposed to him and he gave consent, but when Mr. and Mrs. Gillman heard of the matter they said it would be impossible for them to let him go. Wherever he went, they would have to go too: they could not be separated from him.

Well does Ernest Coleridge, the son of Derwent and grandson of Samuel Taylor Coleridge, say of this wonderful devotion of the Gillmans: —

"With Coleridge's name and memory must ever be associated the names of James and Anne Gillman. It was beneath the shelter of their friendly roof that he spent the last eighteen years of his life, and it was to their wise and loving care that the comparative fruitfulness and well-being of those years was due. They thought themselves honoured by his presence, and he repaid their devotion with unbounded love and gratitude. Friendship and loving kindness followed Coleridge all the days of his life. What did he not owe to Poole, to Southey, for his noble protection of his family; to the Morgans for their long-tried faithfulness and devotion to himself? But to the Gillmans he owed the 'crown of his cup and garnish of his dish,' a welcome which lasted till the day of his death. Doubtless there were chords in his nature which were struck for the first time by these good people, and in their presence, and by their help he was a new man. But, for all that, their patience must have been inexhaustible, their loyalty unimpeachable, their love indestructible. Such friendship is rare and beautiful and merits a most honourable remembrance."

Ernest Hartley Coleridge, who pays this noble tribute to the Gillmans, has given to the world within the last few years the Letters of his grandfather, and has so done his work as distinctly to raise one's estimate of the great poet.

I am glad to note here the following which I find in the Life of Tennyson.

"Arthur Hallam, after visiting Coleridge at Highgate in 1830, wrote: —

> ' Methought I saw a face whose every line
> Wore the pale cast of thought, a good old man
> Most eloquent, who spoke of things divine.
> Around him youths were gathered, who did scan
> His countenance so grand, and drank
> The sweet sad tears of wisdom.' "

Withdrawn as Samuel Taylor Coleridge was, during almost all his married life, from care of his family, his spirit seemed nevertheless to overshadow them; the three children were bound together by the closest ties, and were at one with each other in their feeling for their father. The household life of Derwent Coleridge I looked upon again and again for five and twenty years. It was a home of peculiar intellectual brightness. Books were everywhere, for Mr. Coleridge's library was of eight thousand volumes, and he read in all languages. After twenty-three years of service as Principal of St. Mark's College, the time for retirement had come; his labour had been great, and it had borne abundant fruit, but rest was needed. He accepted the living of Hanwell, a village about seven miles from Paddington, offered him by the Bishop of

London. The rectory, a spacious, rambling building, ivy-covered, with a beautiful lawn and garden, became his home for sixteen years. The parish work was heavy, but the ladies of his family, among them Miss Edith Coleridge, the daughter of Sara Coleridge, were efficient helpers. But a love of teaching was strong with Derwent Coleridge, and at the suggestion of the Rev. Dr. Coit, Rector of St. Paul's School, Concord, he consented to receive into his family a few American pupils. Four or five St. Paul's boys came to him in this way as a beginning. One of them, Mr. Augustus M. Swift, paid a noble tribute to his "dear master" in an address delivered before St. Paul's School in 1880. In it he says: "I shall always count among the greatest blessings and happiest chances of my life my becoming a member of the family at Hanwell Rectory." Mr. Coleridge's drawing toward America was gratified by receiving in succession under his roof ten or twelve American youths. "We were received," says Mr. Swift, "almost as sons into one of the most intellectual and delightful homes in England." They were hardly pupils; Mr. Coleridge was to them as a father and friend. His talk with them at his table and in his walks with them was in itself instruction. The extent of his knowledge, his amazing linguistic attainments, and his delight in giving forth his acquirements made him an incomparable instructor. Dean Stanley said once at a garden party at Fulham Palace, "You young Yankees may not realize that you are reading with the greatest master of language in England." The refining influence of the ladies of the household was no small part of the good which came to these youths. Mr. Swift tells of his having gone to Miss Edith Coleridge for help over more than one difficult passage in Plato. Mrs. Coleridge, with her native grace and dignity, could further her husband in every way in his work of training. It is a satisfaction to me to record her saying to me, in speaking of these youths, that their charge of them had brought them no anxiety. "We could hardly," she said, "have admitted to our family life English young men of the same age." The gentle and courteous ways of the American youths made them agreeable inmates always. They were constant in their devotion to Mr. Coleridge, were eager to do small services for him, to see that his hat and his coat were in proper trim when he went out. They were all delighted to walk with him, and to listen to his talk. In the drawing-room and at the table they were refined and considerate. There is, perhaps, more of the sense of companionship between young men and their elders in America than in England.

I can scarcely refer much in this paper to letters I received from Derwent Coleridge during a long course of years. In one of them, of the date of 1874, he said finely, "As we grow old we get to be more and more content with home comforts, the family circle, the fireside, the returns of food and rest, and, in my case, books, — the only earthly pursuit for which I should desire the assurance of long life." He lived but six years after thus writing, dying in 1880. He was born, as Macaulay was, with the century. One further extract I will give as it refers to the dear friend to whom I owed my introduction to Sara and to Derwent Coleridge as also to Wordsworth. The awful catastrophe of the loss of the *Arctic*, occurring though it did a lifetime since, awakens the keenest sorrow in remembrance even now. Derwent Coleridge wrote to me:—

"You will know how Professor Reed has been mourned by all who knew him in this country to which he did honour, as assuredly he did to his own; he honoured us, I speak advisedly, by his esteem and regard. He was a golden link between us. His knowledge and fine appreciation of our literature (I speak of our modern literature, for our elder worthies of course we share in common) joined to his very attractive personal qualities, made him, as it were, one of ourselves. Yet he was every inch an American. To me, in particular, his loss is irreparable. Yet, while I say this, I do not forget that I have other friends across the Atlantic whom I shall henceforward value more than ever — for his sake as well as for their own."

I add here an extract from a letter of Thackeray to the late William B. Reed, on the tidings of the awful shipwreck reaching England:—

"I have kept back writing, knowing the powerlessness of consolation, and having I don't know what vague hopes that your brother and Miss Bronson might have been spared. That ghastly struggle over, who would pity any man that departs? It is the survivors one commiserates, of such a good, pious, tender-hearted man as he seemed whom God Almighty has just called back to Himself. He seemed to me to have all the sweet domestic virtues, which make the pang of parting only the more cruel to those who are left behind; but that loss what a gain to him! A just man, summoned by God, for what purpose can he go but to meet the Divine Love and Goodness? I never think about deploring such; and as you and I send for our children, meaning them only love and kindness, how much more Pater Noster? So we say, and weep the beloved ones, whom we lose all the same, with the natural selfish sorrow. I remember quite well my visit to your brother; the pictures in his room which made me see which way his thoughts lay; his sweet melancholy pious manner. That day I saw them here in Dover Street, I don't know whether I told them, but I felt at the time that to hear their very accents affected me somehow; they were just enough American to be national; and where shall I ever hear voices in the world that have spoken more kindly to me? It was like being in your grave, calm, kind, old Philadelphia over again, and behold! now they are to be heard no more!

"I only saw your brother once in London . . . I believe I said I should like to be going with him in the *Arctic*, and we parted with a great deal of kindness, please God, and friendly talk of a future meeting. May it happen one day, for I feel sure he was a just man."

There is, indeed, peculiar fitness in the commemoration of Henry Reed in a paper which seeks to do honour to Samuel Taylor Coleridge and his children. Had Professor Reed been brother in blood of Sara Coleridge, there could not have been more of sympathy with her in mind and heart. The "sweet domestic virtues," to use Thackeray's words, were characteristic of both. With both study, intellectual effort, was the law of their being, and with both there was the keenest desire to quicken the interest of others in literature, and to raise the thoughts of men to noble themes. Henry Reed was acquiring always, and was eager always to impart knowledge. He would tell with fine animation of some gem of literature he had lighted upon, seeking to convey to another the pleasure he himself felt in the new acquisition. With his intense interest in English literature, and his sense of fellowship with modern English writers he was in heart and soul a lover of his country. I recall the delight with which he showed me a note which Wordsworth, at his suggestion, had added to the sonnet "To the Pennsylvanians." The sonnet reflected severely on the people of Pennsylvania because of the suspension or delay of payment for a year or two of interest on the State debt; and the note was to the effect that the reproach was no longer applicable. The note was on the flyleaf of the fifth volume of the last edition of the poems published in the poet's lifetime, and was probably the last sentence composed by Wordsworth for the press.

I have spoken of Henry Reed's personal influence and of his desire to awaken in others the interest in literature which so peculiarly characterized him. As a college professor his influence was invaluable, for nothing gave him more pleasure than helping young inquirers in the path of knowledge. But as he moved in society, and as he appeared now and again as a lecturer, an influence for good always went out from him.

Can I ever forget an interview forty-four years ago, in a late October evening, with one of the survivors of the wreck of the *Arctic?* It was at the house of Professor Reed's brother. The survivor was one of a very small number of persons, who by a desperate effort had saved themselves on a miserably constructed raft. Mr. William B. Reed asked Mr. Morton McMichael and myself to be with him when he received the young man. He was shown photographs of Henry Reed and of his sister-in-law, Miss Bronson. He at once recalled them as having been near him at the table; he had never had speech with them. The last sight he had of them they were sitting quietly, side by side, on the deck, in the awful hours of suspense, when they awaited their doom. For four hours they doubtless knew there was no hope. Discipline on the ship there had been none; firemen and crew, with certain of the passengers, had seized the boats, and had gone most of them only to perish. The few that clung to the raft saw the great ship, with its precious remaining freight, sink beneath the waters.

So perished a true scholar and gentleman. One who was the soul of honour, and whose life was pure from all stain. So long as Wordsworth's verse is valued in this land will the name of Professor Henry Reed be cherished as that of his chief American disciple.

As I began my paper with the mention of the friend to whom in all my life I seem to have owed the most, with his name I will make an end.

THE RIGHT HONOURABLE SIR JOHN TAYLOR COLERIDGE AND LORD COLERIDGE

(LORD CHIEF JUSTICE OF ENGLAND)

SIR JOHN TAYLOR COLERIDGE AND LORD COLERIDGE

(LORD CHIEF JUSTICE OF ENGLAND)

THE father and son, whose names I have placed together, figure to me a friendship which I count as among the choicest gains of my life. At my visit to England, in 1855, I had introduction to each, and from each there came prompt and cordial response. They made at that time one household, both in London and at Ottery St. Mary, Devon. John Duke Coleridge, the son, I saw first. Our real knowledge of each other began in a walk from his chambers in the Temple, northward for a mile or more, by Regent Street to All Saint's Church, Margaret Street, a very interesting work of Butterfield's, then nearing completion. I felt instantly at one with my new friend. Life was bright with promise before him; success had already come in his profession, and his future was assured. But it was plain that his supreme love was for literature. A brilliant career at Oxford, and his family traditions, had made intellectual things his chief interest. It was plain to me that he had genius, and that his memory was remarkable, and that he had been an omnivorous reader. Our best American writers were dear to him, and I especially remember his glowing words as to Hawthorne; they brought to me a feeling of self-reproach, for I had hardly at that time taken the full measure of the author of the "Scarlet Letter." But in that first conversation it was the genius of Burke on which my friend dwelt with especial animation; his writings he considered superior to those of any man of his time. It showed, I thought, my friend's fine instinct that at the outset of his own career he should have this devotion to one, who, as philosopher, statesman, scholar, figures to us all excellence as an upholder of Constitutional Government.

The object of our walk was to visit, as I have said, a church in which Coleridge took a deep interest, because of his friendship for Butterfield, the architect, and his admiration for his genius. It was a church of red and black brick, the windows having brown stone mullions and arches, the spire covered with slate. The chief merit seemed to me the skilful way in which the architect had made use of all the ground he had — ordinary building lots in a street of dwelling houses. Tower, nave, and choir were sideways with the street, parish buildings, with gables on the street front at either end of the church lot, leaving space between for the Gothic gateway or portal, and an opening sufficient to disclose the nave windows and the windows of the clerestory. The interior was unfinished, but already there was rich adornment of marbles and alabaster. There could be no east window, but the wall which was in place of it was to be covered with frescoes by Dyce. One, of the Ascension, was already finished. We climbed the long ladder to the platform in front of it; even a near view showed it to be a work of great beauty. The great west window — the chief light of the church — is by Gerente of Paris. The cost of the church up to that time had been £26,000, of which Mr. Beresford Hope had given £5000, Mr. Tritton, a banker, had given the remainder, but his name was for some years unknown. The church for a long time was incorrectly spoken of as Mr. Hope's.

In this year, 1855, the Oxford Movement still had the strongest hold on men who, like Coleridge, had, during their University career, been under its full influence. He spoke of Newman's sermons at St. Mary's, and described the effect produced on the young men who listened; he told of their standing on either side of the path by which the preacher walked as he went from the pulpit, eager to get a near view of his striking face. It was about the time of the closing of Coleridge's Oxford career (1845) that Newman left the Church of England. In 1851 Manning and James Hope (afterward Hope-Scott) went over. It is of this period that Gladstone has spoken as "eminently the time of secessions. Then departed from us James Hope, who may with little exaggeration be called the flower of his generation. The Papal Brief, very closely followed by the Gorham Judgment, was a powerful cause of a blast which swept away, to their own great detriment as well as ours, a large portion of our most learned, select, and devoted clergy." I give this as a somewhat remarkable deliverance of Gladstone, and also as showing what was the atmosphere in the years immediately before the time at which my acquaintance with John Coleridge began.

My first sight of Sir John Taylor Coleridge, better known as Mr. Justice Coleridge, was at dinner a few days after my first meeting with John Duke Coleridge. This was at Park Crescent, the joint home of father and son. The party was eighteen; but the guests of chief interest to me were a young Hindoo and his wife, who were announced as Mr. and Mrs. Tangar. Judge Coleridge introduced me immediately. I said, "You are from the East and I from the West." The Hindoo's reply was, "Sir, England and America and Australia will divide the globe." How often in the more than forty years which have followed has this remark occurred to me; and now, in 1898, has come the practical alliance between England and America which presages a rapid increase in the progress of English civilization over the earth.

My Hindoo friend asked me questions about America, showing wide range of reading; he wished to know whether our Judge Story was a Unitarian. It was perhaps natural that a great writer on Constitutional Government should be of interest to a student; the young man was a graduate of King William's College, Calcutta. He was small, narrow-chested, with straight black hair, and large lustrous eyes. His dress was a black tunic, and he wore a red scarf round his neck. His wife was small and black haired; she wore a dress of green silk, embroidered with gold. As she sat by Judge Coleridge — as he and this young Hindoo woman sat side by side in the midst of a brilliant company — I thought what a contrast they presented; they figured to me the conquering race and the subject one, and the superiority of our own race as to bodily development was strikingly shown. The Judge's face charmed me from the first — a peculiar benignity was expressed, the sweetest courtesy. His hair was grey, but his complexion clear; the look of health which is so much more the characteristic of the English than it is of ourselves. He wore a ruffled shirt — the last I have known of this old-time badge of a gentleman. Alas! that it is no more seen. I remember of the after-dinner talk, Sir Cornewall Lewis's "Credibility of Early Roman History" being a subject, John Coleridge asked, had any one at the table ever read that book? The Hindoo was the only one who answered, he had read it. The English of the young man was perfect; he was fluent, but his language was measured and stately, almost that of books. I may note one of his remarks, though it was not made to myself — an Oriental view of marriage. Referring to his wife, he said with dignity, " I was under obligation to her father, and I married his daughter!"

I saw no more of father or son in that year, 1855. Two years later I enjoyed their joint hospitality, and was further witness to their true companionship of heart and mind. They had kept alive the same love of literature with all their devotion to the profession in which each had achieved such great success. With each, too, there was deep interest in whatever concerned the Church of England. Sir John had been the lifelong friend of Keble, and the son was of the intellectual following of Newman — a feeling which mastered him all his years. Father and son, while manifesting the utmost affection each for the other, argued together as if they were of equal age. Sir John, it will be remembered, had, early in his career, for a short time been editor of the *Quarterly Review*. I refer to this as showing the bent of his mind toward literature as the possible work of his life. His brother, Henry Nelson Coleridge, was another instance of high literary attainment, united to eminence in the profession of the law.

At a dinner in Park Crescent, in 1857, I met Dean Milman and Dr. Hawtrey, Provost of Eton. Sir John told me that these two with himself had been contemporaries at Eton, and, I think, at Oxford. The Dean was a striking personality, small, bent with rheumatism, swarthy of complexion, with bright piercing eyes. In his knee-breeches and his black silk stockings, and his apron, and his great shoe-buckles, he seemed the very pattern of a scholar and a high ecclesiastic. I was opposite to him at table. He talked to me of Panizzi and the struggle it had cost to get him elected Librarian of the British Museum; he was opposed because of his being a foreigner. The Dean had taken the strongest interest in the contest. Already great good had come from the election. The great reading room, the Dean said, was Panizzi's suggestion, the finest single room in Europe, accommodation for three hundred readers, costing £170,000. He complained, half seriously, of the stream of old books, priceless in value, that was now going across the Atlantic, to the great loss of English scholars — books that would never come back. He mentioned as something for me, as an American, to carry away, that he had been at a dinner lately at which there had been present the Chancellor of the Exchequer, Cornewall Lewis, and an ex-Chancellor, Gladstone; and Lord Aberdeen, an ex-Prime Minister, was to have been present, and the occasion of the dinner was that there might be a discussion about Homer. Judge Coleridge supplemented this by saying that pages upon pages of criticism of Homer had been passing lately between Cornewall Lewis and Gladstone, until the former's Budget as Chancellor of the Exchequer came out. Then, said Sir John, Gladstone's knife was at Lewis's throat in a moment.

At another dinner at Judge Coleridge's I met Mr. Butterfield, the distinguished architect of whom I have already spoken. It was curious to me to hear the account which he and John Coleridge gave of the close of the remarkable case in the Court of Queen's Bench in which Dr. Achilli sued Dr. John Henry Newman for having published a defamatory libel. The verdict of the jury had been for the plaintiff — the sentence was a fine of £300. The judgment was delivered by Mr. Justice Coleridge, and was of the nature of a reprimand. The court room was crowded, the deepest interest was felt in the case all over England, and almost to a like extent in this country. Dr. Achilli, an ex-Catholic priest, had been delivering addresses in England denouncing the Church of Rome. On his arriving in Birmingham Dr. Newman published in a newspaper of the city, in great detail, a statement of wicked and loathsome deeds of Achilli, specifying places in Italy and giving dates. The general opinion was that the story thus published was true, and in consequence Dr. Achilli's crusade came soon to an end. All that was left to him was to sue. Dr. Newman was then put to great expense in bringing on witnesses, from Italy and elsewhere. Unfortunately for him evidence in support of many of the charges could not be produced; hence the verdict. The two young men, John Coleridge and his friend, listened with intense interest to the carefully considered, trenchant, and at the same time tender and touching words from the Bench — feeling for the Judge, as well as for the ecclesiastic who was receiving sentence, almost the same reverence and affection. They told me of the half-smile on the lips of Newman as he received the admonition of the Judge, and then, as the final words came, his promptly paying the £300, and, with certain of his friends, going his way.

But however serene might have been Newman's bearing at the close of this passage of his life, we know what the affair had been to him from his dedication of his "Discourses on University Education," published in 1854, "To the Friends and Benefactors who by their prayers and munificent alms had broken for him the stress of a great anxiety."

There are few things in literature or in the history of religious opinion more striking than this judgment of Sir John Coleridge in pronouncing the sentence of the Court of Queen's Bench on Dr. Newman for the misdemeanour of having published a defamatory libel reflecting on Dr. Achilli. Judge and defendant had met early in the race of life; each had won high distinction; and each through all divergence of opinion had retained deep respect for the other. They met now in a court of justice, the one to be condemned by the other. There is a tone of deep tenderness in the Judge's words, while there is no shrinking from duty in his comment on the misdemeanour of which the defendant had been convicted. At the outset there is the very careful statement, that in the opinion of every member of the court Dr. Newman had honestly believed the allegations he had made against Dr. Achilli. But it was then very clearly stated that proof had not been produced for some of the gravest of the charges. There was reproof, moreover, for what seemed the tone in which the allegations were made.

"A spirit of ferocious merriment, partly in triumph, partly in exultation over the unhappy man whose foul offences you were producing before your hearers." "It is sad," Judge

Coleridge continues, "to see that speaking of the Reformed Church you should begin with such a sentence as this — 'In the midst of outrages such as these, my brethren of the Oratory, wiping its mouth and clasping its hands, and turning up its eyes, it trudges to the town hall to hear Dr. Achilli expose the Inquisition.'"

Yet Judge Coleridge refers to writings which had proceeded from the pen of Dr. Newman while he was a member of the Church of England, in which, —

"Great as was their ability, sound as was their doctrine, urgent as they were in teaching holiness of life, nothing was more remarkable than the tenderness and gentleness of spirit that pervaded the whole."

Some of the final words of the judgment were as follows : —

"Firmly attached as I am to the Church of England in which I have lived and in which I hope to die, yet there is nothing in my mind on seeing you now before me but the deepest regret. I can hardly expect that you will take in good part many of the observations I have felt it my duty to make. Suffer me, however, to say one or two words more. The great controversy between the churches will go on, we know not, through God's pleasure, how long. Whether, henceforward, you will take any part in it or not, it will be for you to determine, but I think the pages before you should give you this warning, upon calm consideration, that if you again engage in this controversy, you should engage in it neither personally nor bitterly. The best road to unity is by increase of holiness of life."

John Coleridge, the son, had always an immense drawing to Newman. Better for him it would have been had Keble, his father's friend, been more the guide of his life. In a striking letter contributed by John Coleridge to his father's Memoir of Keble, he speaks of a walk he took with the poet, " He enjoying the sunshine and the air, and I the kindness, perhaps I may presume to say the affection which he showed me then, as always, and which I recall always with a sense of self-reproach." Later on in this letter John Coleridge says: —

"Our conversation fell upon Charles I. with regard to whose truth and honour I had used some expressions in a review, which had, as I heard, displeased him. I referred to this, and he said it was true. I replied that I was very sorry to displease him by anything I said or thought, adding that a man could but do his best to form an honest opinion upon historical evidence, and, if he had to speak, to express that opinion. On this, he said, I remember, with a tenderness and humility not only most touching, but to me most embarrassing, that 'it might be so; what was he to judge of other men; he was old, and things were now looked at very differently; that he knew he had many things to unlearn, and to learn afresh, and that I must not mind what he had said, for that, in truth, belief in the heroes of his youth had become a part of him.'"

I give this as showing what was John Coleridge's reverence of feeling toward his father's friend. When he first went to Oxford Keble was no longer in residence there, and the Newman influence was at its height. The young undergraduate came under the spell of that marvellous rhetoric; he remained under it in a sense for all his life. Coleridge, the father, was of the same entirely religious mind as Keble, whose "Christian Year" shows a devout feeling akin to that of St. Augustine or St. Bernard.

I spent the summer of 1860 in England. John Coleridge had thriven greatly by that time, and had his own establishment in London, his father having retired from the Bench on his pension after twenty-five years of service; he had been sworn in, moreover, of the Privy Council; Heath's Court, Ottery St. Mary, being thenceforth his only home. John, the son, told me of his own great success at the bar; he said he had become the fashion, and retainers were flowing in. So rapidly, indeed, had his reputation risen that he had been offered the Chief Justiceship of Calcutta, at a salary of £8000, with a retiring pension after ten years of service of £3000. Very wisely he had declined this, though he could not have foreseen that in fifteen or eighteen years he was to be Lord Chief Justice of England. In speaking to me of the beginning of his career he said that for the few years that followed his first admission to the bar he had taken charge of the literary department of the *Guardian*, of which his friend Mountague Bernard was the editor. A sharp controversy with Charles Kingsley had arisen because of a review by Coleridge of "Yeast." Frederick Maurice had come to the defence of Kingsley, and it became a fierce passage at arms, leaving, as I know, bitter memories on both sides. The *Guardian* rose rapidly in circulation and influence. John Coleridge's connection with it, no doubt, gave him increased facility as a writer. But his profession soon claimed him. Never, however, did his interest in matters of literature suffer abatement. It could be said of him eminently that he had genius. His brilliant power of talk made him a delight to dinner-table guests at his own house or elsewhere. It was at his table in 1860 that I first met Matthew Arnold. A very brilliant person was Arnold in those days, but of sweet and winning manner; as an especial mark of eminence he was singularly urbane and gracious. Exquisite was he in dress, and his black hair and fine eyes, and his easy bearing and pleasant talk, made him altogether fascinating. The friendship between him and Coleridge was of the closest: it was but the continuing of the almost brotherhood of Mr. Justice Coleridge and Dr. Arnold. One remark of Matthew Arnold at this first meeting I recall. Coleridge had said to his wife from his end of the table, referring to the *Guardian* period, "We were very poor in those days, J——" "Yes, we were," was the quick reply. "Ah," said Arnold, "you talk of having been poor, when at any time you could sit down and in an hour write an article for the *Guardian* for which you would get your ten pounds. Now it costs me a great deal of trouble to write." I have often thought of this in reading the smoothly flowing sentences of Arnold; their very simplicity showing that infinite pains had been bestowed upon them.

With Arnold and with Coleridge there was a peculiar interest in Americans, an eagerness to learn what they could of the civilization across the sea. Coleridge told me of his receiving a copy of Arnold's first published volume of poems — they were anonymous poems by " A." Meeting Arnold soon afterward Coleridge spoke of having received such a volume, — " Ah, yes," said Arnold, " by an American." I mentioned this half seriously at a dinner given to Arnold in Philadelphia, as showing how desirous our distinguished guest had been from a very early period of life to identify himself with our great country!

My first visit to Heath's Court, Ottery St. Mary, was in this year, 1860. I had full opportunity then of observing how close was the friendship, so to call it, of father and son. The fact that the father had been of high distinction as a judge, and that the son was midway in his brilliant career at the bar, made them companions in mind to a remarkable degree. Each was proud of the other. Judge Coleridge was of rare sweetness and nobleness of character, of great refinement of mind, of great literary acquirement, and of an interest in literature which had never flagged in all his professional career. Before his work at the bar had engrossed him he was, as I have said, for a year or two editor of the *Quarterly Review*. Southey helped to obtain his appointment to this position, and expressed his satisfaction at it, for the reason especially that kindlier reference to American writers was thenceforth assured. But John Taylor Coleridge had peculiar qualification for the Bench, and in the roll of English judges there is no more honourable name.

It was a joy to me to be under his roof, and every hour of his society was a delight. Endless was the talk that went on. I could not but be amused at the vehemence with which the son would utter opinions startling to the father; there would be gentle and mild remonstrance, then a further burst from my impetuous friend, but in all the warmth of discussion there was never a sign of any straining of affection.

I was not in England between 1860 and 1865. I had active correspondence, however, in that interval with John Coleridge, and some interchange of letters with his father. Writing under the date of May, 1861, Sir John says:—

"John's progress is all I could have wished — much more than I could have hoped. All through his younger days, at school, at college, and in training, for the law, I used to fancy he was never doing himself justice, always suffering in the next stage from want of due preparation in the one preceding. But he has gone beyond my hopes in the present portion of his career: nothing but doubts as to his bodily strength stand between him and the highest place; and then the older he gets, and the greater, I find him the more loving and considerate."

Sir John speaks in the same letter of his brother-in-law, Sir John Patteson, the father of the Bishop, John Coleridge Patteson:—

"He is dying," he says, "of a hopeless disease, and he knows it, and you could scarcely contemplate a voyage to England with more calmness, hope, and resignation than he does his death and passage to another world. Yet there is not a grain of presumption. . . . He knows whom he has served and in whom he has trusted all his life long. From Eton," he adds, "up to this hour we have lived in unbroken and close intimacy, of the same profession, and on the same Bench, — my brother by marriage, and always living near to each other since we left college, you may fancy what it is to me at seventy-one to part with him." Sir John goes on to say, "I have just lost my nephew, Herbert Coleridge, grandson of the poet, and only son of Henry Nelson and Sara Coleridge. They all sleep side by side, and there could hardly be another plot of ground in which so much genius, learning, and goodness sleep. Herbert Coleridge, owing to circumstances, used to look up to me as what he called his father and mother, and I certainly loved him as my own child."

There is so much that is worth dwelling on in regard to the Coleridge race that I may here insert one or two passages from a paper in *Macmillan's Magazine* of November, 1861, by John, Duke Coleridge on his cousin Herbert. Henry Nelson Coleridge, the father, editor of the works of Samuel Taylor Coleridge, is first spoken of — a person whose intellectual and social qualities were of the highest order — as editor of the *Literary Remains*, the chief contributor to the permanent fame of the poet-philosopher. Sara Coleridge, Herbert's mother, her nephew refers to with great warmth of affection. Her scholarship and wide and varied learning he dwells on, and then adds: —

"And when to these endowments there is added great power of conversation and remarkable personal beauty, it is easy to understand the striking impression she made on the society wherein her lot was cast. Those, however, who only saw her in society could not know how tender and feminine a nature lay under that bright and attractive exterior."

John Coleridge tells in his paper the story of his cousin's achievement in his short life, and then speaks of the strong impression of power and promise he made upon all who knew him well.

"They think," he says, "with a certain sad regret of his unfulfilled renown. They will treasure the memory of his warm heart and affectionate disposition; of his character, temper softened from any harshness, and refined and purified from any selfishness into considerate and almost tender gentleness, by the affliction which he took, as becomes a Christian to take, what it pleases God to send; of his religion, sincere and deep, — thoughtful, as might be expected in the grandson and profound admirer of Samuel T. Coleridge, — but remarkably free from pretence or display; of a man careless, perhaps too careless, about general society and ordinary acquaintance, but giving his whole heart where he gave it at all, and giving it steadfastly."

Returning to my correspondence with Sir John Coleridge, he speaks, under date of September, 1863, of a family reunion they had had at Heath's Court, "For a few days," he says "we had our Jesuit son with us, after some years' absence, and very happy we were together, he as gentle, as natural, as affectionate, as full of old recollections as ever." This was the only reference Sir John ever made either by letter or in conversation to one of the sorrows of his life, — the going away of his second son Henry from the Church of England, — a defection due to the influence of Newman, or rather to the combined influence of certain of the Oxford writers when the Movement was in its period of highest activity. Father Coleridge, as he became, was highly prized in the Roman Communion during the more than thirty years that followed his change; he was editor for many years of the Catholic magazine, *The Month.*

During the period of our war, I had important letters from Sir John; they were admirable in their expression of sympathy with the people of the North, though there were now and then criticisms of our action, and expressions of fear as to the possibility of our success. There was the further foreboding that the restoration of the old Union would be impracticable even in the event of our complete military triumph. Englishmen were slow to realize the strength which the cause of the North had in the leadership of Lincoln. In an interview I had with Mr. Gladstone in March, 1865, I drew from him an admission of the great qualities of Lincoln; but this was just as the war was closing.

In 1867 I made my second visit to Heath's Court. Sir John welcomed me with sweet cordiality. I was more than ever impressed with his simple, natural manner, and the courtesy which influenced every word and action. John Coleridge arrived after I did, from a house he had taken for a time on Dartmoor. Welcomes were said and then followed animated talk on events of the day, and again I looked on at the companionship which was that of the closest friendship between father and son. John was by this time in Parliament, being member for Exeter. I may note as one of the records of the days of my visit my friend's comment on Gladstone from his House of Commons experience of him. (I am writing, it will be remembered, of a period more than thirty years ago.) My friend considered him wanting in worldly wisdom, deficient in skill as a political leader. Mrs. Gladstone, he said, gave him no help in keeping the party together. The two were not to be named with Lord and Lady Palmerston in tact and sagacity as to such management. John Coleridge considered the Liberal Party irretrievably broken up by reason of this imperfection in Gladstone's temperament. Bright, he said, was incontestably the leading mind in the House as to the Reform legislation. John Stuart Mill my friend spoke of with warmth of admiration. "I cannot tell you," he said, "the satisfaction it is to me to sit next him as I do in the House." Mill's shy refined ways attracted him; his quiet humour he dwelt on. Once Mill had to take notice of the frequent quotations members on the opposite side made from his writings in order, really, to badger him. Of course they were passages which these men had seen as extracts and had committed. Mill said, "I feel greatly the compliment paid me by these frequent quotations: it is, perhaps, not good for me to be thus referred to, yet my vanity is kept down by what becomes more and more obvious to me, that honourable gentlemen who thus quote me have really read *no other portions of my writings.*" The House roared at this clever turn, so discomfiting to Mill's assailants.

Of Sir John Coleridge's conversation I have the record of what he told me of Nassau Senior, who was with him at Eton and afterward at Oxford. Senior was of excellent parts, but he professed to care nothing for university honours, said a degree was all he wanted, and accordingly he was idle, but cutting the thing rather too close, he was plucked. This being very mortifying to him he put himself under Whately to be coached. His friends believed in him, and a bet, the curious one of those wine-drinking days, "A rump and a dozen," (a rump steak and a dozen of port) was made that he would still take honours. Sure enough, in six months he had won a place in the first class. He went to the bar afterward and was appointed a Master in Chancery. Subsequently his particular office was abolished, but his salary was continued as a pension. So for the rest of his life he had his £2000 a year with nothing to do. He wasted no moment of his time, however, and as he had to travel a good deal in search of health he kept careful journals, chiefly notes of the talk of leading men. His way was, after a conversation with any one, for instance, with Guizot, to write out what had been said and then submit to Guizot the record, and ask him for his approval of it. Then he would go, perhaps, to Thiers, and say, "Here is what Guizot thinks, what comment have you to make." Of coursé men, knowing they were to be reported, would talk in a less simple, natural way than otherwise; but, as confidence was felt in Senior, things of great importance were said to him. He was received everywhere; he was known to be a very close friend of De Tocqueville, and this gave him distinction in France. It was universally known that at a proper time the Journals would be published. Sir John had seen them and could bear witness to their extraordinary interest.

The Journals of Nassau Senior began to be published some two years after the date of this conversation. They are most valuable as records of the opinions of leading men in all the countries visited. The picture of Egypt of the date of 1856, when the Suez Canal was first projected, is very striking, from the opportunity given for comparison with the beneficent change which has come with the English occupation. It is the glory of England that this benefit has been wrought: well is it for us in America, at the moment when we are undertaking the responsibilities of similar rule, that so noble an example is before us. Hardly since the world began has greater good come to a subject race. India as a whole is a like example, but Egypt, with its ten millions of people is an object lesson from which it is impossible to turn aside.

My last sight of dear Sir John Coleridge was as he gave me his blessing at the end of my visit of 1867.

At a short visit to England of 1869, I dined with William Edward Forster at the Reform Club to meet

Sir John Duke Coleridge, as he had then become, having been knighted on his appointment as Solicitor General. Mr. Forster had tried to get his brother-in-law, Matthew Arnold, also, but telegrams had failed to reach him. The chief subject of talk at this pleasant dinner was the Alabama controversy, which was then at its height. I was put to it to defend our American view against men of such distinction. I could only dwell on the danger to England of her allowing it to stand as a precedent that neutrals could allow warships to go out to prey upon the commerce of belligerents — rather that neutrals were not to be held to account if ships fitted for war escaped from their ports. Forster, I remember, rejected utterly what had been urged in America by Mr. Sumner and others, that England was to be held answerable for the standing given to the Southern cruisers by the acknowledgment of the South as belligerents. He said that he had himself urged on Lord Palmerston's Government this acknowledgment, thinking it necessary on the ground of humanity. I may add that three years later came the settlement known as the Geneva Arbitration, and the payment by England of three millions sterling as compensation to us for the ravages of the Alabama.

Forster and Coleridge, at the time of this Reform Club dinner, were both members of the first Gladstone Government, and were each of great promise of distinction. I saw in Coleridge the fine result of university training founded on unmistakable genius, and in Forster the instinct of rule, rather the quiet inward feeling that the highest position might one day be his. Through all I perceived in Forster an absolute devotion to his country, with a supreme desire for the advancement of its best interests. As I looked on at the intercourse of these gifted men I perceived that Coleridge was fully conscious of Forster's power: he deferred to him, almost unconsciously, as to one who was born to rule.

Four years passed before I again saw Sir John Duke Coleridge. During this period his name had been much in the mouths of people from his having been counsel of the Tichborne family in their famous case. His speech for the defence occupied some twenty days, covering two whole sides of the *Times* daily — perhaps the longest speech on record in a jury trial. His cross-examination of the claimant had lasted fourteen days; that it should have lasted so long was evidence of the cunning and audacity of the claimant. Strange that such a man should have had his upholders among people of education! Coleridge said to me, "Sir Roger Tichborne, who disappeared at the age of seventeen was a proficient in music; when I handed the claimant a music-book, and he held it *upside down*, I thought no further evidence was needed of his being an ignorant pretender." For almost a year the English Courts were occupied with the case, first with the suit brought by the man Orton (the claimant) and then by his trial for perjury. I read almost the whole of Coleridge's speech, as the numbers of the *Times* came here, and found it of remarkable interest. While the case was in progress Coleridge became Attorney General. In 1874, as one of the last acts of the Gladstone Government, which ended in that year, he was made Lord Chief Justice of the Common Pleas and raised to the peerage, becoming Baron Coleridge of Ottery St. Mary. On the death of Sir Alexander Cockburn in the following year, he became Lord Chief Justice of England.

Lord Selborne in " Memorials Personal and Political " (I. 324), writes: —

"In 1874, Sir John Duke Coleridge received with a peerage, the promotion due, not only to his official position and his great powers and services, but to the self-denial with which, when no such prospect was in view, he had declined the Mastership of the Rolls. I rejoiced that his father, my constant friend, then in his eighty-fourth year, should have lived to see these crowning honours of the intellectual eminence, which had descended in that remarkable family through three generations."

Sir John Coleridge's health had begun to fail during the years of his son's rapid advancement. It was at this time that he wrote the " Life of Keble " — a book which was almost of the nature of an autobiography, as he told of the closeness of his personal union with the subject of his Memoir. It remains as a model of sympathetic biography, and as showing that in the busiest career there is abundant opportunity for uplifted thought.

Sir John Coleridge, as I know from Lord Coleridge,

declined a peerage which was offered him by Mr. Gladstone. One of his reasons was that as he had never been in the House of Commons he was without the parliamentary experience needed for debating in the House of Lords. But he was more influenced, doubtless, by unwillingness to exchange the quiet of his Devonshire home for the turmoil of London. It was granted him to decline slowly, preserving his faculties to the last, dying in 1876 at the age of eighty-six. From the letter I wrote to Lord Coleridge on this news reaching me I extract as follows:—

" . . . The sweet graciousness of his hospitality first of all charmed me and then I came to see on what a deep feeling of religious thoughtfulness his character rested. I feel it to be one of the chief blessings of my life to have known him. It was indeed a great privilege to have familiar intercourse with one who had taken part in such important matters — one whose gifts of mind and whose high cultivation, and whose purity of thought made him a guide and example. All this comes to my mind as I think of his long life passed in honour, and of his sweet and noble presence. Even to me the world seems other than it was now that he is gone. What then must be your feeling! I know well what the love was between you — how that besides the affection that was natural, there was deep respect each for the other, and, as one might say, a most tender friendship. What joy for you that your father lived to witness your own high advancement! What joy for you that his help and guidance remained to you so long beyond the time when such strength is ordinarily vouchsafed! But while to you and to all belonging to him he has been thus so priceless a blessing, in another sense he has been to all who have drawn near to him a benefactor of the mind and heart."

Coleridge replied:—

"... I knew that you, and some other brothers across the water, would feel with us and for us in our sorrow—a very great and indeed at times almost a crushing sorrow it is. I think my father was the most beautiful character I ever knew. Looking back on fifty years of life, I really cannot recollect one single thing in which, now, I think my father did or said wrong. His gentleness, tenderness never failed to any one, or under any circumstances, and yet he was as brave and manly a man as ever lived. He never shrank from doing an act or saying a thing, which he thought right, because it might give offence. He was, all his life, the most liberal of Conservatives, and was constantly shocking his High Church Tory friends, by doing and saying things which they could not understand, but which he felt it right to do and say, though it pained *him* to pain *them*. It is quite indescribable the loss he is to me, and even more to my dear sister who lived with him. To her he was the very centre of her life, and her life seems torn up by the roots. To me he was the one person to whom I could turn for sympathy and counsel in all my public and professional life, and never did he fail me: so that a large portion of my life must now needs be lonely, and it is not easy to measure the sadness which this brings with it. To be always looking down instead of looking up, as hitherto I have done all my life, is a solemn change. Our loss had every comfort which such a loss can have; the kindness of friends, the respect and regard shown him by the whole county as evidenced in his funeral are great comforts, no doubt; and the thought that he was fit to go and did not wish to stay is, perhaps, the greatest of all. He did not suffer much pain, not even in the very last illness, but he was weak and weary: his journal shows that life was a sorrow to him, and certainly he was taken when no one who really loved him could wish that he should be left. All this is comforting, and I pray God it may be more so—but *my father is dead.*"

In 1878 a great blow fell upon Lord Coleridge in the death of his wife. His letter in reply to my words of sympathy is an expression of deepest grief, from which I hardly feel that I can quote; it showed what the companionship was that had come to an end. Lady Coleridge was distinctly of genius as an artist. Her first work was in miniature painting; later on she drew, in crayon, life-size portraits, of which the most notable were of her father-in-law, Sir John Coleridge, Cardinal Newman, and Lord Coleridge. These are of remarkable excellence. She drew also for the staircase at Sussex Square — Lord Coleridge's London residence — copies from Michael Angelo, — reproductions in crayon, which, under great sheets of glass, are very striking.

In the Abbey Church of St. Mary Ottery is the memorial by Lord Coleridge of his wife, — a recumbent effigy of singular beauty; at the base is this inscription: —

> "To the fair and tender memory of
> Jane Fortescue, Baroness Coleridge,
> her husband dedicates this marble,
> thankful for his happiness, sorrowing for
> his loss, hoping steadfastly, through
> God's mercy, to meet her when the
> night is passed, in the perfect and
> unending day."

Five years after this bereavement of Lord Coleridge, he made a visit to America. He came in 1838 at the invitation of the Bar Association of New York. The event was important, seeing that he was the highest English official that had ever crossed the Atlantic. His only superior was the Lord Chancellor, but his coming was not to be thought of, considering his solemn charge of the Great Seal. When Lord Brougham was Chancellor, he was meditating a trip to the Rhine, but found he would be unable to leave England unless he placed the Great Seal in commission. The cost of this would have been £1400. I remember hearing Mr. Forster, then a Cabinet Minister, ask in a cheerful way at his own table whether the Lord Chancellor slept with the Great Seal.

The legal profession, wherever Lord Coleridge went in the United States, received him with great distinction. He figured to them the source and centre of their knowledge. He charmed every one by his urbanity, by the silver tones of his voice, by his delightful talk, and his great store of knowledge. Mr. G. W. Russell, a man of great experience of English society, has recently said:—

"I had an almost fanatical admiration for Lord Coleridge's genius; in many of the qualities which make an agreeable talker he was unsurpassed. Every one who heard him at the Bar or on the Bench, must recall that silvery voice, and that perfect elocution, which prompted a competent judge of such matters to say, 'I should enjoy listening to Coleridge if he only read out a page of Bradshaw.' To these gifts were added an immense store of varied knowledge, a genuine enthusiasm for whatever is beautiful in literature or art, an inexhaustible copiousness of anecdote, and a happy knack of exact yet not offensive mimicry. All this, at a dinner table was delightful; and everything derived a double zest from the exquisite precision of English in which it was conveyed."

Lord Coleridge, I am glad to say, was very favourably impressed with the leading lawyers and judges whom he met in the United States. In the West especially, he came to know men who seemed to him of real distinction. Judge Drummond, of Chicago, I remember, impressed him greatly. He had grateful recollection always of the kindness that had been shown him. "I should be afraid to go again," he said, "lest I should be found out." He said also, writing eight years after his visit, "I am never tired of thinking of the noble Americans I met, and whom I shall never see again." It is curious to note, as showing a state of things which we can hope has passed away, that an army officer was detailed by our Government to accompany Lord Coleridge in his journeyings, and detectives also were at hand for his protection. It was the time when Irish outrages were of constant occurrence. It was the wish of his own Government that he should not visit Canada; they thought the danger would be greater there than in the United States. I remember telling him that if a murderous attack were made upon him, there might be consolation in the thought that in America and in England indignation would be so great as to put an end forever to Irish violence. He refused to admit there would be any comfort in this consideration. "You would prefer," I said, "that the risk should be taken by a minor canon?" reminding him of a story of his father's of a meeting with Sydney Smith. A bishop who was present had just finished the rebuilding of his palace, and was doubtful whether it would be safe to occupy it at once. "My Lord," said Sydney, "could you not send down one of the minor canons to begin residence?"

While Lord Coleridge was in America, some family matters, very distressing to him, culminated, making his home dreary on his return. Two years later he married Mrs. Lawford, daughter of an English judge, whose chief service had been in India. Nine years remained to him of life, in which the duties of his high office occupied him, relieved in London by the exercise of a graceful hospitality. His stately home in Sussex Square had the especial adornment of a magnificent library. His chief enjoyment, however, was probably his Devonshire residence, Heath's Court, which he had enlarged and beautified under the direction of his lifelong friend, Mr. Butterfield. There, too, he delighted to show hospitality, entertaining during the long vacation a constant succession of visitors. The drawing-room there remained as it was in the time of his father. The library was new,—a room of great size,—large spaces on the shelves were unoccupied, for the books at Sussex Square were to be placed there on Lord Coleridge's retiring from the Bench. Alas! he did not live to complete the term of service that would entitle him to retire on a pension. The books already in the great room were some 4000 in number, chiefly the collection of his father.

My last visit to Lord Coleridge at his Devonshire home was at the beginning of June, 1891. In his kind note, asking me to come, he said he and Lady Coleridge would be alone there; there would be no other guests; nothing to disturb or distract. So I went, and had three days of the happiest companionship, and was more than ever struck with the affectionate nature of my friend. "Lord Coleridge has been unendingly kind," was the remark of Mrs. Matthew Arnold to me, referring to what he had done for her since the death of her husband. I can add from my own experience that as a friend he was the most steadfast of men.

Within a week after my leaving Heath's Court I was Lord Coleridge's guest in London. He had arranged for my being present at a great dinner in the Hall of the Middle Temple at which he was to preside. The chief guest for this occasion was to be the young Duke of Clarence, the heir to the throne. The company gathered for the banquet in one of the drawing-rooms of the great hall. Each on arriving was announced in a loud voice. All were ready except the chief guest. "How long must we wait for a Royal Highness?" asked Lord Strafford of the one next him. "Oh, till he comes," was the reply. At length came the announcement, "His Royal Highness, the Duke of Clarence and Avondale." A tall youth, self-possessed, his face with a pleasant expression, a broad blue ribbon, I suppose of the Garter, was across his breast. An equerry accompanied him.

Lord Coleridge advanced to meet him. Soon came the great voice at the door, "Your Royal Highness, my Lords and Gentlemen, dinner is served." Then names were called and men walked out two by two. Each guest was assigned to a bencher. What a sight it was as we entered the great hall! The long tables running at right angles to the dais were filled with a great multitude either of barristers or students. All were standing as our procession, headed by Lord Coleridge and the Prince, walked up. I noticed some dark skinned men among the students, one of inky blackness. We took our allotted places at the table on the dais; then grace was read by Canon Ainger, Reader of the Temple — an ancient form. The Prince was on the right of Lord Coleridge; behind his chair was his own footman or servant in the royal scarlet and gold — a fine-looking fellow. In the middle of the dinner came three loud raps on the table from the Master of Ceremonies. "My Lords and Gentlemen, I pray you charge your glasses!" All rose, and Lord Coleridge gave "the health of her Majesty the Queen." A hip, hip, hurrah, followed, and we sat down. A little later came another three raps and another "Charge your glasses," and the health of his Royal Highness, the Duke of Clarence was proposed. The Duke as he sat bowed gracefully and repeatedly from side to side to the standing company. It is the settled rule or understanding at the dinners of the Middle Temple that there are to be no speeches. At a great dinner there of the previous month the Prince of Wales was the chief guest. Lord Coleridge proposed his health, and the Prince, as being above ordinary rules, gave a few words of acknowledgment, and ended by proposing the health of the Lord Chief Justice. Lord Coleridge rose and acknowledged the courtesy, adding, "The text that rises to my mind as I thus return my thanks is—'Put not your trust in Princes.'" He then sat down. The Prince's little scheme failed of success. Later came the loving cup, and at last another rap on the table when all rose and Canon Ainger read a quaint form of words which was the giving of thanks. The dinner was not over, for, Lord Coleridge and the Prince leading the way, we retired from the noble hall, in procession as we had come in, and entered another apartment in which was a table with dessert. Our final move was into a drawing-room where there was coffee.

The Prince and his equerry having at length departed, the rest of the company were free to go their way.

At breakfast, the morning after this Middle Temple function, Lord Coleridge asked me if I would not like to look in on the Gordon Cumming trial—the famous *baccarat* case. I would, certainly. I would not have asked for admission knowing the pressure there had been on the Chief for seats. I drove down with him to the Law Courts. People were waiting to see the Lord Chief Justice arrive. The Chief went to his apartment to put on his robes and wig. I was shown a seat on the Bench. As I entered there was the entire space of the Court filled with barristers in costume sitting closely together, and above was the crowded gallery. A bevy of ladies came in and filled the space on the right of the Judge's seat. My seat, I should say, was on the extreme left. Immediately next the Judge's seat on the left was a red cushioned armchair for the Prince of Wales. Lord Coleridge came in and all in the Court rose. Soon afterward came the Prince of Wales. He bowed pleasantly to the Chief Justice and then to the ladies to the right and to the left. My recollection is that no one rose as he entered except the Chief Justice. I saw his side face as I sat. His bearing was quiet and composed. At eleven Sir Charles Russell (now the Lord Chief Justice) rose to begin his speech for the defence. It will be remembered that Sir William Gordon Cumming was the plaintiff; the defendants were five persons whom he charged with defamation of character. Sir Charles bore terribly upon Gordon Cumming in his speech, which lasted for an hour and a half; his guilt seemed clear beyond question. Yet one hoped against hope for him, for he was a soldier of gallant record and was of ancient family. The first witness for the defence was young Wilson; he had been the first to see the foul play. He told his story well. I could not stay for the cross-examination, nor could I go next day to hear Lord Coleridge's charge. A masterpiece this seemed to me as I read it in the *Times;* it occupied four hours in the delivery. Lord Coleridge, as I know, dreaded having to try the case; but once it was entered upon he gave it the most careful thought.

I may mention that when the Prince of Wales was examined as a witness in the case, the lawyers on both sides forbore to ask the direct question whether he believed the plaintiff was guilty. At the end of his testimony, one of the jury rose and asked, "Your Royal Highness, did you believe Sir Gordon Cumming was cheating?" The Prince's immediate reply was, "I could not resist the testimony of five persons."

I had other experience of the administration of law in England, as I chanced to be Lord Coleridge's guest when he was on circuit,— at Gloucester, at Bury St. Edmund's, and at Manchester. The old-time pomp of these occasions was interesting to me,— the going in state from the Judges' Lodgings to the Court, or, if it were Sunday, to the Cathedral, the new liveries and perhaps the new equipages of the high sheriffs, the javelin men in procession, and the "God save the Queen" from a single trumpet at the departure from the Lodgings, or when the Cathedral or the Court was reached,— all this was striking. The buildings known as the Judges' Lodgings in the Assize towns, though often quaint and ancient, are ample for the exercise of hospitality of bed and board.

Every hour of my stay with my friend was of enjoyment to me, wherever it might be. I have not spoken of the happiness enjoyed by me and mine in receiving him under our roof. He was fascinating to young and old. He could not but feel how absolutely at one with him we all were, and he could feel as to myself, as I did as to him, that friendship had been cemented by a great lapse of years.

Lord Coleridge died in London, on June 14, 1894. On that day I wrote in my journal:—

" . . . The blow to me is heavy. I came to know John Coleridge, as he then was, in 1855. My correspondence with him began in the following year, and has had no check until now. I have kept every letter. I have some of them near me as I write; and as I read them, here and there, he is again before me, and I am listening to the tender, sweet tones of his voice. They are a priceless possession, for, at any moment, I can feel that I am once more with him. I owe to him more than I can say. His fine intellect fascinated me, and gave bent to my thoughts, and left on me enduring impression."

He said to me in almost his last letter, "I have kept all your letters." I have not as yet received these from London, but their return is promised me. It may chance that those who come after me will put in print a correspondence between England and America during thirty-seven eventful years. Whether I receive back my letters or no, there will be safe-keeping here of his. They are more than one hundred in number, and hardly one of them is without passages of distinct literary value.

CHARLES KINGSLEY: A REMINIS-
CENCE

CHARLES KINGSLEY: A REMINISCENCE

The heat of London in the midsummer of 1857, even to my American apprehension, was intense. The noise of the streets oppressed me, and perhaps the sight now and again of freshly-watered flowers, which beautify so many of the window-ledges, and which seem to flourish and bloom whatever the weather, filled me the more with a desire for the quiet of green fields and the refreshing shade of trees. I had just returned from Switzerland, and the friends with whom I had been journeying in that land of all perfections had gone back to their home among the wealds and woods of Essex. I began to feel that sense of solitude which weighs heavily on a stranger in the throng of a great city; so that it was with keen pleasure I looked forward to a visit to Mr. Kingsley. A most kind invitation had come from him, offering me "a bed and all hospitality in their plain country fashion."

At four in the afternoon of a hot July day, I started for Winchfield, which is the station on the London and Southampton Railway nearest to Eversley — a journey of an hour and a half. I took a fly at Winchfield for Eversley, a distance of six miles.

My way lay over wide silent moors; now and then a quiet farmstead came in view — *moated granges* they might have been — but these were few and far between, this part of Hampshire being owned in large tracts. It was a little after six when I drew near to the church and antique brick dwelling-house adjoining it which were the church and rectory of Eversley. There were no other houses near, so that it was evidently a wide and scattered parish. Old trees shaded the venerable, irregularly-shaped parsonage, ivy and creeping plants covered the walls, and roses peeped out here and there. Mr. Kingsley himself met me at the open hall-door, and there was something in his clear and cheerful tone that gave a peculiar sense of welcome to his greeting. "Very glad to see you," said he. Then taking my bag from the fly, "Let me show you your room at once, that you may make yourself comfortable." So, leading the way, he conducted me upstairs and along a somewhat intricate passage to a room in the oldest part of the house. It was a quaint apartment, with leaden casements, a low ceiling, an uneven floor — a room four hundred years old, as Mr. Kingsley told me, but having withal a very habitable look. "I hope you'll be comfortable here," said my host as he turned to go — "as comfortable as one can be in a cottage. Have you everything you want? There will be a tea-dinner or a dinner-tea in about half an hour." Then, as he lingered, he asked, "When did you see Forster last?"

"Six weeks ago," I said — "in London. He had just received news of the vacancy at Leeds, and at once determined to offer himself as the Liberal candidate. He went to Leeds for this purpose, but subsequently withdrew his name. I gather from his speech at the banquet his supporters gave him afterward that this was a mistake, and that if he had stood he would have been elected."

"Ah," said Kingsley, "I should like to see Forster in Parliament. He is not the man, however, to make head against the *tracasseries* of an election contest."

Some other talk we had, and then he left me, coming back before long to conduct me to the drawing-room. Two gentlemen were there, — one a visitor who soon took leave; the other, the tutor to Mr. Kingsley's son. Mrs. Kingsley came in now and shook hands with me cordially, and I had very soon the sense of being at one with them all. Our having mutual friends did much toward this good understanding, but it was partly that we seemed at once to have so much to talk of on the events of the day, and on English matters in which I took keen interest.

India was naturally our first subject, and the great and absorbing question of the mutiny. I told what the London news was in regard to it, and how serious was the look of things. Kingsley said there must be great blame somewhere — that as to the British rule in India, no man could doubt that it had been a great blessing to the country, but the individual Englishman had come very far short of his duty in his dealings with the subject race; a reckoning was sure to come. "Oakfield" was mentioned, — a story by William Arnold of which the scene was laid in India, and which contained evidence of this ill-treatment of the Hindoos by their white masters. Kingsley spoke highly of this book. I said I thought it had hardly been appreciated in England. Kingsley thought the reason was it was too didactic — there was too much moralizing. Only the few could appreciate this; the many did not care for it in a novel.

Our tea-dinner was announced: it was served in the hall. Mrs. Kingsley spoke laughingly of their being obliged to make this their dining room. The talk at the table fell on American affairs. Sumner's name was mentioned. I said he was in London, and that I had had a long conversation with him a few days before. Would I give them his address? they asked: they must have a visit from him. I said he would be glad to visit them, I was sure, for when I told him I was coming here he said he envied me. He was at present engaged in a round of dinners — expected to go to France in August to stay with De Tocqueville, but would be again in England in the autumn. Kingsley spoke of Brooks's death — of the suddenness of it seeming almost a judgment. I said Brooks, as I happened to know, was thought a good fellow before the assault — that he really had good qualities, and was liked even by Northern men. "So we have heard from others," said Kingsley, "and one can well believe it. The man who suffers for a bad system is often the best man — one with attractive qualities." Charles I. and Louis XVI. were instances he gave to illustrate this. A recent article in the *Edinburgh Review* on slavery was spoken of. I said it had attracted a good deal of attention with us, because we saw immediately it could only have been written by an American. Of slavery Mr. Kingsley spoke in calm and moderate words. I told him his introductory chapter to "Two Years Ago" showed that he appreciated the difficulties with which the question was encumbered. He said it would be strange if he did not see these difficulties, considering that he was of West Indian descent (his grandfather had married a West Indian heiress). He admitted that the result of emancipation in the West Indies was not encouraging as it regarded the material condition of the islands, especially of Jamaica, and he was quite able to understand how powerfully this fact would weigh on our Southern planters, and how it tended to close their ears to all antislavery argument. They could hardly be expected to look beyond this test of sugar-production to the moral progress of the black race which freedom alone could insure.

Our pleasant meal being over, we strolled out on the lawn and sat down under one of the fine old trees, where we continued our talk about slavery. Mr. Kingsley said he could quite believe any story he might hear of cruelty practised upon slaves. He knew too well his own nature, and felt that under the influence of sudden anger he would be capable of deeds as violent as any of which we read. This, of course, was putting out of view the restraints which religion would impose; but it was safe for no man to have the absolute control of others.

He left us to go into the house, and Mrs. Kingsley then spoke of his parochial labours. She wished I could spend a Sunday with them—" I should so like you to see the congregation he has. The common farm labourers come morning and afternoon: the reason is, he preaches so that they can understand him. I wish you could have been with us last Sunday, we had such an interesting person here—Max Müller, the great linguist and Orientalist. But we can't have pleasant *meets* here: we have only one spare room."

" How old is Max Müller?" I asked.

" Twenty-eight, and he scarcely looks to be twenty-two."

" How long has Mr. Kingsley been here?" I asked.

" Fifteen years—two years as curate, and then the living becoming vacant, it was given to him."

She told me a funeral was to take place directly—that of a poor woman who had been a great sufferer. "Ah, here it comes," she said.

There was the bier borne on men's shoulders and a little company of mourners, the peasantry of the neighbourhood, the men wearing smock-frocks. They were awaiting the clergyman at the lich-gate. Mr.

Kingsley appeared at the moment in his surplice, and the procession entered the churchyard, he saying as he walked in front the solemn sentences with which the service begins. It was the scene which I had witnessed in another part of Hampshire some years before, when the author of "The Christian Year" was the officiating clergyman. Mrs. Kingsley and I joined the procession and entered the church. It was a small, oddly arranged interior — brick pavements, high-backed pews, the clerk's desk adjoining the reading-desk, but a little lower. Mr. Kingsley read the service in a measured tone, which enabled him to overcome the defect in his utterance noticeable in conversation. At the grave the rest of the office was said, and here the grief of the poor mourners overcame them. The family group consisted of the husband of the deceased, a grown-up daughter, and a son, a boy of fifteen. All were much moved, but the boy the most. He cried bitterly — a long wail, as if he could not be comforted. Mr. Kingsley tried to console him, putting his arm over his shoulders. He said words of sympathy to the others also. They went their way over the heath to their desolate home. Mr. and Mrs. Kingsley spoke of the life of toil which had thus ended, and of the patience with which long-continued bodily pain had been borne. It was clear that the popular author was first of all a parish priest.

We went now into his study, where he lighted a long pipe, and we then returned to a part of the lawn which he called his quarter-deck, and where we walked up and down for near an hour. What an English summer evening it was! — dewy and still. Now and then a slight breeze stirred in the leaves and brought with it wafts of delicate odours from the flowers somewhere hidden in deep shadows, though as yet it was not night and the sweet twilight lay about us like a charm. He asked if I knew Maurice. I did slightly — had breakfasted with him six weeks before, and had seen enough of him to understand the strong personal influence he exerted. "I owe all that I am to Maurice," said Kingsley. "I aim only to teach to others what I get from him. Whatever facility of expression I have is God's gift, but the views I endeavour to enforce are those which I learn from Maurice. I live to interpret him to the people of England."

A talk about the influence of the Oxford writers came next: on this subject I knew we should not agree, though of course it was interesting to me to hear Mr. Kingsley's opinion. He spoke with some asperity of one or two of the leaders, though his chief objection was to certain young men who had put themselves forward as champions of the movement. Of Mr. Keble he spoke very kindly. He said he had at one time been much under the influence of these writings. I mentioned Alexander Knox as being perhaps the forerunner of the Oxford men. "Ah," he said, "I owe my knowledge of that good man to Mrs. Kingsley; you must talk with her about him." We joined the party in the drawing-room, and there was some further conversation on this subject.

At about ten o'clock the bell was rung, the servants came in, prayers were said, and the ladies (Mrs. Kingsley and their daughter's governess) bid us good night. Then to Mr. Kingsley's study, where the rest of the evening was spent — from half-past ten to half-past twelve — the pipe went on, and the talk — a continuous flow. Quakerism was a subject. George Fox, Kingsley said, was his admiration: he read his "Journal" constantly—thought him one of the most remarkable men that age produced. He liked his hostility to Calvinism. "How little that fellow Macaulay," he said, "could understand Quakerism! A man needs to have been in Inferno himself to know what the Quakers meant in what they said and did." He referred me to an article of his on Jacob Boehme and the mystic writers, in which he had given his views in regard to Fox.

We talked about his parish work: he found it, he said, a great help to him, adding emphatically that his other labour was secondary to this. He had trained himself not to be annoyed by his people calling on him when he was writing. If he was to be their priest, he must see them when it suited them to come; and he had become able if called off from his writing to go on again the moment he was alone. I asked him when he wrote. He said in the morning almost always: sometimes, when much pushed, he had written for an hour in the evening, but he always had to correct largely the next morning the work thus done. Daily exercise, riding, hunting, together with parish work, were necessary to keep him in a condition for writing: he aimed to keep himself in rude health. I asked whether "Alton Locke" had been written in that room. "Yes," he said — "from four to eight in the mornings; and a young man was staying with me at the time with whom every day I used to ride, or perhaps hunt, when my task of writing was done."

A fine copy of St. Augustine attracted my attention on his shelves — five volumes folio bound in vellum. "Ah," he said, "that *is* a treasure I must show you;" and taking down a volume he turned to the flyleaf, where were the words "Charles Kingsley from Thomas Carlyle," and above them "Thomas Carlyle from John Sterling." One could understand that Carlyle had thus handed on the book, notwithstanding its sacred associations, knowing that to Kingsley it would have a threefold value. My eye caught also a relic of curious interest — a fragment from one of the vessels of the Spanish Armada. It lay on the mantelpiece: I could well understand Kingsley's pleasure in possessing it.

At the breakfast-table the next morning we had much talk in regard to American writers. Kingsley admitted Emerson's high merit, but thought him too fragmentary a writer and thinker to have enduring fame. He had meant that this should be implied as his opinion in the title he gave to "Phaethon"—

"Loose Thoughts for Loose Thinkers"—a book he had written in direct opposition to what he understood to be the general teaching of Emerson. I remarked upon the great beauty of some of Emerson's later writings and the marvellous clearness of insight which was shown in his "English Traits." Kingsley acquiesced in this, but referred to some American poetry, so called, which Emerson had lately edited, and in his preface had out-Heroded Herod. Kingsley said the poems were the production of a coarse, sensual mind. His reference, of course, was to Walt Whitman, and I had no defence to make. Of Lowell, Mr. Kingsley spoke very highly: his "Fable for Critics" was worthy of Rabelais. Mr. Froude, who is Kingsley's brother-in-law, had first made him acquainted with Lowell's poetry. Hawthorne's style he thought was exquisite: there was scarcely any modern writing equal to it. Of all his books he preferred the "Blithedale Romance."

We talked of Mr. Froude, whom Kingsley spoke of as his dearest friend: he thought Froude sincerely regretted ever having written the "Nemesis of Faith." Mr. Helps, author of "Friends in Council," he spoke of as his near neighbour there in Hampshire, and his intimate friend. Mr. Charles Reade he knew, and I think he said he was also a neighbour: his "Christie Johnstone," he thought showed high original power. Mrs. Gaskell we talked of, whose "Life of Charlotte Brontë" had just then been published: Mr. Kingsley thought it extremely interesting and "slightly slanderous." He told me of the author of "Tom Brown's School-days," a copy of which, fresh from the publishers, was lying on his table. Mr. Hughes is now so well known to us I need only mention that Mr. Kingsley spoke of him as an old pupil of Arnold's and a spiritual child of Maurice. He spoke most warmly of him, and offered me a letter of introduction to him. I could not avail myself of this, having so little time to remain in London.

I must mention, as showing further Mr. Kingsley's state of mind toward Maurice, that he had named his son after him. He spoke of the boy as being intended for the army; the family, he said, had been soldiers for generations. "That is the profession England will need for the next five-and-twenty years." Of Forster he said, "What a pity he had not been put in the army at the age of eighteen!— he would have been a general now. England has need of such men." I note this as showing the curious apprehension of war which he, an Englishman, felt eighteen years ago,[1] and which he expressed to me, an American. How little either of us thought of the struggle which men of English blood were to engage in in three years from that time! How little I could dream that one of the decisive battles of the world was so soon to be fought in my own State, Pennsylvania!

Our morning was spent in all this varied talk, walking partly on the lawn, partly in the study. His pipe was still his companion. He seemed to need to walk

---

[1] Written in 1895.

incessantly, such was his nervous activity of temperament. He asked me if it annoyed me for him to walk so much up and down his study. The slight impediment in his speech one forgot as one listened to the flow of his discourse. He talked a volume while I was with him, and what he said often rose to eloquence. There was humour too in it, of which I can give no example, for it was fine and delicate. But what most impressed me was his perfect simplicity of character. He talked of his wife with the strongest affection — wished I could remain longer with them, if only to know her better. Nothing could be more tender than his manner toward her. He went for her when we were in the study, and the last half hour of my stay she sat with us. She is one of five sisters who are all married to eminent men.

It occurs to me to note, as among my last recollections of our talk, that I spoke of Spurgeon, whom I had heard in London a short time before, and was very favourably impressed with. I could not but commend his simple, strong Saxon speech, the charm of his rich, full voice, and above all the earnest aim which I thought was manifest in all he uttered. Mr. Kingsley said he was glad to hear this, for he had been told of occasional irreverences of Spurgeon's, and of his giving way now and then to a disposition to make a joke of things. Not that he objected altogether to humour in sermons: he had his own temptations in this way. "One must either weep at the follies of men or laugh at them," he added. I told him Mr. Maurice had spoken to me of Mr. Spurgeon as no doubt an important influence for good in the land, and he said this was on the whole his own opinion. He told me, however, of teaching of quite another character, addressed to people of cultivation mainly, and to him peculiarly acceptable. His reference was to Robertson's "Sermons"; he showed me the volume — the first series — just then published. The mention of this book perhaps led to a reference by Mr. Kingsley to the Unitarians of New England, of whom he spoke very kindly, adding, in effect, that their error was but a natural rebound from Calvinism, that dreary perversion of God's boundless love.

But I had now to say good-by to these new friends, who had come to seem old friends, so full and cordial had been their hospitality, and so much had we found to talk of in the quickly-passing hours of my visit. Mr. Kingsley drove me three miles on my way to Winchfield. His talk with me was interspersed with cheery and friendly words to his horse, with whom he seemed to be on very intimate terms. "Come and see us again," he said, as we parted; "the second visit, you know, is always the best."

OXFORD, AND THE AUTHOR OF "THE CHRISTIAN YEAR"

OXFORD, AND THE AUTHOR OF "THE CHRISTIAN YEAR"

It was on a bright morning in June, 1852, that I left London for my second visit to Oxford. The fifty miles journey was made in little over an hour, and soon afterward I was comfortably quartered at the quaint old inn, " The Mitre."

I found the streets well filled; it was term-time and the undergraduates, as well as the Fellows, and other university men were everywhere to be seen; their caps and gowns, which by rigid law they are compelled to wear, adding much to the quaint old-time look of the city.

I called in the afternoon at Oriel College to deliver a letter of introduction to the Rev. Charles Marriott, Fellow of Oriel and Vicar of St. Mary the Virgin's — the successor of Mr. Newman, holding precisely his position in the university, and occupying his rooms. Not finding him, I went at four to the cathedral, which is really the chapel of Christ Church College, to evening service. I had the hope that Dr. Pusey would be there. The small congregation had already assembled. I was shown by the verger to one of the high stalls. There were several of the canons, or students of the college, answering to the Fellows of other colleges, present, but no one of these could be Dr. Pusey. At the very stroke of four a quick step was heard, a man of middle age, of grave countenance, pale, but seeming vigorous, came in and went to a stall very near me. He wore, as the others did, a surplice and rose-lined hood. When the service was over he passed me in going out, and I had a full view of his countenance. I was struck with its intellectual expression — his serious thoughtful look. " Is that Dr. Pusey ? " I asked the verger at the door. " Yes," said he, and so my wish was gratified. I had felt for him, for years, admiration and reverence ; the sight of him, though it was nothing more, gave me pleasure. Already he had become the most conspicuous figure at Oxford, though the period of which I write was forty-seven years ago ; and this in spite of his shrinking from any personal distinction, or even notice. It was a true instinct of the popular heart that affixed his name to the great movement of 1833, although Newman had more to do with its actual beginning than he. Dr. Newman informs us that he felt for him, as early as 1827–28, enthusiastic admiration. He adds, " His great learning, his immense diligence, his scholar-like mind, his simple devotion to the cause of religion overcame me." Newman speaks of him further, of the date of 1834, as having a vast influence in consequence, in part, of his deep religious seriousness, and the munificence of his charities.

But to return to my passing sight of him. He was joined as he crossed what is known as the " Tom

Quadrangle"—so called because of the great bell, "Tom of Oxford" that sounds over it from its cupola, — by a youth whom I noticed in the cathedral, who was quite lame; also by a young lady. The two were, as I afterward learned, his son and daughter. His wife had died ten years before. I stood looking after them until they had reached the opposite side of the Quadrangle, and entered their own apartments — that part of the old range of buildings which constituted Dr. Pusey's residence as Canon of Christ Church.

I may note here that Dr. Pusey's weight and influence in Oxford was at the first in some degree due to the fact of his holding a professorship, and also to his family connections. He was of an ancient family; his brother, the late Philip Pusey, of Pusey, Member of Parliament, and a great agriculturalist, was long at the head of it. At a celebration some fifty years ago, of the thousandth anniversary of the birthday of Alfred, the Pusey horn was produced — a precious possession, the tradition being that their direct ancestor, then a boy, had sounded it from a hill-top to give notice of a Danish invasion.

Dr. Pusey's son, whom I have spoken of as accompanying him, bore the name of Philip. He was very lame, in fact deformed. It is probable that on this account he did not take Orders. He became, however, as I have understood, a man of curious learning and especially an authority in regard to the text of the New Testament. He made journeys to the Levant and elsewhere, spite of his infirmities, in search of manuscripts. A visitor at Mt. Athos was inquired of by the monks, some years after one of young Pusey's visits, for tidings of " Philip of England."

To return to my narrative. Later in the afternoon I wandered from one college to another, entering the Quadrangles, and studying the architecture, and looking at the old statues of founders, many of them crumbling away under the gnawing tooth of Time. The spire of St. Mary's I stood long to admire; it had just been almost completely rebuilt — one of the most beautiful spires in England, not lofty, but of admirable proportions. The High Street, the noblest, perhaps, in Europe, with colleges and churches on either side, was the one along which I was walking. I reached Magdalen, and passing through the Quadrangle came at length to the gardens, and the famous water-walk along the banks of the Cherwell. The noble trees formed a green archway. As I walked along I thought of the many to whom these sweet shades had brought peace, and with it elevation of mind. Addison's name is perhaps the most famous in literature of the students of Magdalen (*Maudlin*, as it is mostly called). Besides this water-walk there is a park connected with the college grounds. There were many deer under the noble trees.

I met by chance Mr. Marriott in the Chapel of Merton, with some friends to whom he was showing the beautiful restorations in this chapel. He had been to " The Mitre " he said, to look for me. He welcomed me cordially. His manners were grave and quiet. He pointed out to me the beauty of the chapel we were in, and afterward some very ancient parts of the college—perhaps the most ancient architecture in Oxford. We went into the library where there were some books chained to their shelves. Thence we walked to Christ Church meadows and along the banks of the "Silver Isis." A boat-race was going on, and a large number of the young Oxford men were gathered, representing, doubtless, some of the best blood of England. We stood to watch the gay scene, and I thought of Wordsworth's lines referring to a similar scene at Cambridge

> "Who . . .
> Could have beheld,—with undelighted heart,
> So many happy youths, so wide and fair
> A congregation in its budding time
> Of health, and hope, and beauty, all at once
> So many divers samples from the growth
> Of life's sweet season—could have seen unmoved
> That miscellaneous garland of wild flowers
> Decking the matron temples of a place
> So famous through the world?"

The beautiful tower of Magdalen was often in view as we followed the windings of the water-walk; it seemed almost to move as we did, and ever to end the prospect. We had some pleasant talk. One subject was Mr. Gladstone, and the canvass which was then going on at the University; a general election was at hand. The Oxford men were beginning to be restive under the leaning toward liberal opinions which they discovered in their then representative.

Mr. Marriott said he was going in the evening to Dr. Acland's — afterward Sir Henry Acland — a son of Sir Thomas Acland, and that he would be glad if I would accompany him. I accordingly joined him at his rooms at a little after eight. His study, as I have said, was once Mr. Newman's: here the Parochial Sermons were written, those remarkable productions which to so many persons stood for years in the place of a living teacher. Principal Shairp, who heard these sermons, has said of them: —

"The look and bearing of the preacher were as of one who dwelt apart; who, though he knew his age well, did not live in it. From his seclusion of study, and abstinence and prayer, from habitual dwelling in the unseen, he seemed to come forth that one day of the week to speak to others of the things he had seen and known. To call these sermons eloquent would not be the word for them; high poems they rather were, as of an inspired singer, or the outpourings of a prophet, rapt, yet self-possessed. And the tone of voice in which they were spoken, once you grew accustomed to it, sounded like a fine strain of unearthly music. After hearing these sermons you might come away still not believing the tenets of the High Church system; but you would be harder than most men if you did not feel more than ever ashamed of coarseness, selfishness, worldliness, if you did not feel the things of faith brought close to the soul."

I had never myself the happiness to hear Mr. Newman, but the associations of the room in which I found myself were of strange interest. Books were everywhere in the apartment, so that there was, indeed, but little space left for the piano and table which were in the middle of the room. Music appeared to be the one recreation of Mr. Marriott's studious solitude.

We set off soon on our walk. The spire of St. Mary's we looked at long as we drew near to it in the evening light; the reflected glow of the western sky was upon it, tinting it with pale gold. It was in this church that Mr. Newman's sermons were preached. At Dr. Acland's I met agreeable, cultivated people. The Rev. Sir George Prevost I had much talk with. I enjoyed the quiet evening extremely; it was yet another glimpse to me of the best household life of England — an experience of the sort from which an American traveller may gain a true knowledge of "Our Old Home."

I breakfasted the next morning with Mr. Marriott to meet Sir George Prevost and a few others, one of them the Rev. Charles Page Eden, editor of the new edition of Jeremy Taylor. I had wondered, when Mr. Marriott had asked me, the evening before, how he could entertain us in his room in which books had so much the upper hand; but, behold! his large library table had been cleared of its usual occupants, and a cloth was spread, and there was promise of a substantial meal.

Mr. Marriott made the coffee and the tea, for there was fire on the hearth. His "grace" was *"Benedictus benedicat,"* a form of words which has been in use at Oriel since the Middle Ages. There was animated talk, chiefly upon Church matters, though many questions were asked me about America. Mr. Eden I was glad to meet; he had just completed a stupendous work, — verifying every quotation made by Jeremy Taylor, giving the reference at the foot of each page — a task requiring almost the learning of Jeremy himself.

Sir George Prevost in parting asked me to visit him in Gloucestershire, and offered to introduce me to his brother-in-law, the Rev. Isaac Williams, author of "The Cathedral" and other poems, and one of the leading Oxford Tract writers — a man for whom I had high admiration. This visit I was unable to accomplish, nor did I ever see afterward Sir George Prevost. He was a baronet as well as a clergyman, and had always much weight and influence in the English Church. He was very simple and gentle in manner.

When our pleasant breakfast party was over I walked for a while in the beautiful gardens of New College. Never was there richer green than that of the turf on which the shadows of these colleges, and their walls and towers, now and again fall, and never fuller, richer, more abundant foliage.

I returned to Oriel to take my leave of Mr. Marriott. He inquired very kindly as to my further journeying in England, and offered me introductions, among them one to Mr. Keble. I gladly accepted this, and he then wished me God-speed and I went my way. I must note that he died some years afterward, and what was printed in regard to him at the time showed that his life had been saintly in its zeal and devotion. He impressed me as a man of great singleness of mind, of high and unworldly aims.

My thoughts had been, naturally, much of Mr. Newman while I was in the room which spoke so continually of his presence. But indeed the whole air of Oriel College seemed to tell of him. In the very year of my visit he uttered this half-wistful recollection of it, speaking with something of the narrowness which had come to him with his new faith.

"In the heart of Oxford there is a small plot of ground, hemmed in by public thoroughfares, which has been the possession and the home of one Society for above five hundred years. In the old time of Boniface the Eighth and John the Twenty-second, in the age of Scotus and Occam and Dante, before Wiclif or Huss had kindled those miserable fires which were to be the ruin of souls innumerable down to this day, an unfortunate King of England, Edward the Second, flying from the field of Bannockburn, is said to have made a vow to the Blessed Virgin to found a religious house in her honour if he got back in safety. Prompted and aided by his almoner, he decided on placing this house in the City of Alfred; and the Image of Our Lady which is opposite its entrance, is the token of the vow and its fulfilment to this day. King and almoner have long been in the dust, and strangers have entered into their inheritance, and their creed has been forgotten, and their holy rites disowned; but day by day a memento is still made in the Holy Sacrifice by at least one Catholic priest, once a member of that College, for the souls of those Catholic benefactors who fed him there for so many years."

Against this passage, with its strangely uncharitable words, I place one other showing Newman's deep love for Oxford as a whole, and what a wrench it must have been to his spirit to leave it.

"There are those [he says] who, having felt the influence of this ancient school and being smit with its splendour and its sweetness, ask wistfully if never again it is to be Catholic, or whether at least some footing for Catholicity may not be found there. All honour and merit to the charitable and zealous hearts who so enquire! Nor can we dare to tell what, in time to come, may be the inscrutable purposes of that Grace which is ever more comprehensive than human hope and aspiration. But for me, from the day I left its walls, I never, for good or bad, have had anticipation of its future; and never for a moment have I had a wish to see again a place which I have never ceased to love, and where I lived for nearly thirty years."

It was with the sweet influence of Oxford still upon me that I arrived at Winchester on a Saturday afternoon, intending the next day to present myself at Hursley, the home of Mr. Keble. But Winchester had its own attractions, chiefest of all the cathedral. I found the same open space of greensward about it, which adds so much to the beauty of the English cathedrals as compared with those of the Continent. I entered by the west door, and was delighted and astonished at the grandeur of the nave. It is as long as that of York, 250 feet; the extreme length of the cathedral is 560 feet. The noble pillars, white and fair as if the work of yesterday, and the view of them from the west door with the vista of the distant choir opening beyond, and the aisles in like manner, with their springing arches in long perspective, afford a whole which it is a deep delight to look upon. Hawthorne says of York that it is the most " wonderful work that ever came from the hands of man, seeming indeed like a house not made with hands, but to have come down from above, bringing an awful majesty and sweetness with it." He adds, "I thank God that I saw this cathedral again, and I thank Him that He inspired the builders to build it, and that mankind has so long enjoyed it, and will continue to enjoy it." One may not go beyond such glowing words as these, and yet the interior of Winchester surpasses in some respects that of York.

I was taking my full of pleasure as I walked slowly up the nave, and I had paused opposite the chantry and tomb of William of Wykeham, when the verger approached and asked me to join the party to whom he was then showing the cathedral. We went into the choir, and there the first object that struck me was the tomb of William Rufus. I was rather fresh at the time from Lingard, and so I looked with peculiar interest on the very spot where the hasty burial took place, in the year 1100, of the second of the Norman kings. His life, Lingard says, had been base and impious, and so there were no religious rites.

"... they laid him in the Cathedral Church
Because he had been a King.

"But never a heart at his death was sore
And never an eye was dim;
The Church bells toll for rich and poor,
But they never toll'd for him."

And here is this further record of him from Neale's version of the old chronicler's story:—

> "There was never a night but he lay down
> A worse man than he rose;
> And never a morning but up he sprung
> Worse than at evening's close."

Another interesting historical association of Winchester Cathedral is the fact that there, at the high altar, the marriage of Philip and Mary was solemnized. In the south transept under a plain slab in the pavement lies Izaak Walton, and not far off is a monument to Jane Austen. Such are the contrasts of an English cathedral — the associations utterly separated as to time and strangely various in character.

After my dinner at "The George," I walked in the sweet summer evening to the hospital of St. Cross, about a mile distant. This is one of the quaint relics of the Middle Ages which happily are still preserved in England: originally called "The Almshouse of Noble Poverty," it is a house for a certain number of poor men. The buildings are of the thirteenth century and are of curious interest. At the porter's gate a dole of bread and beer is given to all who apply for it — until the supply for the day is exhausted. Some years after the date of my visit, an immense stir was made about this endowment, and its perversion from its true use, by the then Earl of Guilford. Mr. Trollope's novel, "The Warden," is based upon the story of this old foundation, and the abuses of long years which were brought to light at the time of which I speak. As I saw the hospital of St. Cross it was wonderfully picturesque, and nothing indicated to me the sham and hypocrisy that I suppose it really was. The beer did appear to me of the smallest as I tasted my pilgrim's share of it.

I was up betimes the next morning, Sunday, that I might attend morning prayers at the cathedral at half past seven. I was shown to one of the high stalls in the choir. Somehow in the freshness of the early morning there seemed a sublimer beauty in pillar and lofty arch. The service was short, — morning prayer only, as far as the litany, — but it seemed to give a glory to the day.

Two hours later I started for Hursley, five miles distant — the parish of which Mr. Keble was vicar. I had a delightful walk over the Hampshire hills. Now and again I came upon a flock of sheep with a shepherd and his dog attending them — quiet pastoral scenes. From the first ridge or eminence after leaving Winchester I had a fine view of the town with the cathedral in its majesty rising far above all the other buildings, seeming to gather them under its sheltering arms. It was interesting to think of the importance of the city in the old days and of the great things which had come to pass there. It was a most important post or encampment of the Romans, and when their power passed away it fell into the hands of the Saxons and became the capitol of Wessex. Alfred held his witan there; and there in 1522 the great Emperor Charles V. was entertained by Henry VIII.

It was eleven o'clock when I reached the village

church at Hursley — a new and beautiful church, built in the main, as I afterward learnt, out of the profits of "The Christian Year." I could give no study to the exterior, for service had begun. The church was well filled; the men and women sat on different sides. The men were for the most part the peasantry of the neighbourhood, wearing the white smock-frock peculiar to this part of England. There were no pews, so that rich and poor were in a true sense met together. The psalms for the day were chanted, and I noticed that the entire congregation seemed to take part in the singing. There were three clergymen in the chancel, and one of them I saw at once was Mr. Keble. A print of him which I had long possessed, from a portrait by Richmond, guided me, though the picture was of twenty years earlier date — the period indeed of his prime. Now his hair was grey, and the spectacles he wore gave a further look of age. The choristers had their seats in the chancel — boys in white surplices. I mention this fact because of a little incident of a later period of my narrative. Mr. Keble read the litany and a part of the ante-communion service, but he did not preach. To my disappointment, one of the other clergymen, also grey-haired, went into the pulpit. But the sermon was excellent, plain, and earnest, and quite of the character of those of Mr. Keble's I had read.

I lingered for a while in the church and church-yard when the service was over, and then entered the garden or grounds of the vicarage. Mr. Keble at the moment appeared at the hall door, and I delivered in person my line of introduction from Mr. Marriott. "What a pleasing countenance!" I said to myself, as I thus saw him. "What a look of gentleness and benignity!" He led me to the drawing-room, and then asked me about my travels. There was a certain shyness or half timidity of manner at the first, but this soon passed off. I was struck with the brightness of his eye, and at the same time with his look of purity and guilelessness. The print, of which I have spoken, gives with remarkable fidelity the sweet smile and the lustre of the eye, which, as it were, constituted the charm of his countenance. I thought I had never seen a more winning look in one on whom age had begun to tell. The room was pretty and bright, looking out on the garden, which was gay with its summer bloom, and across to the church and churchyard. On the walls were some fine prints, among them the Dresden Madonna engraved by Müller. Books were there in abundance, showing that the library had overflowed into the drawing-room.

I had no thought of making my visit other than a call, but, when I rose to go, Mr. Keble rose at the same moment, and, taking my hat from me, said, "You will stay and take luncheon with us, and dinner afterward at six, after Evening Service." The invitation was in the light of a command, and I was only too happy to obey. Soon afterward luncheon was announced. Mr. Keble said: "Let me explain to you whom you will see. My wife will be at the head of the table; the gentleman is my brother, the elderly lady is my sister, two of the young ladies are my brother's daughters, the other is Miss Richards. Except the last, the names are all Keble." So we went to the dining room, and I was duly presented. I was struck with Mrs. Keble's sweet expression of countenance. Mr. Keble's brother proved to be the preacher to whom I had just listened,— the Rev. Thomas Keble, vicar of Bisley. Somehow I felt drawn to him at once. I knew of him as having been one of the Oxford Tract writers. The meal was informal, and I think no servant was present. Mr. Keble himself went round the table offering wine to his guests. There seemed something characteristic in this simple act.

When we returned to the drawing-room, Mr. Keble soon said that he had his school to look after, but that his brother would remain with me. So for an hour or two I talked with the good vicar of Bisley, and was charmed with his quiet humour, and the quick intelligence which was manifest under the quaint simplicity of his manner. He asked me many questions about my country, but our talk was chiefly about Church matters. I felt at the time lively interest in the Oxford Movement, and was especially curious to know about Hurrell Froude, who was the bosom friend of Keble and of Newman, and who was as much answerable as any man for the great awakening, so to speak, of 1834. "A man of the highest gifts," Newman testifies; "so truly many-sided," he says, "that it would be presumptuous in me to attempt to describe him." "Would he have been likely," I asked, "if he had lived, to follow Newman in his great change?" "A question difficult to answer," said the good vicar of Bisley, with a smile. "Newman thinks he would certainly have gone with him, but I believe myself that he would have remained with my brother and Dr. Pusey." He added that Froude had never been betrayed into sharp denunciation of Rome, as Newman had, so there was no rebound of feeling. Mr. Keble said further that there was something of strangeness in Froude, and that people did not at first understand him; he had been himself a little afraid of him, because of his abrupt way of speaking, but, as he came to know him better, he saw the essential nobleness and beauty of his character.

The afternoon service was at three o'clock, and was well attended, and this time the sermon was by the author of "The Christian Year." It was very simple; the text was, "Heaven and earth shall pass away, but my word shall not pass away." There was no gesture, nor were there any high-wrought expressions; the tones of the preacher's voice were touching in their earnestness, but the matter of the discourse was level to the understanding of the most unlearned of his hearers. He held his manuscript in his hand as he read, but his manner now and then had a sort of plaintive tenderness which compelled attention. It was impossible not to feel that he was speaking to those whose inmost souls lay open to him. The people of the scattered hamlets which formed the village of Hursley were almost as his own household. I had been told I should find him a pattern vicar, and that Sir William Heathcote, his lifelong friend and the lord of the manor, might well be considered a pattern squire. Certainly everything in the church and out of it seemed to speak of watchful care and guidance.

Service being over, I remained in the church to study the windows, which are beautiful; the designs for them were contributed by various artists, Copley Fielding, Mr. Dyce, and others. The church itself was paid for, as I have said, almost wholly out of the profits of "The Christian Year," and the cost of the windows was in part defrayed from receipts from the same source. Mr. Keble had told me there would be a funeral shortly, and in a few minutes I saw him standing at the lich-gate to meet the mourners. From a distance I looked on. The procession came very slowly up the avenue of old trees, the vicar repeating at intervals the solemn sentences with which the burial service begins. It was the funeral of a child; they were poor people who followed, women chiefly, with black dresses, but wearing white veils or hoods, and the coffin was covered with a fair linen cloth. Mr. Keble looked upward to the clear heavens, and seemed as if awed by the solemnity of the duty he had to perform; certainly if it had been a child of the noblest of the land he could not, with more touching earnestness, have uttered the consoling words of the service. The sweet summer afternoon, and the beautiful church, and the quiet country around made the scene memorable to me.

I returned to the vicarage, where I had some further talk with Mr. Thomas Keble. I may note that I afterward learned in regard to this good man that he exercised much influence on those associated with him, though modest and retiring to an extreme degree. He was but two years younger than his brother. Dr. Pusey said of him that, though known to the world only as a simple parish priest, he exercised a silent and unconscious influence on such a mind as Newman's. "It used to be noted at an early period," Dr. Pusey says, "that a visit to the vicar of Bisley was attended by the unconscious reappearance of some of his thoughts in the pulpit of St. Mary's."

At six o'clock the same company that I had met at luncheon assembled in the drawing-room, and dinner was announced. Mr. Keble had been occupied with the duties of the day up to this time, but now his work was over and he seemed happy to be again with his family and friends. His poet's eye was bright and his countenance gay and smiling. Mrs. Keble seemed to me a charming person, sympathizing with her husband, I could readily see, in all his thoughts and feelings. She was some fifteen years younger than he. She seemed frail in health. When the ladies left us, Mr. Keble took his wife's place at the table, and thus I was close to him. The talk which went on was free and flowing. I mentioned my having lately seen Dr. Pusey, and that I thought his appearance was that of vigorous health. Mr. Keble said he was stronger than he had been for a year or two previous. He had felt deeply "the cruel attacks" upon him of Mr. Dodsworth and others — men who had gone over to Rome, and had alleged Dr. Pusey's influence as a cause, and had upbraided him for not accompanying them. One of these men, Mr. Keble said, had been greatly beholden to Dr. Pusey, — and then came the half involuntary ejaculation, "Nasty conceited prig!" Mr. Keble turned to me, after he said this, with a pleasant smile, as if apologizing for his vehemence. The two brothers talked further of certain persons who, while they had not gone over to Rome, were very harsh in their judgment of matters in England, speaking, Mr. Keble said, in a "miserably undutiful way of the English Church." Manning's going over had taken place a year or two before; I had alluded to this and to the pain it had caused in America. Mr. Keble said there had, of course, been great feeling in England. "But," he added, "the strength of the Church of England is not with her leading men; there are old women in my parish, please God, with whom I should far rather say is found the true life of the Church; such as they are our true witnesses, — the simple-hearted poor."

I have mentioned in speaking of the morning service at the church that the boy choristers had their seats in the chancel. While I was sitting with the two brothers in this after-dinner talk, Mr. Keble in drawing his handkerchief from his pocket found a knot in it. He seemed to puzzle over this for a moment, and then said, "Oh, I remember. One of the boys of the choir was eating an apple while the service was going on, fancying that nobody could see him. I put a knot in my handkerchief that I might remember to tell his mother to give him no more apples for a while." I felt a certain pity for the small offender, and I thought the incident showed, as in the case of the sharp remark before quoted, something of the severity which Mr. Keble was no doubt equal to on occasion. But I fancied he was half amused, all the same, at the young rogue's delinquency.

In Mr. Thomas Keble there was a rich overflow of this kindly humour which went far, no doubt, to make him dear to his friends. But in England a quick sense of humour is very often to be found in highly educated men. As I sat by the two brothers, I felt strongly that matters of the deepest and gravest thought were unceasingly present to them, and yet with them both there was a sort of sunny radiance that gave a peculiar charm to their conversation. In looking as I have done since I began to copy out these notes, at that delightful book, Sir John Coleridge's "Life of Keble," I find a passage in a letter of Mr. Keble's of a date some years later than that of my visit; he is speaking of a visit he had paid his brother at Bisley, and of their going together to the Musical Festival at Gloucester Cathedral, where

"The Elijah" was given, and "where," to quote his own words, "the two old codger Kebles were seen sitting side by side."

I may note that the more than brotherhood of these two extended over a period of seventy years and upward. Thomas Keble survived the poet five or six years. Each was the main help and stay of the other. They were the children of a clergyman whose living was of small value, but who, educating them himself, as far as preparation for college went, so fitted them that each won scholarships. Moreover, John Keble, when scarcely eighteen, obtained a double First Class, a distinction which up to that time no one had earned but Sir Robert Peel, with whose examination the University was ringing, Sir John Coleridge says, when Keble began his Oxford residence. Keble's success was the more remarkable because of his youth, and of what might well have seemed his imperfect preparation for college. It was understood that his father had never compelled him to study, and that he was taught only when he liked to learn.

As I draw to an end with my own very slight narrative, I recall a remarkable incident which is told by Sir John Coleridge,— the visit of Dr. Newman to Hursley in the last year of Keble's life. The account is mainly given in a letter of Newman's to Sir John. He came without being expected. Mr. Keble was at his door speaking to a friend. He did not know Newman, and asked him his name. What was more wonderful, Newman did not know him, though he had come purposely to see him. He gave him his card without speaking. Then they found each other out, and Keble with that "tender flurry of manner" which Newman says "he recollected so well," told him Pusey was there. Then came the meeting of the three. They had not seen each other for twenty years — they who had been so closely united for so many years. Four or five hours passed in this renewed intercourse. Newman tells very little of their talk. Dr. Pusey, he says, was full of the question of the inspiration of Holy Scripture, and Keble expressed his joy that it was a common cause on which there could be substantial agreement. Pusey left them, and Keble and Newman walked a little way, and "stood looking," the latter says, "at the church and churchyard so beautiful and calm." Newman adds that Keble began then to converse with him with more than his old intimacy, as if they had never been parted. Newman went away to the Isle of Wight, intending to repeat his visit, but Mrs. Keble's illness prevented. Many notes, he says, passed between him and Keble about this time; in one of them the latter made a reference to the lines in "Macbeth": —

> "When shall we three meet again?
> When the hurly-burly's done,
> When the battle's lost and won."

The date of this remarkable and last meeting of the three was September, 1865; the following April Keble was gathered to his rest.

I have little more to tell of my own day at Hursley. Mr. Keble asked me to visit them again on my return from the Continent. Mrs. Keble, too, said some kind words to me, and then the two brothers walked with me to the wicket-gate, and, with the blessing of the elder, I went my way.

THE OXFORD COMMEMORATION,
1860

THE OXFORD COMMEMORATION,
1860

DURING a visit to Oxford in June of 1860, I witnessed a " Commemoration." I was a guest of one of the Fellows of St. John's College, Mr. William West Jones — a Fellow, as I have said, though still an undergraduate. He looked to taking orders, and certainly there was everything in his personal bearing to make this seem natural. May I say it, his sweet cheerfulness of spirit betokened a purity of heart and mind which was of rich promise for his future life. The years have brought their fulfilment, for my kind host of those days became afterward bishop of Cape Town and Metropolitan of South Africa.

On the Sunday morning of that Oxford visit we went to St. Mary's to hear the sermon to be preached before the University — the last of the Bampton Lectures of that year. Many of the Dons were there; the Vice-Chancellor in a pew raised above the others and sitting alone; the proctors and heads of houses around him. A large congregation was present. It was eleven o'clock; there was no service because in all the colleges there had been morning service at eight. A metrical psalm was exquisitely sung by the choristers present, and then the preacher read that admirable collocation of words — the "bidding prayer." It is a calling upon men to pray for the sovereign, for the nobility, for the magistrates, for the institutions of learning, for all, in short, who are in any way in authority, and for every earthly means through which blessings can come; and then there is a giving of thanks for all the good which has flowed to men in times past — for the great departed whose labours have blessed the world — "and herein I am especially bound to name the founder of the college of St. John, and Dr. William Laud and Dr. William Juxon, successively heads of that college, and Archbishops of Canterbury." These last are some of the words I recall of this impressive prayer. The preacher was of course a member of St. John's College.

On the Monday there was a visit to the Bodleian, where wonderful manuscripts were shown us, and where various portraits by Holbein looked down upon us from the walls. I lunched with my kind host at St. John's on that Monday with a small party; we had some of the old college plate — huge tankards of silver, and wine-coolers; and the cheer was bountiful as well as scholastic. I should mention that our host, while he entertained us with university gossip, was briskly compounding the love cup. It proved a delicious beverage, and it contained the borage, which is, I believe, indispensable to give mystic significance to the draught. The tankard used for it was especially antique in form, and so heavy that the two handles had to be grasped to raise it to the lips.

Of the procession of boats on that sweet summer evening — one of the spectacles of Commemoration week — and of the flower-show the next day in the gardens of Worcester College, where the Woolwich band was in attendance, I need say little. All Oxford was gay with the company which the coming ceremonies had gathered. I may mention my dining on the Tuesday with my friend Mr. Jones in the hall of St. John's. A curious Oxford scene that was: the Dons, at the high table on the dais at the upper end of the hall, and also at a table at right angles with it extending down the centre, had their friends with them, many of them ladies, who had come up for the Commemoration. Among the dignitaries present was Professor Mansel, the chief ornament then of St. John's, afterward dean of St. Paul's — a robust, well-looking man. All the college plate was displayed, and there were flowers and other decorations. From the walls portraits of Laud and Juxon and others looked down on the scene, and far above was the open-work roof. My place was with J—— at the undergraduates' table, where there was perhaps a trifle more freedom than at the high table. My companions were certainly a jolly set. One of them declared that the president of St. John's — the august head of the college — had just sent for "gooseberry fool" for himself and his especial guest, and that the order which went sounding from the hall to the buttery adjoining was "president and friend, two fools." We adjourned before long to Jones's room, and then followed what is known as an Oxford wine. J——'s scout was sent out to order dessert, and soon oranges and ices were brought, and sherry-cobblers were made, and claret was produced, and talk went on, and the thing was like a chapter out of "Tom Brown." There is the utmost freedom with each other on the part of the Oxford men, but there is courtesy and evident good feeling. They love Oxford intensely and all belonging to it. The wine-drinking, I may say, was very moderate.

At length the great day dawned — Wednesday. I breakfasted with Mr. Mountague Bernard at All Souls' — Professor of International Law at Oxford and a very accomplished man. He was a Fellow of All Souls'; this college has the distinction which I am sure all professors elsewhere will thoroughly appreciate, that it has no students. Such was the case at the time of which I write. But a period of change was then beginning, and the stately leisure of the All Souls' Fellows and professors may have since been encroached upon. (I may mention that Mr. Bernard twelve years later was one of the High Commissioners who arranged the Geneva Arbitration.) The time came for us to go, and my host, putting on his cap and his embroidered gown — being that which his professorship entitled him to wear — conducted me to the entrance to the theatre. All was excitement there. A mob was assembled to see the privileged ones go in, and carriages were going about, and there was all the movement and stir that marks a great day. Under Mr. Bernard's protection I passed safely through the files of university police and entered the theatre. What a scene it was! A huge semicircular room with seats all around it, those in the middle being for ladies, tier above tier. And over their seats a gallery in which the undergraduates were gathered, piled, as it were, thick upon each other, and roaring and yelling like madmen. My place was on the floor — standing-room only — there were no seats. It was ten o'clock; the ceremonies would not begin until eleven. The ladies were nearly all in their places, but a few who were late came dropping in. Of course the undergraduates thought it necessary to remonstrate with them for being late; they thought it right also to urge the proctors to find seats for these fair ones without delay. "Do your duty, Ben!" was their cry addressed to the warden of Wadham, who in his red robes of office was the chief figure in conducting these late comers. The ladies themselves, on whom all eyes were thus turned, looked sufficiently uncomfortable. Then the attention of the young men would be drawn to persons entering the theatre without uncovering. "Hats off!" was the peremptory cry. Once a straw hat was observed. "Out with that straw! Officers, do your duty!" was the long-continued shout. Names were called to be cheered. The "Bishop of Oxford" (Wilberforce) was among the first proposed; then "Garibaldi," who had just begun his splendid Italian career. Gladstone's name was much disputed over—cheers and groans. Groans for John Bright were given very heartily. It was the period when the aristocracy of England had little love for that great man. Cheers for the "ladies in pink," "in mauve," for the "ladies under twenty-one"; tremendous cheers for the "Prince of Wales"; then "for ourselves"; "for everybody"—"except John Bright," a single voice added.[1] It was all very exciting. The ladies assembled showed lively interest in all that was going on; they were a brilliant company, their costumes making a splendour of colour in the midday light.

The Vice-Chancellor's seat was, as it were, flanked by the seats of the ladies, and it was directly opposite the grand entrance. I may mention that the Vice-Chancellor is the head of the whole University. The Chancellor is always a nobleman of the highest rank, but he appears only on great occasions, and at rare intervals. The Duke of Wellington was Chancellor for many years; at the time of which I write the Earl of Derby held the office; it is now held by the Marquis of Salisbury. To the right of the Vice-Chancellor's chair was a seat on the back of which was a gilt crown or crest surmounted by gilded plumes. It was the chair used by the Prince Regent at the visit of the

[1] Some twenty years later Oxford did honour to itself by conferring its degree on John Bright. Time had wrought its wholesome change in opinion. The appearance in the theatre of the great Liberal chief in his doctor's robes was the signal for a tempest of cheers; the new generation showed themselves of one mind in their wish to do him honour.

Allied Sovereigns, and was now to be occupied by the Prince of Wales.

Eleven o'clock at length struck; the great doors were thrown open, and "God save the Queen," was given forth by the organ. First of all in the procession, as ranking all, came the Prince — a fair, slender boy. True, he was between eighteen and nineteen, but he had a very youthful look. (It will be perceived I am speaking of a period nearly forty years ago, when the Prince was an Oxford student). His face had a certain sweetness — a grave, pensive expression. He smiled pleasantly as he bowed. There was little that was intellectual in his countenance, yet he seemed interested in what went on around him. I fancied in him a certain repose or serenity befitting a royal personage. To me there was, at that time, a fascination about the youth. Doubtless it was the remembrance of the long line of kings from whom he has sprung, and there was something, too, in the thought of his tender years, and the cares which were by and by to come on him. A storm of applause greeted him as he ascended to his seat. The ladies, and all the company, stood up. He bowed again and again to those of them he knew. Mrs. Gladstone, who was nearest him, he shook hands with — a handsome woman, sprightly in manner.

The Vice-Chancellor took his seat, and the other dignitaries, all in grand costume, ranged themselves in their allotted places. Canon Stanley, as he then was, afterward the famous Dean, was in professorial robes of scarlet, or black and scarlet. The first business of the day was the reading by the Vice-Chancellor of a Latin paper setting forth the especial claim or merit of the persons on whom degrees were to be conferred; and then the proposing to the members of the University their names for approval or otherwise, "*Placetne Vobis Domini Doctores?*" said he, addressing the Doctors present, and then "*Placetne Vobis Magistri?*" turning to two Masters of Arts who stood in cap and gown to figure that entire portion of the academic body.

Lord Brougham was one of those who were that day to be honoured. The time had at length come when Oxford was willing to recognize the eminence of the great Whig leader. When his name was read in the list there was tremendous applause, and it was some time before the Vice-Chancellor could go on. The Swedish Ambassador and some other foreign dignitary were two of the names read and accepted without much disturbance. Next in order was the name of Sir Richard Bethell. No sooner had this been uttered than shouts of dissent came from the galleries, and there was prodigious uproar. The undergraduates, it was plain, were utterly opposed to this Whig lawyer's receiving a degree. He was obnoxious to the Conservative party as being a leading member, in the Whig interest, of Lord Palmerston's Government, and as the author of the Divorce Bill. I may add that he was afterward Lord Chancellor under the title of Lord Westbury.

The Vice-Chancellor waited, as well he might, for no word of his could have been heard. At length there was a slight lull; the "*Placetne Vobis*," was hurried over as quickly as possible, but not without the yells of disapproval being again sent forth. Then came the name of Sir Leopold McClintock — discoverer of the remains of Sir John Franklin's expedition — an adroit arrangement this, for a popular name would appease the incensed crowd. Instantly a shout of approval burst forth, and cheer after cheer was given. Last of all was the name of John Lothrop Motley; this was received respectfully but calmly.

Now came the entry into the theatre of the men who were to be thus honoured. Each was in flowing robes of scarlet. The Regius Professor of Civil Law, Dr. Twiss, conducted them singly toward the Vice-Chancellor, and then in sonorous Latin set forth their achievements or their fame. First, the Swedish Ambassador; his merits having been recited by Dr. Twiss, the Vice-Chancellor addressed him as " *Vir illustrissime*," and then conferred the degree. The Ambassador wore his scarlet robe over his foreign uniform, or court dress. He ascended the steps, and the Vice-Chancellor gave him his hand, and he took his seat among the other dignitaries. Lord Brougham was the next, and his appearance was the signal for such a frenzy of cheering as, I fancy, had not often before been heard within those walls. I was close to the old man, and watched the play of muscles in his countenance, as with downcast eyes he received the recognition of the young men of England of his great name and fame. He was then over eighty, and his hair was entirely white. I thought, as I looked at him, of the great part he had played in modern English history — of the trial of Queen Caroline, the stormy debates in regard to Catholic Emancipation and the Reform Bill, the long struggle for the freedom of the West Indian slaves. I could not foresee that in the very next year, when the great cause of emancipation in my own country was in sore need of moral support from Lord Brougham, that support would be coldly withheld. But it is charitable to suppose that age had in those last days dimmed faculties that were once so bright.

At length the Professor of Civil Law was allowed to go on. When the Vice-Chancellor addressed the venerable man, there was a renewed burst of enthusiasm, and when he gave him his hand, there was another. Turning round and facing the assembly, the aged peer bowed with dignity in acknowledgment of his great reception. At length there was quiet. Now appeared Sir Richard Bethell. At once there were groans and hisses and cries of all kinds — a fearful din. Again I watched the countenance of the man who was standing thus, the object of all eyes and of every one's thoughts. His brow grew dark. I feared that the proceedings might be brought to a sudden end. Dr. Stanley had told us, at his breakfast-table the day before, that the Vice-Chancellor had resolved, if the uproar exceeded a certain limit, he would at once break up the convocation. By and by there was a pause; hastily the concluding words of the orator were said, and quickly, too, the Vice-Chancellor did his part; then Sir Richard ascended the steps, and, turning round, looked up at the galleries and bowed, as though he had something to thank the young men for. This unexpected act seemed to awaken their better feelings, and there was at once applause. And so the matter ended better than it began.

What a contrast there was when McClintock appeared! The Oxford men appreciate hardihood; here was a hero they could thoroughly understand. I thought what a reward it was for long trials and endurance to receive honours from this renowned University. McClintock was a small man, unpretending in look. He wore his naval uniform under his doctor's robes. When he ascended the steps, it seemed difficult at first to find a place for him. He took a low seat, but immediately room was made for him higher up, quite among the ladies. "None but the brave deserve the fair," came in a clear voice from the undergraduates' gallery, and immediately there was a shout of laughter and cheers.

Mr. Motley was next in order, and with him the list of doctors closed. His form and features are familiar to us now, but to me he was until then a stranger, and I certainly saw no finer face in all that company than his. The young Oxford men seemed to know little of him (only his "Dutch Republic" had then appeared), for they received him with but moderate cheers. I should mention that when, at the beginning of the proceedings, the Vice-Chancellor recited his claim to the honour it was proposed to confer, and dwelt on his merits as an author, he used the word *luculentissime* (most luminous, perspicuous), and for some reason or other it caused a laugh. The Vice-Chancellor himself smiled. Whether it was that the phrase was a stilted one, the learned must decide. I remember further that when the question *Placetne* was put, "Oh, by all means!" was the prompt reply from the gallery.

I must mention here a little incident as showing how pitiless young men are. One of the eminent personages on whom a degree was to be conferred — indeed it was Mr. Motley — had as a measure of precaution brought his umbrella in with him. He might cling to it any day of that rainy summer of 1860. He doubtless thought he had it well hidden under his scarlet robes, but a quick-sighted and unmerciful youth in the gallery got a glimpse of it, as the new-made D. C. L. was taking his seat, and at once there came the shrill cry, "Three cheers for the umbrella!"

The conferring of degrees had now ended, but the address which gives title to the day was yet to be delivered — an address commemorating Founders and Benefactors. There was stir and confusion, for people were arranging to depart. The address was to be in Latin. Matthew Arnold was the orator;

he appeared in a reading-desk or pulpit projecting from a side gallery, and began his task. Nobody seemed to listen, but Mr. Arnold's manner gave one the impression that he did not in the least expect attention would be paid to him. With the ending of his address, the proceedings closed.

I have said little of Oxford as a whole, for I shrink from attempting to define its especial dignity and charm. Again and again I have been there, and each time, "smit with its splendour and its sweetness," I have felt envy of the men whose minds have been moulded under influences so peculiar and so enduring. I have experienced what Newman describes as the fascination which the very face and smile of a University possess over those who come within its range. Oxford has indeed attractions quite indescribable; and it would be well if more of our countrymen would seek to enter into the spirit of the place, and experience, as they assuredly would, its manifold impressiveness. At the visit of which I have now told, certain ladies were my companions. From a letter from one of them I give the following, which I deem a fit ending of my story.

"Surely never was there a place that had such a subtle charm as that old city, sitting like some ancient sibyl among her deep, flowery meadows and embowering trees, with such a mystery of learning and wisdom in her musing eyes."

THE RIGHT HONOURABLE WILLIAM EDWARD FORSTER

THE RIGHT HONOURABLE WILLIAM EDWARD FORSTER

On my first visit to England in 1849, among my letters of introduction — in those days a very important part of one's preparation for travel — was a letter to Robert Forster of Tottenham, a leading member of the Society of Friends. I was received by him and his four sisters very cordially, at their pleasant home in one of the quietest of the small towns of the London radius. They were all past middle age, and none of them had married. Their elder brother, William, had married a sister of Sir Thomas Fowell Buxton, and the son and only child of this marriage, William Edward Forster, was then beginning to make himself a name. He was the one representative of his generation, of this excellent family, and it is of him that I have now chiefly to speak. I was greatly impressed with the purity and uplifted souls of this Tottenham household — their interest in works of charity of every kind, and their deep sense of religion. The saintly life has its illustration in quiet and retired family groups everywhere — here it was peculiarly manifest. Robert Forster I sat with, in a summer-house of his garden, late in the sweet June evening, and it was natural to me to open, in a way, my mind to him. It was interesting to him to know how it was that as my family had been Friends from almost George Fox's time, I had strayed from the fold. I made what explanation I could, and at the end, the good old man put his arm round my neck, saying, almost with emotion, "I hope thou wilt keep thy mind open to conviction." I felt in regard to him and his, I can truly say, after this first meeting, that they were a family which had been "ennobled by purity of moral life for many generations."

Some three years later I was travelling in Switzerland, and at Interlachen met again Robert Forster and his four sisters. I was with them for a day or two, and felt once more the influence that went out from them, making it good to be near them. They were kind to me in every way, regarding me, perhaps, as a "proselyte of the gate." They said to me, "Thou must know our nephew, William Edward Forster; we will write to him, and will hope thou canst make him a visit." I was only too glad to respond to this, for I knew of him, and of literary work he had already done, and I had read especially his reply to Macaulay in defence of Penn — a vigorous and convincing pamphlet, showing that questionable acts attributed by Macaulay in his history, to William Penn, were really the work of quite another person, a certain George Penne. I knew also of William Edward Forster's keen interest in all political matters in England, and in the great question of slavery in America. I knew, too, of his having been, on his first coming of age, private secretary to his uncle, Sir Thomas Fowell Buxton. This, in fact, had been the beginning of his efforts to fit himself for the career of a statesman. I was eager, therefore, to meet one from whom I could learn so much, and whose future seemed to me so full of promise. I knew that he had married, a year or two before, the eldest daughter of Dr. Arnold of Rugby; this fact was of great interest to me.

On my return to England I received a note from William Forster, asking me to come to them at their Yorkshire home at Burley, in the valley of the Wharfe. I replied that I should arrive at Ben Rhyding, a watering-place within a mile or two of their residence, on a Saturday night, and should perhaps see them at church the next day. I was early at the church, and, as I sat on one side of the main aisle, a young lady of slight and graceful figure passed me, and took a seat on the opposite side, higher up. I knew by a sort of instinct that this was no other than the daughter of Dr. Arnold. Soon a tall man, thin and wiry, with a resolute expression, walked up and took a seat beside her; this was Forster, I felt no doubt. The service went on. At the end of the sermon, as it was a Communion Sunday, many of the congregation went out — Mr. Forster among them. I remained for the second service. He stopped for a moment where I was sitting, told me his name, and said his wife would remain, and asked if I would walk with her to their home. At the church door my acquaintance with this admirable person began — now forty-six years ago; her age then was about thirty. My instant feeling was that intelligence, refinement, high and pure thought, met in her, together with all feminine charm. Long afterward I learned that Wordsworth had said that in all that went to make up excellence in women Jane Arnold was as fine an example as he had known.

What a vision it is for my memory, that pretty home at Wharfeside, where I first came to know William Edward and Jane Forster! Never was there closer intellectual companionship; each, as it were, supplementing the other — his rugged strength, his quick mind, his wide knowledge of books, of men, and of affairs — her keen intelligence, her grace of manner, her sweet dignity, her tenderness of feeling.

The pretty river, the Wharfe, flowed at the foot of their grounds, and soon after our pleasant meal we went out on its waters — Forster rowed, Mrs. Forster and I sitting in the stern. I remember his saying to me, "I understand you have become an Episcopal — that is, that you have given up a religious fellowship in which there were no slaves, for one in which there are more slaves per head than any other." His wife reproved him for his seeming discourtesy, but, as his look showed anything but malice, I could forgive him. The remark showed where we were in that year of grace, 1852. It was the year of the "Uncle Tom's Cabin" excitement. I may mention that I arrived at Liverpool at the end of April of that year, and told of that remarkable book in various households in which

I had chanced to visit. These friends have always since maintained that I brought the news of the book to England. Certainly, when I came back from the Continent at the end of four months, I found the whole land ringing with it.

Another characteristic remark of Forster's was — after inquiring after my Aunt Lucretia Mott — " I remember listening in London in 1840 to a discussion between Mrs. Mott and a Reverend Someone, I think an American, on the woman question." After a pause, Forster added, "She whipped him to everlasting smash." Mr. Forster perhaps thought it polite to use the language of my country in telling me of this incident.

The few days of my visit went quickly by, and every hour was of enjoyment. The evening talks in the library — a large room which was, at the same time, the drawing-room — gave me the keenest pleasure. The walls were covered with books, showing interest in literature of the widest range. But it was plain that all literary interests were subordinate to a deep concern in questions of politics and Government. My new friend was to me a striking example of a man of affairs, a man giving close attention to business, and yet securing to himself always the infinite solace of books and study. Yet it was clear that the hope ever before him was the taking part in Government. He caught eagerly at every opportunity of informing himself on all matters of public concern, on all Colonial questions, on our American slavery, and on subjects of chief discussion and controversy in the United States. He seemed from the first to have a vague feeling that America was to go hand in hand with England in influencing the future of the world. With his wife he was absolutely one in thought and feeling, and she "forwarded him unweariedly," to use Carlyle's words, "as none else could in all of worthy he did or attempted." She had come to him from an atmosphere purely intellectual. Fox How had been the gathering place, always, of men of distinction — Bunsen and Whately, Julius Hare, Wordsworth, Mr. Justice Coleridge, Hartley Coleridge, Frederick Faber, Crabb Robinson, Caroline Fox, Mrs. Fletcher, Dr. John Davy, Lady Richardson, and Harriet Martineau, are the names that rise first to one's mind. But Wordsworth was the commanding figure to whom all paid instinctive reverence.

Dr. Arnold stood for literary cultivation as much as any man in England; his name had become a household word in America from the wide circulation of "Stanley's Life" — far wider, owing to the cheap reprint, than had been reached in England. Mrs. Forster seemed to me peculiarly to reflect her father. When I came later to know her sisters at Fox How, one of them said to me; "You know the one of us who most resembles our father." I felt from the first how remarkably she was fitted to be the wife of a statesman. She could well cherish the hope that when the opportunity he longed for came to her husband, she could aid him in work which would have been dear to her father's heart.

I took my leave after this first visit, trusting a beginning had been granted me of a friendship that would endure. It did last until Forster's death thirty-four years later, and now twelve more years have passed, and I can count as a blessing which remains to me, my friendship with Mrs. Forster. Three of my children, too, have seen and known her, and I can truly say for them their feeling is altogether that of reverent affection and admiration.

My second visit to Wharfeside was in 1855. I rejoiced to take part once more in that keenly intellectual life. My friends very kindly went with me on a visit to Fountains Abbey — as glorious a ruin as any in England. I remember noticing that in the group of persons who were that day making the round of the Abbey there was an unconscious leadership on the part of Forster; I was strengthened by this in the feeling that rule or government would one day fall to him. It was something, as I have said, unconscious on his part — the bearing of a born ruler of men. It was at this visit I asked him whether he did not look to entering Parliament. He said he did, but that as yet he was hardly well enough off. It was clear to me that during the interval of my visits he had been steadily preparing himself for the work of a legislator. He had written for the *Westminster Review* a paper on "American Slavery" in regard to which I had had correspondence with him. In common with all thoughtful men, he was considering what could be the outcome of the slavery agitation in America, which was each year becoming more acute. As yet the war was five years distant. But the Crimean war was at that time a subject of keenest interest and anxiety. Gladstone and Lord John Russell had just retired from the Aberdeen Government, declaring that peace ought to be made, although Sebastopol had not as yet fallen. I find in my journal the record that Forster was furious against Gladstone especially, for thus abandoning his colleagues, he having been answerable equally with them for the beginning of the war.

I remember asking Forster whether he could look forward to a time when John Bright would become a member of the Government. He said the question was a difficult one because of Bright's views as to war and in regard to the Church. He added, however, his conviction that whatever Government Bright became a member of he would practically control — so great, he considered, was his ability. Some twelve years afterward, Bright did become one of the Ministry, and the Irish Land Bill of 1870 was his work; this, with the Bill for Disestablishing the Irish Church, and Forster's Education Bill, were the chief acts of the Gladstone Government of 1868–1874.

Forster, at the time of my visit of 1855, was employing in his mills some eight hundred people, —

he and his partner,—and yet in some way he seemed to secure a good deal of leisure, and to be able to give thought to literature and public concerns. He was fortunate then, and later, when he entered Parliament, in having a partner who was willing to release him for public duty, taking upon himself the full burden of their important manufacturing operations. These operations prospered, however, through all, and Forster, when he became a member of Parliament and afterwards of the Government, was wholly without anxiety as to his business affairs.

But at my visit of 1855, the prospect of a seat in Parliament was as yet remote. The work of preparation was going on unceasingly, so that delay was only fitting him more for the position he could feel sure would be his, if life lasted. I may note here a prediction of the first Sir Fowell Buxton in regard to his nephew Forster, then twenty-two. "I shall not live to see it, but that young man will make his mark." I give this from the "Life of W. E. Forster," by Wemyss Reid. I can truly say that a like conviction was never absent from my mind from my first knowledge of my friend.

In this waiting time of 1855, literary matters could claim much of Forster's attention. In that month of August "Maud" had just appeared, and had caused a great stir. I remember that in railway carriages you constantly found people reading it. Much talk of it went on at Wharfeside. The "Ode to the Duke of Wellington," which appeared in the same volume, impressed Forster profoundly. I remember the feeling with which he read it aloud to us — that and the "Charge of the Six Hundred." The two poems seemed to go to his inmost heart. Charles Kingsley, whom I came to know in 1857, said to me Forster should have gone into the army: "He would have been a major-general by this time." But he was an Englishman before all things, animated by an extreme desire for liberal progress and for the true advancement of his country.

The Crimean war ended, and our slavery matters were more and more occupying the attention of statesmen on both sides the Atlantic. I was in England again in 1857, and was staying at Fenton's Hotel, St. James's Street, London. A knock at my door in the morning — there was my friend! He had come up to London suddenly, because of a parliamentary vacancy which had just occurred. He had seen my name on the books of the hotel. He had strong hope of securing the nomination, but, by some chicanery of a committee, it was given to another. As I have already quoted from Charles Kingsley, Forster was hardly the man to deal with the *tracasseries* of an election contest; his time of waiting and of preparation was to go on for yet three years.

In a month or two I was once more at Wharfeside. I found there Thomas Arnold, Mrs. Forster's brother, with his wife and little children, fresh from Tasmania. Arnold's history, as Forster informed me, was that, after a distinguished career at Oxford, he went out to New Zealand, Dr. Arnold having bought land there. The young scholar gave himself to sheep farming. Happily, before much time had been wasted on this occupation, Captain Owen Stanley, brother of the afterwards famous Dean, calling at Auckland in command of one of her Majesty's ships, heard of young Arnold, and, meeting him, saw at once how unfitted he was for bucolic pursuits. Captain Stanley's next call was at a port in Tasmania then known as Van Diemen's Land. He told Sir William Denison, the governor, of Arnold. Sir William at once sent for him and made him Inspector of Schools for Tasmania. He remained there, and there also became a Roman Catholic. I asked Forster if this change was the result of Oxford and High Church influences. "Quite the contrary," said Forster; "it was a reaction from Latitudinarianism." My impression is that Jowett had more influence on him than any one else in his Oxford days. His wife had not followed him in his change. Mrs. Forster remarked to me that, though it would seem strange for her to say it, she could almost regret that her sister-in-law had not gone with her husband. The little children who were playing there were too young for me to take much note of. One of them is now Mrs. Humphry Ward.

I had delightful walks and talks with Forster and his brother-in-law—"our Papist brother" he called him. I was much impressed with Thomas Arnold;

he seemed a keenly intellectual man, and to have deep conviction of the truth of the opinions he had embraced. He is, I think, the only man I have ever known, who has made that change, who awakened any questionings in my own mind. He had made sacrifice, I think, of his worldly fortune by his change.

I remember Forster's saying to him one day after dinner, "Tom, I had an experience lately at a meeting to consider my nomination for Parliament. A story had got about that I had High Church leanings, and that as my brother-in-law had turned Papist, I might go the same way. I was anxious to meet this, so I arranged for some one to put the question to me. The meeting, however, silenced the questioner at once, and my little scheme failed."

But the animated conversations on political and literary matters in the large drawing-room-library are the chief memory for me of my visit of that year. Each evening the talk went on, Mrs. Forster making tea for us. The Indian mutiny was of absorbing interest, the arrival of the *Times* in the early afternoon being the chief event of the day. William Arnold, another brother of Mrs. Forster, was at that time Inspector of Schools in the Punjaub. Letters from him were read showing his forebodings of three months before; his latest letters were read, also showing his belief that the Punjaub would be a tower of strength to the English rule in India. The Punjaub, under the lead of Sir John Lawrence, did, in fact, save India.

Ireland was another of the subjects of our talk, then, and for long years before, of chief concern to English legislators. Forster had been Carlyle's companion on a short Irish tour in 1849. But Carlyle's feeling at the misery they witnessed was more of wrath than of pity, for to him the suffering was but the people's deserving. Forster, who had seen the famine of two years before, and had taken an active part in administering relief, was shocked at the almost exultation of Carlyle at the wretchedness of the people. The travelling companionship soon came to an end, and the intercourse between the two thereafter was slight. A scene described by Forster in a letter may be worth quoting here, of the date of 1847, some years before his marriage. Mr. and Mrs. Carlyle were Forster's guests at Rawdon for three weeks. He took them to the Derbyshire region, and at Buxton at a *table d'hôte* Forster was at the bottom as last comer, Mr. and Mrs. Carlyle at his right, and a tall, starched, gentlemanly Irish parson on his left.

"For a time all went on easily [says Forster], in silent feeding or low grumbling, till at last Carlyle began to converse with parson, then to argue with him on Ireland, then to lose thought of all arguments or *table d'hôte*, and to declaim. How they did stare! All other speech was hushed; some looked aghast, others admiring; none of them had ever heard or seen anything approach to such monster. We remained *incog* the whole time, spite of all the schemes of the guests, and the entreaties of the waiter to book our names, and my proposal to Mrs. Carlyle to save our expenses by showing him at so much a head."

Another incident of this visit of the Carlyles to Forster was his being thrown from a gig when driving with Mrs. Carlyle. The horse took fright and dashed down a long hill. Mrs. Carlyle showed wonderful presence of mind — turning her back to the horse and embracing the gig, and so when it was overturned, rolling out without being hurt. Forster was a somewhat reckless driver. He tells himself this further story of his bachelor days. He had picked up an old man, one of his work people. "The pace down the hill astonished the old man, who shut his eyes and clenched the seat in mortal fear. He reached his home, however, safely, and soon after his son came in looking very glum: 'What's t' matter with thee, lad?' 'What's t' matter with thee, feyther? Why could na' thou see me, a bit sin'? Thou might have taken notice of thy son, though thou was in Mr. Forster's gig.' 'Eh, bless thee, lad; I had more to do than to take notice of thee. I was ower throng (busy) making my peace with my Maker!'"

Forster's comment on Carlyle after the three weeks' visit was: "He certainly is a most delightful companion, a rich store of hearty, genial, social kindness shining through his assumed veil of misanthropy, and often the more conspicuous from his efforts to conceal or disown it, and his eccentric humour, striking laughter out of all manner of every-day, trivial occurrences."

A proposal to abolish the Lord Lieutenantship of

Ireland was a subject of discussion in 1857, and I remember Forster's taking down from his shelf Thackeray's Ballads and reading with inimitable effect "Molony's Lament"—

> "O Tim, did ye hear of thim Saxons,
>   And read what the peepers repoort?
> They're goan to recal the Liftinant,
>   And shut up the Castle and Coort!
> Our desolate counthry of Oireland,
>   They're bint, the Blagyards, to desthroy,
> And now, having murthered our counthry,
>   They're goin' to kill the viceroy,
>   Dear boy;
> 'Twas he was our proide and our joy!"

and again:

> "And what's to become of poor Dame Sthreet,
>   And who'll ait the puffs and the tarts,
> When the Coort of imparial splindor
>   From Doblin's sad city departs?
> And who'll have the fiddlers and pipers,
>   When the deuce of a Coort there remains?
> And wher'll be the bucks and the ladies,
>   To hire the Coort-shuits and the thrains?
>   In sthrains
> It's thus that ould Erin complains!"

Forster had a true sense of humour; I remember the delight with which he read, at a later visit, bits from Artemus Ward. But the conversation on Ireland, at the time of which I speak, and the quotation from Thackeray, were of peculiar interest to me in recollection thirteen years later, when my friend had taken on himself the awful burden and responsibility of the government of that unhappy country.

In my visit of 1857, I saw in Forster's intense interest in all that concerned his country how much there was in him of the making of a statesman, and I longed more than ever for his entry into Parliament. In February, 1861, he was returned for Bradford, and that constituency he represented for five and twenty years — though he had contest after contest to sustain.

My correspondence with my friend continued after my return to America in 1857. The clouds were gathering, and it was plain that momentous days were at hand. The nomination of Lincoln in 1860, or, perhaps I should say, the debate between Lincoln and Douglas in Illinois in 1858, was the first signal of the great conflict. No Englishman had more thoroughly informed himself as to the question involved in the great struggle. Our war went on, and its varying fortunes were watched by Forster with intense solicitude, and both in Parliament and before his constituents his voice was raised in our behalf. No one, except Mr. Bright, was more conspicuous than he in our defence, for no one spoke with fuller knowledge. He felt, as Mr. Bright did, that the cause of free institutions was involved in the issue. He was vigilant in the House of Commons in making head against the men who were in sympathy with the South. I regret to say that Lord Robert Cecil, now the Marquis of Salisbury, was very prominent among the friends of the Confederates. Few men in public life have advanced more, morally as well as intellectually, with advancing life, than the present Prime Minister of England.

William Forster was in constant communication with Charles Francis Adams during the war, giving him all the aid he could. Mr. Adams told me this, and especially of his suggestion to him of a legal adviser when, as to the matter of the *Alabama*, it became necessary to employ English counsel. The opinion then given compelled the English Government to act — though all too late.

Forster made his mark in the House very early, though he was not what would be called a good speaker. His force of character, his clearness of mind, and his wide knowledge were at once recognized. In 1865, he had been four years in Parliament; before the year closed he was a member of the Ministry. Lord Palmerston had died and Lord Russell was once more Prime Minister. The Reform Bill the Government brought in failed because of the defection of Robert Lowe. Lord Russell resigned and Lord Derby came in. Disraeli, as leader of the House in the new Government, brought in another Reform Bill more advanced than the one which had been defeated. Disraeli's object in this measure was to "dish the Whigs." "Household suffrage," Sir Henry Maine says, "was introduced into towns to dish one side, and into counties to dish the other." Sir Henry Maine makes the further acute remark that "universal suffrage in England would have prohibited the spinning-jenny and the power-loom." " A leap in the dark," Lord Derby called this bill of Disraeli's, but, all the same, he accepted it as a party measure, and the Tories and landed proprietors voted for it, and it became law. I was present at the final vote on this measure in the House of Lords in August, 1867. I had my own thoughts at this further widening of the suffrage in view of our American experience. "Shooting Niagara," Carlyle called it, saying, "it is well that he they call Dizzy is to do it — a superlative Hebrew conjuror, spellbinding all the great Lords, great Parties, great Interests of England, to his hand in this manner, and leading them by the nose, like helpless, mesmerized, somnambulant cattle."

I anticipate events by stating that while Disraeli's bill became law, he did not remain long in power. The Liberals came in and went on with reform in their own fashion. In 1872 there seemed a pause, and Disraeli took the opportunity to say in a speech at Manchester: —

"As I sat opposite the treasury bench the Ministers reminded me of those marine landscapes not unusual on the coasts of South America. You behold a range of exhausted volcanoes. Not a flame flickers on a single pallid crest. But the situation is still dangerous. There are occasional earthquakes, and ever and anon the dark rumbling of the sea."

Walter Bagehot said of Disraeli, "His wheat is worthless, but his chaff the best in the world." Of this latter the above is a fine example.

I had but brief sight of William Forster in that

year, 1867. In 1868 Gladstone came into office for the first time as Prime Minister, and Forster was made vice-president of the Council, though, to the surprise of many, he was not of the Cabinet proper. It was not until the death of Lord Clarendon in 1870, that he was sworn in as one of the group of ten or twelve men on whom the Government of England rests. I had companionship with him in this year, and looked on for a night or two as he was carrying through the House his great Education Bill, — a measure to give common school education to the English people. I remember a speech from below the gangway on the Government side, which was flowing and eloquent and which was in support of the bill, though it closed with the offer of an amendment. The speaker was Sir William Harcourt. When he sat down Forster rose, and said he must express the satisfaction of the Government at the support of the honourable and learned member, but that this satisfaction would have been greater if the support had been offered at an earlier stage of the bill. With regard to the particular amendment offered by the honourable and learned member he must take leave to say that no amendment had been offered that had less to recommend it. I saw plainly enough from Forster's remark that there was something of political rivalry between these two eminent men.

The Education Act of 1870 was the especial work of William Edward Forster. Again and again schemes for common school education had been brought forward, and again and again there had been failure. The leading feature of Forster's plan was the recognition of the schools which had been established by the different religious bodies of the country, for the education of the poor — continuing them and subsidizing them. Wherever there was no school, the Government would establish and maintain one, the local authority directing it — such school to be known as a Board School. Forster had full charge of the difficult work of carrying through Parliament this great measure. He told me he had always the cordial support of Gladstone, as his chief, but the measure was essentially his, and he had ever to be on the watch to meet opposers. Alas! for human weakness, the Nonconformists raised the cry that the Church of England would receive benefit from the measure. Members of the Church had been far more active than the Dissenters had been; hence the Government aid would seem to be especially extended to them. Forster knew that this would be complained of, but he knew also that there would be no possibility of carrying through a scheme of education for the whole of England except by the plan he proposed. Any other plan would have involved the building of schoolhouses everywhere, and the throwing over of the schools, which, as works of charity and religion, had already been set up. William Forster was not himself a Churchman; he was aiming before all things to educate the people; in no other way could he accomplish this. He saw how seriously his personal popularity would be affected by the course he took, but he acted in the light of duty. His scheme, moreover, involved the recognition of religion as a primary influence in the beginning of education. His heart was made heavy by the outcry that was raised. He told me the opposition of the Nonconformists was a blow struck at once at religion, and at education. Even John Bright was not free from what I must call sectarian prejudice, in the half-hearted support he gave to Forster. Yet Forster was almost of the same faith as Bright. He told me that, while he had ceased to be in formal membership with the Society of Friends, he could never be of any other religious body. The Friends, he said, had disowned him for the best act of his life, which was his marriage (marrying, as the phrase is, "out of meeting"). This in no way affected his feeling for them. The memory of his father was, moreover, to him almost a religion. William Forster the elder was a man of saintly life, considering, through all his days, the supreme duty laid upon him to be the deepening a sense of religion in the souls of men. I must add, however, a remark once made to me by Forster: "It was hard on my mother. I was but a year old when my father made his first religious visit to America, and he was gone five years." His mother remained alone in a cottage in Dorsetshire with her young child, and, though frail in health, made occasional religious journeys; for she too was a minister among Friends. Forster used to tell of an incident of his childhood. He was travelling in a coach in the charge of his nurse when a benevolent old gentleman began to talk to him. "Where is your papa, my dear?" said his fellow-passenger. "Papa is preaching in America," was the reply. "And where is your mamma?" continued the gentleman. "Mamma is preaching in Ireland," was the answer which the astonished stranger received.

It will readily be seen how strong were the influences favourable to Quakerism in his youth, and how closely he was bound to that religious body in heart and mind. It was not from them that opposition came to his education measure, but from the class that Matthew Arnold called "Political Dissenters." Very serious to Forster was this opposition. He had ambition, a passion which, as Burke has said, is the instinct of all great souls, indeed a necessary qualification for a statesman. His rise in the House of Commons had been so rapid that his reaching the leadership had seemed altogether a possibility. Now arose a cry against him which could not be disregarded. He went on, however, without faltering, and his bill became a law. For several years there was no relaxing of the opposition. In 1872, Lord Salisbury spoke as follows:—

"Nothing is more surprising to me than the plea on which the present outcry is made against the Church of England. I could not believe that in the nineteenth century the charge against the Church of England should be that churchmen, and especially the clergy, had educated the people. If I were to fix on one circumstance more than another which redounded to the honour of churchmen it is that they should fulfil this noble office, and, next to being 'Stewards of Divine Mysteries,' I should think the greatest distinction of the clergy is the admirable manner in which they have devoted their lives and their fortunes to this first of national objects. I have due and great respect for the Non-Conformist body. If I could have found that, in the Education Act, any injustice had been done to the Non-Conformists, I should have voted with them."

I quote this because it bears on the opposition the Education Act had, in its first years, to meet with. In the year 1874 the Gladstone Government came to an end. In the next year (1875) Mr. Gladstone by reason of his *then advanced age* retired from the leadership of his party. He felt admonished, he said, by declining strength, to betake himself somewhat to seclusion and study. (A pretty lively hermit he was, we must all admit!) A successor had, however, to be chosen. Forster's name was the only one mentioned in opposition to Lord Hartington; but for the education matter the contest would have been close. The result seemed the loss to Mr. Forster of the chief place, when next there was a change of government, but as Gladstone very soon resumed, practically, the leadership, Lord Hartington's position became altogether nominal.

As proof of what I have stated as to the high position Forster had reached in the country, I may cite here a passage from the diary of the late Dr. Norman Macleod of the date of 1872. "At Balmoral I met Forster, the Cabinet Minister. He, and Helps and I, had great arguments on theological subjects till very late. I never was more impressed by any man as deep, independent, *thoroughly* honest, and sincere. I conceived a great love for him. I never met a statesman whom for high-minded honesty and justice I would sooner follow. He will be Premier some day."

In visits to England of 1869 and 1870, it was a peculiar satisfaction to me to see my friend at last in his true position as a member of the Government. At his table in London there was naturally talk of the heated feeling which remained in America growing out of the *Alabama* matter. I could report the universal opinion with us that the position of England was one of peril so long as the dispute remained unsettled — that while the *Alabama* precedent remained, our Government could not prevent the going out of privateers in case of England being at war with a Continental power. I remember a singular offhand reply of Forster's — hardly a serious one — that this risk could be covered by insurance, and that the cost to England would not be greater than the loss which had been caused by the Overend-Gurney failure. All the same, no man in England worked harder than Forster did to bring about the great settlement. Charles Sumner by his elaborate, but unwise, speech demanding that the indirect claims should be presented at Geneva, among them a claim for an enormous sum for England's having acknowledged the South as belligerents, caused intense excitement and indignation, making it doubtful whether the English Government could proceed with the arbitration. Forster made a very careful speech in reply to Sumner, whom he knew personally, and had regard for. Then as a member of the Cabinet he laboured with the utmost ardour to prevent the abandonment of the arbitration. "As toward America," as has been well said, "his record was clear, for no American could doubt his sympathy with the party and the Government which had triumphed in the war. On the other hand his English self-respect was clear." Gladstone, to his great honour, stood firm, and the Court of Arbitration met. It is proper to add that at this supreme crisis in the history of the two countries, Grant and Fish displayed conspicuous wisdom. The English Cabinet awaited news of the first proceedings at Geneva with anxiety, — Forster with breathless interest. At length the tidings came: "The indirect claims ruled out." This was for Forster one of the happiest moments of his political life.

In 1874, when the Gladstone Government went out, Mr. Forster took advantage of his leisure to pay a visit to America. A chief object was to visit the grave of his father, who had died in Tennessee when on a religious visit some twenty years before. Forster's companion was his cousin, Sir Fowell Buxton, grandson of the first Sir Fowell, now the governor of South Australia. I cannot but record here that my wife, who saw Mr. Forster then for the first time, had an instant sense of his power, while she saw very plainly the tender and loving traits there were in him.

Writing to an English relative, my wife said: —

"Mr. Forster strikes me as a man a head and shoulders, morally and intellectually, above other men. His individuality is singularly strong, and you are instantly at rest with him because he is so true and single-hearted. He impresses you immensely as a man of character, a man entirely himself, not influenced by those around him; but he has deep feeling and refinement, and a shrinking from display of all kinds.

"He has met many of our political men while in this country; some, I hope, have felt, from personal intercourse with him, how grand and great the office of a statesman is when the heart is pure and true and duty-loving. There is a beautiful sermon of Maurice's, which I remember reading years ago, in which he says how different rulers and those in authority would be if they but realized at all that it was God who was allowing them to help Him to govern the world."

Every one who saw him was impressed by him. I remember a dinner at Mr. John Welsh's, a party of sixteen, which lasted for four hours and was extremely pleasant. Mr. Welsh placed Mr. Forster at the middle of the table on one side, Sir Fowell Buxton at the middle on the other, himself and Mr. William Welsh were at the two ends. The talk was general. Men of distinction were present. I mention only the names of Judge Sharswood and Morton McMichael. Mr. Forster said to the company that his wife in a late letter had asked the cause of the political change here as shown by the elections then just over. Many replies and explanations were given. At the end Forster said: "Gentlemen, this is all extremely interesting, but what am I to write to my wife?" Forster enjoyed the occasion much. He said to me afterward Judge Sharswood was the strongest man of all that company.

Forster made two speeches in America, one here in Philadelphia at the celebration of the fiftieth anniversary of the founding of the Historical Society, the other before the Union League of New York. The burden and drift of each was a plea for the essential union and co-working of English-speaking men. This I may say was the dream and desire of his whole political life. My own sight of my friend ended with his visit here of 1874. I was not in England between 1874 and 1886. Two of my children received kindness from him in London and were greatly impressed by him. He introduced my eldest daughter and a friend to the Ladies' Gallery of the House of Commons. As they followed him up the narrow staircase my daughter said she felt as if she was being conducted by a friendly lion. His tall figure had by this time become broad, and he was, perhaps, somewhat shaggy, but there was that in him always that denoted distinction. My eldest son, then nineteen, was much touched by the gracious kindness of his manner toward him; he cherishes this as among his best recollections. In early life Forster was long-limbed and slim, and seemed loosely knit together, his look of a half-humorous sternness. Mrs. Forster once asked me if I did not think he looked like an American. Though born in the South of England, and resident there through all his youth, he had the look of Yorkshire; it used to be said of him that he was a very "stage Yorkshireman."

Of the years that followed 1875, I need not speak

at length. He was not wholly of accord with Gladstone in regard to the Bulgarian question. He travelled through Servia, Bulgaria, and Turkey, to see with his own eyes the state of things there. He felt the utmost horror of Turkish oppression and misrule, but could hardly give assent to the " bag and baggage " policy until he saw what was to take its place. He was especially cautious as a statesman — wise in judgment — and was misunderstood, because of his determination to hear both sides, by men of extreme opinions. His training as a man of affairs had taught him this wisdom. His constituents, again and again, complained that he was not true to his party. Caucus rule, a system which had been begun at Birmingham, sought to establish itself at Bradford. Forster made strenuous resistance to this from the first; he stood for the absolute independence of a member of Parliament, and fought against the rule of wire-pullers, which he saw would result from caucus supremacy. The very moderation of his position in 1877 and 1878 made his influence the greater in opposing Disraeli's policy of that period, which threatened to involve England in war with Russia in behalf of Turkey.

In 1880 came the overthrow of Lord Beaconsfield's Ministry and the accession of Gladstone. Forster, it was generally thought, would be Secretary for the Colonies. But the Parnell agitation in Ireland was then at its height, and a statesman of the first class was needed for the Chief Secretaryship — the Chief Secretary being practically the chief ruler. Forster took the place because, as he said, he thought it would have been his father's wish that he should do so. Then followed two years of storm, and anxiety, and peril, on which I need not now dwell. Mrs. Forster said, in a letter to me from the Chief Secretary's Lodge, it was hard there should be all this crime and outrage to contend with when a Government was in power every member of which was pledged to do all that possibly could be done for Ireland. Again and again assassins lay in wait for Forster, their plans only failing by strange accident. His courage never forsook him. In the very height of the agitation he made a journey to the Tipperary region, County Clare, — the most disturbed district, — without guard of military and scarcely of police. He addressed the people several times and no harm came to him. In a speech he made to his Bradford constituents soon afterward, he spoke of his journey and of his safety in it. His sense of humour would not, however, allow of his failing to tell them of resolutions which had been passed by the women's branch of the National League at a place not far from Tipperary. These resolutions were in stern condemnation of the Tipperary Nationalists, that they had allowed the opportunity to pass of dealing with the Chief Secretary as he deserved, adding that if the "old gorilla" would come their way they would show him!

Gladstone's policy of surrender to Parnell, which began with the Kilmainham Treaty of 1882, Forster was wholly unable to acquiesce in; he retired from office with great dignity, accepting calmly isolation, and what to many seemed the closing of his political career. No one of his colleagues accompanied him. Strange to say Chamberlain, afterward to be so eminent in opposing Gladstone's Irish policy, was a leader who was behind Gladstone in refusing to support Forster. In less than three years Gladstone's complete surrender was made, and then Bright, Chamberlain, Lord Hartington, Goschen, the Duke of Argyll, Lord Selborne, nearly all the great chiefs of the Liberal party, were by the side of Forster, being absolutely one in mind with him in opposition to Gladstone. Bright wrote to Gladstone that if any one else had proposed the Home Rule scheme there would not have been twenty men in the House of Commons, apart from the Irish members, to support it. I dwell on this Irish matter to illustrate the wisdom which I have maintained was Forster's characteristic. He was before all men in noting the limitations of Gladstone — "a bewitching, a fascinating personality," to use Matthew Arnold's words, "but a dangerous minister."

The subject of Imperial Federation, as yet but a shadowy beginning, occupied much of Forster's attention during the period of his retirement from office. South Africa and Egypt were also matters of close study to him. The vacillating policy of the Government in regard to Egypt he strongly condemned in the beginning of the session of 1884. His anxiety in regard to Gordon was then very great; he was maddened by the delay of the Government in despatching an expedition for his rescue. Finally he delivered himself in the House of Commons as follows. Speaking of the danger of Gordon's position, he said: "I believe every one but the Prime Minister is already convinced of that danger, and I attribute his not being convinced to his wonderful power of persuasion. He can persuade most people of most things, and, above all, he can persuade himself of almost anything." The words made a profound impression, although party leaders at the time condemned them.

I may venture to add the following as almost a personal confirmation of this charge of Forster's that the delay of the starting of the Nile expedition was due to Gladstone. My son, then nineteen, at the end of June, 1884, sat alongside Sir Redvers Buller at dinner in an English country house. Sir Redvers Buller was next to Lord Wolseley, in command of the expedition. He said, "I have always been a Liberal, but I cannot, for the life of me, understand why the Government delays ordering the expedition to start." Two months were yet to pass. The starting was in September. Alas! for the result.

The Queen, in writing to Gordon's sister when the news of his death came, said, "That the promises of support were not fulfilled, which I so frequently and so constantly pressed on those who asked him to go — is to me grief inexpressible, indeed, it has made me ill." These words seem to me to imply censure for inexcusable delay.

But almost as I write my eye falls on a copy of the *London Times* in which I read that at a dinner given in Edinburgh to Lord Wolseley, the Earl of Wemyss, who presided, said that Lord Wolseley dined with him shortly before starting on the Nile expedition. Lord Wolseley said to the lady next to him at that dinner, "What would I not give for those three months when Gladstone was trying to make up his mind." I have reason to believe that Gladstone gave reluctant consent to the sending out of Gordon; he clung, too, to the belief that, if he had to abandon Khartoum, he could escape to the southward.

I cannot but add, as some relief to the painful story on which I have been dwelling, the following, which was told me by an eminent London artist, Edward Clifford. Gordon sat to Clifford for his portrait just before starting for Khartoum. He said to Clifford he had one objection to the expedition on which the Government was sending him, viz.: that if he succeeded, they would be giving him one of their "beastly titles."

To return to Mr. Gladstone. Forster was as sensible as any man of his great qualities, but, as I have said, he noted very early certain intellectual deficiencies. When he became associated with him as a ministerial colleague, and especially when he was under him as his chief, his feeling for him was of affection, as well as respect and admiration. But the trial to Forster was great when suddenly his chief refused longer to support him. He could but retire and await, but with a heavy heart, what the future would bring. This was in 1882. In 1886 I chanced to hear Dean Burgon say to Sir Thomas Acland, referring to Gladstone, that it was " the great moral fall of the age." The dean was a man of learning and ability, but unrestrained in speech; Sir Thomas was Gladstone's lifelong friend; he smiled at the vehemence of the dean. It was a parting shot of the sturdy ecclesiastic. I visited Mrs. Forster soon afterward at Fox Ghyll, and mentioning to her the dean's remark, she said in her gentle way, " Perhaps a better word would be a *moral deterioration.*" Then she added, holding her hand before her, " Mr. Gladstone when he decides on a view or opinion or course of conduct will listen to no contrary views or arguments, he will see only the line he has determined to take."

I venture to think that the late Bonamy Price, a distinguished Oxford professor, stated with wonderful clearness Gladstone's chief characteristic: " Gladstone sees every side of the truth, but he only sees one side at once. You will find him fervent on one side; a little time goes by, and that whole point of view has passed away from him; he has forgotten that he ever held it; with equal fervour and perfect sincerity, he urges a quite different side. He never balances the two together. I call that a dangerous faculty."

At the end of December, 1885, when William Forster was on what proved to be his death-bed, a rumour reached Mr. Gladstone that he might not be unfavourable to the Home Rule scheme which was about to be brought forward. A letter came to him from Mr. Gladstone, expressing a hope that this report had foundation. Forster dictated a reply, acknowledging the kind tone of Mr. Gladstone's letter, adding, however, this distinct utterance:—

"This Irish matter is indeed most full of difficulties, and I wish to say that I have looked at Home Rule with a most earnest endeavour to form an impartial judgment. I have employed hours, I may say days, in overhauling my previous views, but I cannot come to any other conclusion than the one I gave in a late-published letter." In this letter he had stated, explicitly, that he believed a Parliament in Dublin would be fraught with danger to both England and Ireland.

In Mrs. Forster's very touching account of her husband's last illness, there is a record of a fortnight later date than that of the letter to Gladstone, which is as follows:—

"*January* 15, 1886.— This afternoon I read him a letter I had had from Mr. Tuke, in which he said that he thought Mr. Forster would like to know that in the Friends' 'Meeting for Sufferings' his recovery had been earnestly prayed for. My beloved husband was greatly moved. 'The Church of my fathers has not forgotten me!' he said, bursting into tears."

William Edward Forster died on the 5th of April, 1886. His death made a profound impression. At the suggestion of the *Times*, a funeral service was held in Westminster Abbey, which was attended by a vast throng of his old political associates and friends, by representatives of the Colonies, and by the general public. The next day, April 10th, there was the simple Quaker funeral on the hillside burying-ground at Burley, near the home he had loved so well. His biographer says of those who stood around on that wild winter's day, that they witnessed "the last farewell to the friend and neighbour, who had risen high in the councils of the State, but whose heart had remained unaffected by all the changes of fortune; who had never varied in his affection for the friends of his youth, or in his bearing toward the humblest of those among whom his lot was cast; whose temper had not been soured by trials, nor his sympathies narrowed by the growth of years; whose spirit had remained young whilst his head grew grey; and the horizon of whose mental vision had seemed ever to grow wider and brighter as he drew nearer to the end of life."

William Forster was childless, and was the last of his race. In 1859 he adopted the four orphan children of his brother-in-law, William Arnold; their mother had died in the Punjaub, their father at Gibraltar, on his way to England. Forster at once took upon him the whole charge of these children; they grew up to be, to both Mr. and Mrs. Forster, as if they had been of their own blood. Never had a good action received an ampler reward, and never was there a fuller return of love and gratitude. One of these adopted sons, Mr. Oakley Arnold-Forster is a member of Parliament of distinction and promise, and a writer of ability. One of the daughters is married to a nephew of Aubrey de Vere. This lady, then Miss Florence Arnold-Forster, tells in her journal of Mr. Forster's energy and enthusiasm as a traveller, his eagerness to obtain information. She says: —

"Whether it was with an enthusiastic Czech professor at Prague, or with a cultivated Austrian merchant returning to his home in the Bukowina, or a gentlemanly whist-playing Pole at some German watering-place, or a party of Russian volunteers going to help the Servians, or a Hungarian Honved officer, or a government official in a Roumanian railway carriage, or a shrewd English man of business in the fair at Nijni Novgorod, or some high diplomatic magnate at Constantinople or Vienna, or an active politician and deputy at Berlin, Pesth, or Athens — wherever or with whomsoever it might be, my father seemed always to have the faculty of getting straight on to some topic that thoroughly interested both himself and the man he was talking to, if it was only for a five minutes' conversation."

In what I have written in regard to William Edward Forster I have had chiefly in mind the example which his career affords for instruction here. The fact that he always spoke of himself as a politician shows the meaning which the term bears in England in contrast with the lower meaning which attaches to it in this country. With us it has become almost a term of reproach. But no words can be better than his own to illustrate this contrast. In 1876 he was chosen Lord Rector of the University of Aberdeen. In the address he made there, he thus summed up the qualifications of the true politician:—

"There remain these two absolute necessities — the knowledge, the quick perception, of right and wrong; and the desire to do right. It is not for me to turn this address into a sermon, or to attempt to preach the lessons which many a man here has learned in his Highland home from the Bible read by the father or mother; but remember this, that the politician you have so kindly heard to-day declares that, of all possible occupations, politics is the most unprofitable, the least worth following, if for any personal, or still more tempting party object its true aim be forgotten; and that true aim is this — the fulfilment by our country of her duty, by which fulfilment, and by which alone, can be secured her power and her superiority and the well-being of her sons."

ENGLAND AND THE HOUSE OF COMMONS IN THE CLOSING DAYS OF THE AMERICAN CIVIL WAR

ENGLAND AND THE HOUSE OF COMMONS IN THE CLOSING DAYS OF THE AMERICAN CIVIL WAR

I SAILED from New York for Liverpool on the *Australasian* on the 22d of February, 1865. Our voyage was prosperous, and on the tenth day we were in sight of land. Some hours later we were following the line of the Irish coast, looking with keen interest on the green, treeless headlands. The sea was calm and the sun was bright, and there was the peculiar gladness in one's heart which comes from the thought of the safe passage over the great waters. I know few sights which are more exhilarating, and of which the recollection is more vivid, than that of the Irish coast after a voyage from America. But now we had the further pleasure of being the bearers of news of victory. It was the year before the laying of the Atlantic cable.

When we were perhaps a hundred miles from the entrance to the harbour of Queenstown, a small steamer was seen to put out from the shore and head toward us. Soon a tin box with a long float of wood was brought on deck, and, when the little steamer was near, the box or canister, with its long pole attached, was thrown into the sea. We saw the little steamer hook it up, and then turn and make for the land. We knew that the box contained despatches with the latest war news, and that in an hour London and Liverpool and all of Europe would know of the fall of Charleston.

I landed in Liverpool on March 4 — the day of Mr. Lincoln's second inauguration. I had occasion to remain there for a few days, and was glad of the opportunity of conferring with the small group of persons who, in that city, had been in sympathy with the North from the beginning of the war. Mr. Dudley, our consul, lived chiefly in the society of this handful of persons. He could look for little other companionship as opinion then was. Perhaps his high-tariff principles helped to make the Liverpool merchants shy of him. But hardly anywhere in England was there stronger desire for the success of the South than in that busy city which owed so much of its growth and prosperity to American cotton. Mr. Dudley told me of the hard life he had led there in the watch he had to keep over the efforts of the Confederates to get out their cruisers. He said he had also to keep up the hopes of the friends of the North as well as he could, during the long period of our adverse fortune. Mr. Bright, he said, had several times come to him with a feeling almost of despair. He spoke of the mass of testimony he had sent to Mr. Adams in London to support the representation the latter had constantly to make to Lord John Russell, then

Foreign Secretary, in regard to the action of Confederate agents in Liverpool in violation of international law. Mr. Dudley's whole soul was enlisted in the effort to resist these Confederate schemes; and his skill and experience as a lawyer made him an efficient representative of our Government in that period of its trial.

I remember one dinner-table experience in Liverpool, when I was in an atmosphere entirely hostile to the cause of the North. Our host and all the guests but myself were in sympathy with the South. Our host, I should say, was an old friend of mine, — an agreeable and cultivated man. The talk at the beginning was chiefly in regard to the war. Our host was careful to ground his opposition to it on what he called its fratricidal character. He said the spectacle in this age of the world was a sad one truly — the bloody strife of men of the same brotherhood; that all war seemed contrary to the spirit of the present day. He hoped we would soon see our way to the settling of our contest and letting the South go. The others at the table supported this advocacy of peace, and especially a legal gentleman who urged it with great zeal and earnestness. Talk took another direction; and, some little time having passed, I referred to the *Trent* matter, and asked my legal friend whether he really thought there would have been war if the United States had refused to deliver up Mason and Slidell. He replied instantly that England would have given her "last man and her last shilling" to compel the surrender of the envoys. The very mention of the matter seemed to set his soul on fire. "Oh," I said, "then you think it would be the duty of a nation to carry on a contest at any sacrifice of life because two men, not its own citizens, had been taken from one of its mail steamers, but that it is not right for people to resist by force of arms the dismemberment of their country — the blotting out of their national existence." Our host laughed, and upbraided his legal guest at having so seriously damaged himself and the common cause by his unfortunate admission.

I reached London within a week from the time of my landing. I soon saw my friend, then of many years, William Edward Forster, and had a prolonged conversation with him in regard to our war. He had been our strenuous defender through the whole of it, and had greatly aided our minister, Mr. Adams, in the heavy work which had been upon him from the moment of his reaching London.

I was with Mr. Forster the day before he was to speak on the general subject of the relations of England with America. The particular occasion was this. Lord Derby, in the House of Lords, had called upon the Government to see to it that Canada was provided with adequate defences as against attack from the United States. He had urged that hostility to England was deep-seated in America, and that, as the war was probably drawing to a close, there was imminent danger that the forces which would then be free to act elsewhere would be turned against Canada. The *Times* had taken up this foolish cry, and at the moment the excitement which had been caused was sufficient to affect the funds. I could, of course, tell Mr. Forster how absurd such a suggestion was, that the one desire of the people of the North was for an honourable peace; that such a peace would be welcomed with passionate joy, and once it was secured armies would disband. Mr. Forster fully understood this, and was eager to reply to Lord Derby and the *Times*. The opportunity offered in a debate which was appointed for March 13 on the Canadian Defences Bill. My friend kindly arranged for my being present at that debate, and for my having a seat upon what is called the floor of the house. I went in with him at four o'clock, and was taken to a bench at the end of the house, immediately fronting the Speaker. There were two benches there precisely alike.

I may mention here a slight incident showing the curious care of the House of Commons to magnify the office of the Speaker as a mode of maintaining their own dignity. In one of the pauses of the proceedings of the evening a member, with whom I had slight acquaintance, very civilly came to shake hands with me. He was behind me and I turned half round to talk with him. When he was about to go I rose to say good-by to him, turning fully round. Instantly with a look of alarm he said to me, "Don't turn your back on Mr. Speaker." I am told that when the Speaker proceeds from the House to his apartments persons of whatever dignity who may be in the corridors are swept from his path by men with great staves of office who exclaim with solemnity, "Make way for Mr. Speaker!"

From my excellent seat I looked on for near an hour on what to me was an interesting scene, though the immediate proceedings were not wholly intelligible. Name after name was called by the Speaker, and a member would rise and say a few words rapidly, and then descend, with what appeared to be a petition, to the clerks' table. Then one member after another rose to ask a question, notice of which he had given previously, and a short reply was at once made from the Treasury Bench. I was glad to hear on one of these occasions the clear, ringing voice of Mr. Gladstone, then Chancellor of the Exchequer. During this time the House was gathering, and it was evident from the full attendance that an important debate was expected. A flood of mild light poured suddenly on the scene near five o'clock; it came from the ceiling through squares of ground glass, and thus was everywhere diffused.

I noticed that members entering the House, or going out, were always uncovered, and that when they took their seats they generally put their hats on. If a member rose to speak to another only a few feet distant he instantly removed his hat. This little custom is, however, well known. Side by side, sitting closely together, were the men from England, Wales, Scotland, and Ireland, who were the real rulers of England — Sovereign and Ministers being but the servants of their will. As I looked I could well understand why to be a member of Parliament was so extreme an object of desire.

At five o'clock Mr. Fitzgerald, from the front Opposition bench, rose to begin the evening's discussion; his seat was next to that of Mr. Disraeli. In his opening remarks he showed much solicitude lest offence should be given to the Americans. But he urged upon the Government increase of energy in the construction of fortifications at Quebec and elsewhere. He said England was especially bound to defend Canada against the Americans, because it was only the conduct of England which had excited American hostility. It was England, and not Canada, that had precipitately given to the South belligerent rights, and it was England, and not Canada, that had suffered the *Alabama* to escape. Remarkable language this, I thought, to come from the Tory side of the House; it amounted almost to a confession that these particular acts could not be defended. The whole speech was based on the idea of there being irritation against England in America which might at any moment lead to war. It was admitted that good feeling between the two Governments then existed, this being largely due to the " wise, discreet, and prudent conduct " of the American representative in England, who had done more than any man living to preserve peace between the two countries. Cheers came from both sides of the House at this reference to Mr. Adams. Mr. Fitzgerald went on to point out how imperfect were the present defences of the Canadian frontier; how feeble the force on the Lakes. He said the Guards were in Canada, the flower of the army; that there were in all 8,000 or 10,000 troops; that had war broken out during the previous three years the only counsel to be given to these troops would be to take to their ships. He suggested, in conclusion, that, in the intoxication produced by a successful ending of the war, the population of the North might insist on attacking Canada under the belief that she was incapable of making any defence.

While Mr. Fitzgerald was speaking a slight movement on the bench immediately before the one on which I sat led me to glance that way. A young man was sitting down and several other persons were rising as he did so. "Do not move," he said quietly, and all was still again. Another glance at the side face of the young man thus taking his place as a peer to listen to a debate in the Commons House of Parliament confirmed my first thought — it was the Prince of Wales. The expression of his countenance was pleasing; it was to me that of a man of kind heart. This, too, was my feeling when I saw him five years before at Oxford and in Philadelphia.

Mr. Forster was given the floor to reply to Mr. Fitzgerald. He remarked first that the expense of fortifications as proposed would be enormous, and that there was no feeling in America toward England that would justify the outlay. He said the alarm that prevailed was due first to the speech of Lord Derby, and next to the leaders of the *Times*. In a late article there had been this passage, "If the Federals can go to war with the prospect of success, they will go to war;" the article concluding with the expression of the hope that the present contest in America might continue so that the Northern people might become exhausted and unable to attack. Mr. Forster admitted that articles hostile to England had appeared in the American papers, but he asked whether what the English papers had said at different times was not a fair offset to them. He attributed the then excitement to the influence of Confederate agents and Confederate sympathizers who sought, as a last effort, to frighten England into some action hostile to the North; and, further, to the efforts of persons who had foretold from day to day the miserable failure of the Federal power, and who now sought to divert attention from their mistakes by urging that the success of the North would but herald war with England. He said the people of the North were not greedy of empire and of dominion; they were fighting to prevent the destruction of their country; neither were they vindictive, and eager for revenge; nor was it true that their Government was unable to control them. Further, the Americans could not but appreciate the adherence of the Lancashire operatives to their cause. He said: "For one man in this country who has deluded himself into the belief that the greatest experiment of modern times is a failure, there are a hundred who have hoped from the beginning that the great Republic would come out of the struggle unscathed, and who rejoice now that it seems likely that she will emerge purified from that slavery which has been her weakness and shame, because it has been her sin." Mr. Forster concluded by saying that peace in the United States would be the best defence for Canada; that the prosperity of the country North and South, which would surely follow, would put away all thought of war; that the time, he trusted, was at hand when all English-speaking men, either in the British Islands or their dependencies, or in the great Republic, would feel themselves so bound together by common interests, by ties of language, blood, faith, and common freedom, as to make them essentially one people and brotherhood.

Mr. Disraeli was one of the next speakers; he said he was not one of the mortified and baffled prophets to whom the honourable member (Mr. Forster), had referred. "Now the right honourable gentleman opposite" (Mr. Gladstone) "made the most confident predictions of the success of the South." He sought also to defend his chief, Lord Derby, by saying that living, as he did, with that eminent statesman in perfect confidence, he could declare that they shared the same sentiments as to American affairs. He said he had from the first been of opinion that the Government of the United States, under circumstances of unprecedented difficulty, had conducted itself with great energy and great discretion. He thought there was no immediate danger of war; the Americans of the North were a sagacious people, and were not likely to seize the moment of exhaustion as the one most favourable for beginning another contest. The talk of some of their newspapers — rowdy rhetoric he might call it — was no more to be considered the settled judgment of the people, than the strange and fantastic drinks of which England heard so much were to be regarded as their ordinary potations. The American democracy, he said, was a territorial democracy; he added, "Aristotle, who has taught us most of the wise things we know, never said a wiser thing than that the cultivators of the soil are the class least inclined to sedition and violent courses."

But, he said, a strong central government would be necessary in the United States to preserve order in the South, and an army would be required to uphold it. This might entail danger to Canada. It was England's duty to defend Canada so long as she desired to continue her connection with the mother country. On this general ground he was in favour of greater energy in carrying on works of fortification.

Disraeli was followed by Mr. Lowe — at that time a distinguished member of the House — a man of the most acute and vigorous mind. He spoke with extraordinary rapidity and animation. He urged the House to take a common-sense view of matters; said that it was impossible to cope with the Americans on the Lakes; that in 1813 and 1814 they, the English, had got well thrashed there. Then there were no railways; now by means of the New York Central and the Erie Railroads the Americans could put ten gunboats on Lake Erie or Lake Ontario to the Canadians' one. As to troops, the Americans could invade with ten times the number that Canada could bring into the field. "Could anything be more wild," he said, "than an attempt to vie with America on her own ground?" He reminded the House that General Montgomery, in the War of Independence, had to struggle through almost impenetrable woods, in the depth of winter. America, he said, now has railways which could transport to the frontier any number of men she pleased. In regard to Quebec, he said General Wolfe cannonaded it from Point Levi, three quarters of a mile from the town, even with the artillery of that day. If Point Levi were seized, it was certain that, with modern artillery, Quebec would be absolutely at the mercy of the enemy. He said he had never seen a place which seemed to be commanded from more points. When Wolfe attacked it and gained the Heights of Abraham, Montcalm judged it prudent to march out into the open field instead of awaiting the assault behind his fortifications. Mr. Lowe added, what sounded oddly to me after all this, that he would not object to improving the fortifications, but he thought it impossible, when the troops were once hunted into Quebec and Montreal, that they should ever escape again. It had been assumed, he said, that you could only make war in Canada during the summer, and then ships in the St. Lawrence could aid in the defence; but General Montgomery, who besieged Quebec, had made his way through Maine in the depth of a severe winter. He assaulted the city at that time of year, and if an extraordinary casualty had not happened — if he with seventeen of his staff had not been killed by the discharge of a single cannon — he might have taken Quebec, and the destinies of Canada might have been entirely changed. Mr. Lowe urged the withdrawal of the British troops from Canada because their presence there would be an incentive, in America, to war — the desire to capture a small army and lead it in triumph through the States would be irresistible. He said he grudged the Americans this gratification, and he wished to take away every motive for war. War with America he said, in conclusion, would be the greatest calamity that could befall either country, perhaps the whole human race.

Mr. White, member for Brighton, who was one of the next speakers, referred to the satisfactory tone and temper of the Opposition speeches of the evening, as contrasted with the speech of their leader, Lord Derby, in the House of Lords. He thought that noble Lord would not have ventured on such inflammatory language had he regarded his early return to power as probable.

One of the most sensible things said in the debate was a remark of Mr. Ayrton's, viz., that, instead of fortifying Canada, it would be better to yield to the American demand for arbitration — that Lord Russell's refusal to entertain this was the real cause of irritation in the United States; the demand would be repeated when the United States had again become strong, and then England might have to yield it or go to war.

Prophetic words these were, for though six years later the Government of Mr. Gladstone, to its great honour, yielded to the demand, unaccompanied by a threat of war, yet England had come to see the perilous position she was in by allowing it to stand as a precedent that the escape of the *Alabama* was not a matter for which she was to be called to account. To Mr. Gladstone the credit of the great act of the Geneva Arbitration is mainly due; this is some offset to what was the prodigious error of his previous political life — the public and confident prediction of the success of the South.

Lord Robert Cecil, now the Marquis of Salisbury, spoke next; he scouted the idea of arbitration, and urged the most vigorous efforts for the defence of Canada. At eleven o'clock Mr. Bright took the floor, beginning what proved to be one of his greatest speeches — the last, I think, of the splendid orations by which that eminent man upheld the cause of the American Union during the period of its awful trial. He addressed himself to the particular matter of the vote asked for, and said at once there was no power in the United Kingdom to defend successfully the territory of Canada against the power of the United States. He begged honourable gentlemen not to talk folly, and be called afterward to act folly. He said there was not a man in the United States whose opinion was worth considering who desired to attack Canada; nor had the Canadians any real hostility to their neighbours. They had been unwise in not preventing the raids which bands of Confederates had made across the frontier; but the Government of Canada was now doing all in its power to check these raids. All was calm in that region, and the United States was making no complaint. It was plain then that if war broke out it would be because of hostility between America and England, between the Government of Washington and the Government of London. Was there any one in that House, he asked, who desired such a war? He noticed with delight the change which had come over the House in regard to American questions. Honourable members had come to the conclusion that England was not in favour of war with America. The Government had preserved, in the main, its neutrality during the struggle; it had resisted a motion to break the blockade; it had resisted the efforts of the Confederate Government to obtain recognition, although France had urged England to join her in granting this. The question then came up: Did the United States wish war? Mr. Bright maintained that the relations between the two countries were entirely amicable, and had been growing more and more so during the past months. He said there never was an administration in the United States, since the time of the Revolutionary War, more favourable to peace with England than the Government of which President Lincoln was the head. Not a line of President Lincoln's could be shown, since his accession to power, which betrayed anger against England. But if the United States did not want war, and Canada did not, and England did not, whence was it to come? Why the anxiety? People said "the City" was alarmed. Well, he never knew the City to be right. As to the newspapers, he agreed with Mr. Forster in thinking the course they were taking showed a wish to hide their own confusion. Mr. Bright asked the House whether they had not in their heart of hearts a feeling that their course in the past four years had not been fair toward the United States — whether some stings of conscience were not the cause of the uneasiness which was felt.

He proceeded then to review some of the acts of England of which America, he said, had cause to complain. First the acknowledgment of the belligerent rights of the South. He did not condemn the Government for this action, except on the ground of the undue haste of it. Fort Sumter was fired on on the 12th of April, 1861. Mr. Dallas, the then American Minister, declined to discuss any important matter with the Government, as he did not represent the President; his successor was on the way, and would arrive on such a day. Mr. Adams did arrive on the 13th of May, and, on opening his newspaper the next morning, he found the proclamation of neutrality, and the acknowledgment of the belligerent rights of the

South. Mr. Bright said the Government should have awaited Mr. Adams's arrival in order to explain the need of the action they contemplated, and that they might thus disclaim unfriendly feeling toward the United States Government. Their not doing so made the act seem to the Americans almost hostile; it caused grief and irritation at the North, while it gave comfort and courage at Richmond.

Then, as to the *Trent* matter, undoubtedly the Americans were wrong in seizing the envoys. True, there were English precedents for such action, but they belonged to the long past. The Government was right in demanding explanation, but no defence could be made for their instant conclusion that the United States Government would justify the act, nor for their at once preparing for war. There was not the slightest evidence that Captain Wilkes had acted under orders from Washington. But this was not all. It became known later that the American Secretary of State, Mr. Seward, the moment the news of the seizure reached Washington, wrote to Mr. Adams informing him the Government had not authorized it, and that they were ready to enter into consideration of it with the British Government. The despatch was communicated by Mr. Adams to the Foreign Secretary, and was conclusive as to the fact that the Americans were ready for friendly discussion of the matter. The Government, strange to say, withheld from the public the knowledge that such a despatch had been received, and went on with war preparations. Further than this, a journal, supposed to be the organ of the Prime Minister (Lord Palmerston), had denied with solemnity that any such despatch had been received. The result was that for almost a month the English people were allowed to remain in full expectation of war. It might almost have seemed that the purpose of the Government was to fan the flames of war, even when the ground for it had been removed.

I may mention here that I had myself evidence of this withholding of important evidence of the friendly feeling of the Americans at that critical time, for a copy of the newspaper of the date of about December 15, referred to by Mr. Bright, containing a denial of the report that a despatch friendly in tone had been received by Mr. Adams, was sent to me from London. It was on November 15 that news of the seizure of the envoys was received in America, and late in the month the news reached England. The despatch of Mr. Seward to Mr. Adams reached him about December 10. News of the settlement at Washington of the *Trent* matter reached England about January 10, 1862.

I may venture further to interrupt my abstract of Mr. Bright's speech, by quoting two passages from letters of mine to the London *Guardian*, one bearing date before the settlement was accomplished, the other when the crisis was at an end. On December 17, 1861, I wrote:—

"The news which has come to-day has caused indescribable excitement, for it seems almost to amount to a declaration of war by England. The law officers of the Crown, it is said, have decided against us; and at once, without awaiting the reply of our Government, vast military preparations have been ordered. One statement is that our very forbearance in not stopping the voyage of the *Trent*, and sending her into port for adjudication, makes our act illegal. Thus, on a lawyer's opinion that our exercise of the belligerent right of search has in this instance been marked by some circumstance of informality, England is about to begin a war with a nation allied to her in blood, and at a time when she was especially bound to show that nation forbearance and consideration. Long ago I ventured to express the opinion that we were fighting England's battle, inasmuch as our domestic contest was to prevent the spread of slavery. Of late it has seemed that slavery would everywhere cease in this land unless the men who had taken up arms to extend and strengthen it should prevail in the struggle, and unless England should interfere in their behalf. This latter contingency, it may be, is now to become a reality, and the ruin, for a time, of my country and the triumph of slavery to be hereafter on the consciences of Englishmen. In the awful solemnities of the hour you will not deny me the utterance of these sad forebodings, if so be that a single voice might help to stay a fearful wrong. A demand made on this country for the surrender of the men taken from the *Trent*, with war as the alternative of the refusal, must, of course, have but one reply. We cannot yield to menace, when we consider law to be on our side, and expect to hold hereafter our position among the nations. Widespread ruin may, it is true, follow to all our material interests, but we shall not be alone in our suffering. England has vast interests in this country which will at once be imperilled; the market here for her products will cease to exist; her commerce in every quarter of the globe may be assailed. The little navy, which the *Times* says can be swept so quickly from the seas, is one that has grown in seven months from 46 vessels to 264. But it is distressing to write such words as these; and they lead one away from the question of chief concern to Christian men. Is England about to begin an unjust war? I think our people would be willing to refer the case to any impartial umpire, or even to a neutral prize court. Everywhere I hear suggestions like these, while the opinion is universal that to yield simply to a display of force is utterly impossible."

On the 6th of January, 1862, I wrote:—

"Although the case of the *Trent* is settled and beginning to fade from the remembrance of people here, it is proper I should state the fact that much soreness of feeling toward England remains. The conviction that we had overstepped the limits of law does, it is true, gain strength, but men are unable to see that the offence was such as to warrant an instant beginning of war by England. We cannot but consider, too, that there was little of the charity that hopeth all things in the action of your Government, presuming, as they seem to have done, that this country would not listen to reason, and was incapable of wishing to make reparation if wrong had been done. The hasty embarkation of troops for Canada, and the vast warlike preparations of every kind, of which each steamer now brings us accounts, leads us the more to dwell on this low view of America which has been taken by England. We ask ourselves further, what must be the judgment of the world on the spectacle which has been presented to it? What effect, it might be questioned, has Christianity had upon the nations, if the two of all others the nearest allied in blood, and in which it is claimed that religion has most influenced the lives of men, are ready on so trivial a pretext to rush to arms?"

I have given the above passages because they show plainly enough the fever of excitement in which we all lived in those days. It is not to be forgotten that two ill-judged actions on our part afforded some justification for the steps taken by England. One was a hasty letter of our Secretary of the Navy, Gideon Welles, commending the action of Captain Wilkes; the other, a public meeting in Boston, in which a Judge of the United States Supreme Court took part, the purpose of it being to express approval of the seizure of the envoys. The sober second thought of the people of this country was, I think, to the effect that while, by British decisions and British precedents, the act of Captain Wilkes might readily be defended, it failed of justification under that interpretation of international law for which the United States had always earnestly striven.

The final remark to be made on the *Trent* matter is that it was given to Prince Albert to do a service to civilization as great as any man has been able to perform in these latter times. The despatch in which the surrender of the envoys was demanded being submitted to him, he insisted, on behalf of the Queen, on such modification of it as would remove from it everything which was of the nature of menace. It may well be said that by this change war was averted.

To resume my notice of Mr. Bright's important speech. He took a final opportunity of referring to Mr. Laird, the builder of the *Alabama*, "a member of the House who is careful not to be present this evening." He said, "I do not complain of the friendship of that honourable member for Captain

Semmes, who might be described, as another sailor once was, as "the mildest-mannered man that ever scuttled a ship"; but he did complain that he, a member of Parliament and a magistrate of a county, should, by his building of the *Alabama*, drive England into an infraction of international law. He referred to a retort of Mr. Laird's to him, Mr. Bright, of two years before, that he would rather be the builder of a dozen *Alabamas* than be one to stir up class against class, — words which had been received with repeated cheering on the Opposition side of the House. He referred to the fact that this same gentleman or firm, after they had seen the peril into which the country was drifting on account of the *Alabama*, had gone on audaciously to build the two rams. These great vessels, Mr. Bright said, the Government had only summoned up courage to seize when war was on the eve of breaking out on account of them.

Mr. Bright made impressive allusion to the steadfastness of the bulk of the great counties of Yorkshire and Lancashire under their sufferings from the failure of the cotton supply. Not an expression of sympathy with the Confederacy could ever be wrung from them. Indeed, the fact that peace had been preserved between England and America was due more to the laborious millions than to the wealthy and the cultivated.

Very striking was the conclusion of this great speech. "Nature," he said, "will not be baffled because we are jealous of the United States. The decrees of Providence will not be overthrown by aught we can do." He dwelt then on the certain growth of population; it was then 35,000,000; the increase would be more than a million persons per year. Jealousies were sure to disappear; there had been undue excitement in America, and there had been inadequate knowledge of the real state of events in that country since the beginning of the war, even among persons high in rank and distinguished in culture in England. Mr. Bright said finally:—

"It is on record that when the author of 'The Decline and Fall of the Roman Empire' was about beginning his great work, David Hume wrote a letter to him urging him not to employ the French, but the English tongue, because, he said, our establishments in America promise superior stability and duration to the English language. How far that promise has been in part fulfilled, we who are living now can state; but how far it will be more largely and more completely fulfilled in after times, we must leave to after times to tell. I believe that in the centuries which are to come, it will be the greatest pride and the highest renown of England that from her loins have sprung a hundred millions — it may be two hundred millions — of men who dwell and prosper on that continent which the old Genoese gave to Europe. Sir, if the sentiments which I have uttered shall become the sentiments of the Parliament and people of the United Kingdom — if the moderation which I have described shall mark the course and Government of the people of the United States — then, notwithstanding some present irritation and some present distrust, and I have faith both in us and them, I believe that these two great commonwealths will march abreast, the parents and the guardians of freedom and justice, wheresoever their language shall be spoken and their power shall extend."

A day or two after the important debate of which I have been telling I had an interesting interview with Mr. Adams. As I looked forward to meeting him, I recalled what Mr. Sumner told me seven years before, that Charles Francis Adams, having finished the Life of his grandfather, was about to enter public life — that he was to be elected to Congress; and that he was as great a man as his father or his grandfather. I little foresaw the great service he was to render to his country, as her representative in England, at a time when only the highest wisdom would avail for the duties of an American Minister. I found him hale and cheerful, with a serenity of bearing, indeed, which told of difficulties overcome, and a pathway now clear. I could not but endeavour to express to him, almost at once, the feeling of gratitude toward him common to us all at the North for the great work it had been given him to perform in London. I might have said, indeed, that he had seemed to me, from the first, to have the same marvellous qualifications for his high and difficult position, that Mr. Lincoln had for the Presidency. But I did say to him that it was a great pleasure to me to hear, as I had a night or two before, in the House of Commons, the cheers which came from both sides of the House at every mention of his name. He replied: —

"Oh, the English have always been kind to me personally. One matter which occurred early helped me with them. My letter of instructions I had been ordered to read to the Foreign Secretary on my first interview with him, and to give him a copy of it. But as I read this paper of Mr. Seward's myself carefully, I felt satisfied that portions of it would give offence. I was certain that in the extremely delicate condition of our then relations with England, it would be dangerous to lay before the Foreign Secretary a document in which our attitude toward the British Government, and the demands we made, were stated so uncompromisingly — indeed, in almost the language of menace. I accordingly determined to disobey this particular of my instructions, although I knew I ran a risk in doing so. I resolved to make my communication to Lord John Russell in my own words, rather than in Mr. Seward's. Of course I had fully possessed my mind with the substance of the letter. I soon had my interview with the Foreign Secretary; I was with him for three hours, and was able, I thought, to remove many wrong impressions which he had received, and under which the Government had been acting. The truth is that Lord Lyons had misled them. Living as he did at Washington, where the controlling influences of society were distinctly Southern, and seeing how resolute the Southern leaders were, and how intense was their feeling, it was natural for him to make up his mind that the slave States would certainly succeed in establishing their separate government. Such, clearly, had been the tenor of his despatches on the breaking out of the war, and for months preceeding it. All this, I had to show Lord John Russell, was a hasty conclusion, not warranted by the full facts of the case. I was satisfied with the impression I made, and felt that I had done all that I could be expected to do, as I had been permitted to state thus fully the grounds on which the North built their hopes of success. I, of course, acquainted our Government with the fact that I had withheld the letter. I was aware that letters or despatches addressed by the Secretary of State to a foreign minister are sometimes intended mainly for the home public; such, I supposed, might be the case in this instance. I took a similar responsibility, to this that I have stated, by withholding the full text of Mr. Seward's instructions to me in the event of the refusal of the British Government to prevent the going out of the two rams from the port of Liverpool. In this latter case Mr. Seward, finding I had not given to the Foreign Secretary copies of the despatches he had addressed to me, ordered them to be published. They appeared, accordingly, precisely as though they had been communicated to Lord John Russell. At once there were stern enquiries in both Houses of Parliament how it was that the Foreign Secretary had allowed such language to be laid before him. Lord John made the quiet reply that no such words had been submitted to him, that he saw them then for the first time. The fact that I had withheld them was considered to my credit, and strengthened the good feeling of the English toward me."

I said to Mr. Adams it had been matter of great surprise to me that the Government had allowed the building of the two rams to go on so long as they did; their being ships of war without any armament made their very preparation so flagrant a violation of international law. I asked whether he thought there was real danger of their being allowed to go out. He said certainly there was; he had again and again submitted evidence to the Foreign Secretary showing the character of the vessels, and always the reply was that Government was assured they were private property, and therefore they could not interfere. One final batch of testimony, Mr. Adams said, he submitted, intimating plainly that his instructions were to demand his passports in case the vessels were allowed to go out. Lord John replied that he saw no more in the evidence submitted than in that which the Government had already considered. Mr. Adams then replied briefly that this was war. On receipt of these very serious words Lord John summoned Lord Palmerston, the Prime Minister, to London, and the result of the consultation was that an order was issued to seize the rams. The precise words of Mr. Adams, in the note referred to, as I learnt afterward, were as follows. After expressing profound regret at the conclusion to which her Majesty's Government had come, he added, "It would be superfluous in me to point out to your Lordship that this is war."

Mr. Adams went on further to explain to me in regard to the action of the Government, that they had, from the beginning of the war, been compelled to proceed warily; the Opposition were constantly on the watch to trip them up on the American Question; the Tories, as a party, were in sympathy with the South.

Some curious particulars Mr. Adams mentioned in regard to the tardy efforts of the Government to prevent the going out of the *Alabama*. He said Mr. Dudley brought him some evidence, which they both thought was conclusive, as to the character of the vessel; it was not stronger than other evidence which Mr. Adams had submitted to counsel, with no satisfactory result; he hesitated about throwing away more of the money of the American Government in lawyer's fees. Just then Mr. Forster came in, and Mr. Adams asked his advice. He said he thought Mr. Collier, who was a member of the House and an eminent Queen's counsel, would give a good opinion.

Mr. Adams submitted the evidence, which Mr. Dudley had brought, to Mr. Collier, who soon gave the opinion that if the Foreign Enlistment Act was not sufficient to hold the vessel it was no better than waste paper. Fortified with this, Mr. Adams made a further appeal to the Foreign Secretary. By him the papers were referred to the Advocate General, and exactly at this point of time this functionary became insane. A delay of a few days followed, and this was one of the causes of the escape of the *Alabama*. She went out, as is well known, under pretence of a trial trip, and did not return.

I had a few other meetings in London which were of much interest to me in those days of March, 1865, when here, on this side the ocean, the great drama of war was drawing toward its closing scene. At Mr. Forster's table I had the happiness to find myself next to John Bright. I could tell him of the gratitude which was felt toward him in all loyal American hearts. He remarked to me that the American war had caused him more anxiety than any event of his whole political life. I understood him to mean that he felt that the cause of free constitutional government was staked on its issue. Of the company present was Matthew Arnold, and I remember being struck with the fact that he and Mr. Bright met then for the first time. Next to me on my right was a clergyman, a Mr. Fraser, of pleasing manners, and as I felt, from my talk with him, of high intelligence. Five years afterward I again met him; he was then

Bishop of Manchester. He died but a few years ago, after a distinguished and honoured episcopate of fifteen years. It was Mr. Forster to whom his elevation was chiefly due. He selected him, when only the vicar of a country parish, to go out to America to examine as to our common-school system. The report he made drew Mr. Gladstone, the Prime Minister's attention to him; he was made Bishop of Manchester. He threw himself into his work with such ardour, and with so truly catholic a spirit, that by some one's happy instinct he was designated as the "Bishop of all Denominations." But I recall his saying to me when I met him, after his elevation, that he would have preferred to remain in his simple way of life.

On the 28th of March I was present at another field-night in the House of Commons. It was a debate on the Church Establishment in Ireland. Very important this proved in its after results. I went between four and five. Members with their hats on were sitting carelessly on the cushioned benches, and others, hats off, were moving about. There was the hum of conversation everywhere, and somehow there was that in the atmosphere which betokened a stirring debate at hand. At five o'clock a certain Mr. Darby Griffith, member for Devizes, rose, and at once there broke from every part of the House cheer after cheer. There was something peculiar in the sound, and yet it was natural for me to suppose that here was some notable member appearing after a long absence, and greeted accordingly. I soon found my mistake; the cheers were ironical, and the House was merely expressing its vexation at the thought of the infliction that awaited it; the member for Devizes was an insufferable bore. He stood firm, notwithstanding the ridicule thus levelled against him at the outset. At length there was a pause, and he began with entire calmness his dreary harangue, and maundered on, spite of efforts, again and again renewed, to stop him. Conversation went on at a high key during such intervals as there were between the bolder efforts at interruption. The drowsy "Order, order," of the Speaker had little effect to restrain the House. For three quarters of an hour the infliction lasted.

The speech of Mr. Dillwyn, with which the debate of the evening opened, was rather a halting one; its purpose was to show that the Irish Church Establishment was a great wrong to the body of people. An Irish member, known as "The O'Donoghue," seconded the resolution with which Mr. Dillwyn's speech had closed. Sir George Grey on the part of the Government opposed the motion. His speech was fluent and very direct and clear; it was that of a practised debater, to whom long years of parliamentary life had given grace of manner. He admitted there was a grievance, but urged that to attempt to redress it would involve the country in dissensions which would be totally destructive to peace and progress. Mr. Gathorne Hardy followed in what struck me as a brilliant oration, lasting for an hour and a half. He spoke from the front Opposition bench. He urged that to attack the Irish Church was to attack the English; but he seemed sincere in his conviction that the continuance of the Establishment in Ireland was for the good of the Irish people. There was a charm in his readiness and his perfect self-possession. I listened without a thought of fatigue, though it was nine o'clock when he came to an end.

Five hours had now passed. Members who had gone away for dinner were returning. I noticed, however, that Lord Palmerston and Mr. Gladstone had scarcely been absent at all. The Speaker left the chair, and there was a pause of ten minutes. Then Mr. Gladstone took the floor. For one hour this great orator enchained the attention of the House, controlling it in part by his eloquence, and in part by the interest which was excited by the desire to know what line he would take in regard to the perplexing subject under discussion. To the surprise of, I think, most of those who listened, he gave his adhesion, clearly and distinctly, to the statement that the condition of the Irish Church Establishment was unsatisfactory. He stated that condition to be this: in a nation of between five and six millions of people, about 600,000 or 700,000 had the exclusive possession of the ecclesiastical property of the country intended to be applied to the religious instruction of all. He argued that this state of things could not continue, but he denied that the time for dealing with the question had yet fully come. The speech seemed eminently wise, and it was uttered in an earnest way, enforcing one's assent. The moment he came to an end, an eminent Opposition orator, Mr. Whiteside, started to his feet, and, with the air of a man confident in himself and rejoicing in his opportunity, addressed himself to the work of a reply. It was a splendid arena on which he looked round, for the House was now crammed, and it was evident the speaker was one to whom all delighted to listen. He spoke mainly from the inspiration of the moment, for Mr. Gladstone's speech was in great part his text. He knew well the importance of the declaration to which he was thus replying, and he was conscious, too, that the great body of his Tory supporters, sitting in close phalanx behind him, relied on him to do his best. So his Irish blood, one could suppose, was all aglow at the thought of his being thus a recognized champion in what was likely to prove a memorable contest. Not for a moment did he pause to collect his ideas, but, starting at once in a high strain of eloquence, he swept on with irresistible force and effect. It was a flood of denunciation and of sarcasm, and there was withal a sort of rollicking humour showing itself through the scholarly refinement that really characterized his speech. Once the House was moved to uncontrollable laughter at the orator's expense; he was betrayed into the curious Hibernian statement that the province of Ulster returned thirty members to this House, some of whom had sat in Parliament for two centuries. He explained, in some adroit way, his meaning as soon as the House would listen, and the flow of his eloquence swept on. He closed his speech soon afterward in a tempest of cheers.

It was after eleven o'clock when he sat down, and the chief interest of the debate was now over. What gave great importance to the evening's discussion was that it had been the occasion of one of the memorable declarations of Mr. Gladstone's life, committing him further as a Liberal, but involving the sacrifice of something dear to him, his seat as a member for the University of Oxford. The honour he lost in the general election of 1868 was bestowed upon his opponent in this debate of 1865, Mr. Gathorne Hardy. It has been sometimes charged against Mr. Gladstone that he assailed the Irish Church, and urged disestablishment, when he was out of office, and as a means of recovering power. The record of this debate shows that he pronounced against it in 1865, when he was in office. The bill for disestablishment was passed in 1869.

The day after the debate of which I have been telling, I had the great satisfaction of an interview of an hour with Mr. Gladstone. He had appointed half past ten for my call at Carlton House Terrace. As I entered the wide hall he was entering it from the staircase. He had a book or review in his hand. As the House had sat late, it was natural that his face should show signs of short hours of sleep. He led me at once into the library, a large room, and gave me a seat near the fire. He referred, of course, very soon to the war, and asked me what I thought was likely to be the course of it. I said it was plain to me it was near its close. But, he asked, had not the South still resources to draw on; he had seen the statement that they were about themselves to declare the slaves free, and put arms in their hands. I said this suggestion was really one of despair, that a Confederate officer had told me it came from Mr. Benjamin, who owned no slaves himself. Moreover, I said, the blacks knew the North to be their friends. Northern soldiers escaping from prisons at the South had always been helped on their way by the slaves. I then added that two governments were really impossible within the limits of the United States. He asked at once why they were impossible, and rather held me to precise and definite objections. I said there was no natural boundary; that the West and Northwest could never allow the mouth of the Mississippi to be beyond their control; that New Orleans could never be surrendered by the Federal Government, nor could the control of Chesapeake Bay be given up. I referred to the fact that separate governments would imply frontier fortresses and separate fleets.

Mr. Gladstone then referred to his own state of mind in regard to the war; said he had thought the North was attempting the impossible; he had never opened his mouth on the merits of the contest. He added with warmth that it was a vulgar error to suppose that any but the most inconsiderable portion of the English people desired the downfall of the United States. He went on to say that he, with many others, thought our system of government was not capable of bearing the strain of a great civil war; that the States seemed too loosely knit together. "But," he said, speaking with great animation, "in the constancy which has been shown, the fortitude, the self-sacrifice, I for one perceive the extraordinary strength which is given by free institutions." He said further, though I cannot give his precise words, that the love of country which had been exhibited had given to the world a very striking lesson. He qualified this by saying that a similar heroic spirit had been shown by the South.

It was natural for me to wish to obtain from Mr. Gladstone some expression in regard to Mr. Lincoln. I said I hoped he appreciated the advantage the United States had had, in this great crisis, in the gifts of mind of the President and his singleness of heart. He replied at once, with his peculiar animation, almost vehemence of manner, that he did most fully. He had always, he said, thought well of Mr. Lincoln, and considered that he had high qualities as a leader; but his Inaugural Address, which had just come, filled him with admiration; he saw in it evidence of a moral elevation most rare in a statesman, or indeed in any man. "I am taken captive," he said in substance, "by so striking an utterance as this. I see in it the effect of sharp trial when rightly borne to raise men to a higher level of thought and feeling.

It is by cruel suffering that nations are sometimes born to a better life; so it is with individual men. Mr. Lincoln's words show that upon him anxiety and sorrow have wrought their true effect." Mr. Gladstone spoke with approval of Mr. Forster's bearing in regard to the war. "Mr. Bright," he said, "does cruel injustice to the South." This remark I thought showed that Mr. Gladstone's sympathies had been with the South, though they might, if the phrase is allowable, be called unconscious sympathies.

I cannot forbear to give here those last words of President Lincoln which made so profound an impression on Mr. Gladstone, and which will cause men to lift up their hearts while our English tongue endures.

"The Almighty has his own purposes. 'Woe unto the world because of offences, for it must needs be that offences come,' 'but woe to that man by whom the offence cometh.' If we shall suppose that American slavery is one of these offences, which in the providence of God must needs come, but which, having continued through His appointed time, He now wills to remove, and that He gives to both North and South this terrible war as the woe due to those by whom the offence came, shall we discern there any departure from those divine attributes which the believers in a living God always ascribe to Him. Fondly do we hope, fervently do we pray, that this mighty scourge of war may speedily pass away. Yet if God wills that it continue until all the wealth piled by the bondsman's two hundred and fifty years of unrequited toil shall be sunk, and until every drop of blood drawn with the lash be paid by another drawn by the sword, as it was said three thousand years ago, so still it must be said, that 'the judgments of the Lord are true and righteous altogether.'

"With malice toward none, with charity for all, with firmness in the right as God gives us to see the right, let us finish the work we are in, to bind up the nation's wounds, to care for him who shall have borne the battle, and for his widow and his orphans, to do all which may achieve and cherish a just and a lasting peace among ourselves and with all nations."

On the 3d of April England was startled by news of the death of Richard Cobden. In the House of Commons Lord Palmerston and Mr. Disraeli spoke, the same evening, in sober and graceful eulogy of him; the latter characterized him as, without doubt, the greatest political character the pure middle class of England had yet produced. Mr. Bright's few and, I think, broken words were as follows:—

"Sir, I feel that I cannot address the House on this occasion; but every expression of sympathy which I have heard has been most grateful to my heart. But the time which has elapsed since in my presence, the manliest and gentlest spirit that ever tenanted or quitted a human form took its flight, is so short that I dare not even attempt to give utterance to the feelings by which I am oppressed. I shall leave to some calmer moment, when I may have an opportunity of speaking before some portion of my countrymen, the lesson which I think may be learned from the life and character of my friend. I have only to say that, after twenty years of most intimate and almost brotherly friendship with him, I little knew how much I loved him until I found that I had lost him."

On the 8th of April I embarked at Liverpool for my return voyage, and on the 19th, at six o'clock in the morning, we took on board a pilot, who brought us news of the fall of Richmond and the surrender of Lee. Although we were but one hundred miles from New York, the intelligence we thus received only reached to the date of Friday, the 14th. The Americans on board had six hours of high rejoicing over our glorious successes, little knowing what a terrible calamity had, on the night of that same Friday, befallen the country. Our good ship, the *Persia*, steamed rapidly on, and the American coast grew more and more distinct. The day was of marvellous brightness, and most of the passengers were on deck to enjoy the interesting approach. All, too, were happy in the thought of the speedy ending of a prosperous voyage. We paused off Sandy Hook, just at the entrance to the Narrows, for there we were to deliver a letter bag to be put on board the *China*, the steamer of that day for Europe, and which was already under way. I leaned over the ship's side, watching the approach of the small boat which was thus to convey letters from one steamer to the other. Slowly it came over the bright waters; the bag was thrown down to it, and some late English newspapers; and in return a New York paper of that day was handed up to our captain. Looking from above, I saw that the paper was in mourning. Something very serious, it was plain, had happened. An Englishman near me suggested that the mourning might be for Cobden. "No," said I, "that cannot be the explanation." Fifteen minutes passed before Captain Lot, who had taken the paper to his cabin, returned with it, and handed it to his passengers, with its terrible announcement. Then the tidings went instantly from one to another, "Mr. Lincoln is dead, he has been assassinated." Who that was of sufficient years to understand the meaning of the words can ever forget the shock and horror of them! To us, on the ship, there was the further element of bewilderment that the when, where, and how of the murder were still unknown to us. The one newspaper we had was chiefly filled with details of the pursuit of the assassin, and the acts of the new President, Johnson. This suspense lasted for an hour or two. With the coming of the quarantine officers we received the full tidings.

I landed, and everywhere signs of sorrow met my eye. It was the day of the funeral at Washington; and, in town and country, work and business were alike suspended. Other days of lamentation followed, for in every household the feeling was that of personal bereavement.

The funeral at Washington was the beginning of the slow, solemn tread of a procession which went from city to city, awakening grief anew, as one eager waiting multitude after another was reached. I saw, in Philadelphia, the hearse drawn slowly onward along the same streets by which the living man had gone, attended by rejoicing multitudes, to begin his solemn work. He had uttered here on that memorable occasion, in front of the Hall of Independence, words which almost expressed foreboding of his doom. Momentous years came and went; his steady hand guided us through our awful danger, until at last his country's deliverance was wrought. Then to his great and pure soul came the release, the relief — shall we not say the reward — of death.

INDEX

Abbotsford, built by Blore, 131.
Aberdeen, Lord, 151, 248.
Aberdeen, University of, 277.
Achilli, Dr., sues Dr. Newman, 151-154.
Acland, Sir Henry, 204.
Acland, Sir Thomas, 204, 273.
Adams, Charles Francis, 257, 282, 287, 288, 296, 297, 298; interview with, 304-308.
Adams, John Quincy, 5.
Addison, Joseph, 202.
Æschylus, 38.
Ainger, Canon, 176, 177.
Aira Force, 62.
Alabama Controversy, the, 166, 257, 264, 265, 287, 301, 302, 307, 308.
Alfred, the thousandth anniversary of King, 201; City of, 207, 211.
All Saints' Church, the building of, 145, 146, 147.
All Souls' College, 228.
Allibone, S. A., 21.
Allston, Washington, 124.
"Alton Locke" (Kingsley), 192.
Ambleside, 33, 61, 75, 86, 94, 98.
Ambleside Church, memorial window to Wordsworth in, 56-57.
American Literature, how treated in the *Quarterly Review*, 158.
"Ancient Mariner" (Coleridge), 63.
Antislavery movement, 6-7.
Arctic, wreck of, 55, 139, 141.
Argyll, Duke of, 270.
Aristotle, 291.
Arnold, Frances, 75, 76, 81-82.
Arnold, Jane, see Mrs. W. E. Forster.
Arnold, Matthew, 26, 95, 157, 158, 166, 236, 237, 262, 270, 308.
Arnold, Matthew (Mrs.), 175.

Arnold, Thomas, 86, 90, 95, 250-252.
Arnold, Thomas (Dr.), 76, 82, 96, 194, 243, 246.
Arnold, Thomas (Mrs.), 75, 76, 79, 80, 82, 87, 88, 89, 90, 95, 96, 98.
Arnold, William D., 89, 186, 252, 275.
Arnold-Forster, Florence (Miss), 276.
Arnold-Forster, H. O., 276.
Ashburton, Lady, 19.
Atlantic cable, laying of the, 89, 281.
Auckland, 251.
Australasian, steamship, 281.
Ayrton, his part in a debate in the House of Commons (1865), 293.

Baccarat case, the, 177-179.
Bagehot, Walter, 258.
Baillie, Joanna, bust of, 70.
Balliol College, Oxford, 59.
Balmoral, 263.
Bampton Lectures, 225.
Bannockburn, 207.
Bassenthwaite, Lake, 85.
Beaconsfield, Lord, 268.
Belligerent rights of the South, English acknowledgment of, 296-297.
Ben Rhyding, 243.
Benjamin, Judah P., 314.
Bernard, Mountague, editor of the *Guardian*, 156, 157, 228.
Bethell, Sir Richard, 232, 234, 235.
Bhow Begum, 64.
Bidding Prayer, the, 226.
Binney, Horace, 11.
"Biographia Borealis," 121.
"Biographia Literaria," 105, 106.
Birmingham, 152, 268.
"Bishop of all Denominations," the (Bishop of Manchester), 309.
Bishop of Cape Town, 225.

Bishop of Oxford, 229.
Bisley, Vicar of, 214, 215, 217, 219.
Black Heath, home of John Stuart Mill, 24.
"Blithedale Romance" (Hawthorne), 193.
Blore, architect of Abbotsford, 131.
Board Schools, 260.
Bodleian Library, 38, 226.
Boehme, Jacob, 191.
Bolt Court, Rogers's visit to, 127.
Boniface VIII., 207.
Borage, the, 226.
Borrowdale, 68.
Bowman, Bishop, 12.
Bradford, 268, 269.
Brathay, 56.
Bremer, Frederika, 6.
Bright, John, 163, 230, 248, 256, 261, 270, 282, 294-298, 301-303; interview with, 308; 316.
British Museum, reading room, 150-151.
Bronson, Miss (sister-in-law of Henry Reed), 55, 141.
Brontë, Charlotte, life of, 193.
Brooks, Preston S., 186, 187.
Brotherswater, 61.
Brougham, Lord, 5, 18, 172, 232, 233, 234.
Broughton, 83.
Browning, E. B., 127, 132.
Browning, Robert, 127.
Brydges, Sir Egerton, 74.
Bulgarian atrocities, 268.
Buller, Sir Redvers, 271.
Bunsen, 246.
Burgon, Dean, 273.
Burgoyne, Sir John, 14.
Burke, Edmund, 146, 262.
Burley, W. E. Forster buried at, 275.
Bury St. Edmunds, 179.
Butterfield, architect of All Saints' Church, 145, 146, 151, 174.
Buxton, 253.
Buxton, Sir Thomas Fowell, 241, 249, 265.

Calcutta, 148; chief justiceship of, 156.
California, the settlement of, 35.
Campbell, Lord, 21.

Canadian Defences Bill, 284-285, 287-296.
Carey, Henry, 15.
Carlisle, 102.
Carlton House Terrace, home of Gladstone, 313.
Carlyle, Jane Welsh, 253, 254.
Carlyle, John, translator of Dante, 63, 64.
Carlyle, Thomas, description of Wellington, 18, 19; allusion to Mrs. Taylor, 24; 112, 192, 246; visit to Ireland, 253; Forster's comment on, 254; 258.
Carter, Mr., secretary to Wordsworth, 59, 60, 71.
Catholic emancipation, 5, 20, 234.
Cecil, Lord Robert, see Marquess of Salisbury.
Chalmers, Thomas, 19.
Chamberlain, Joseph, 270.
Chancellorship of Cambridge University, 38.
Chancellorship of Oxford University, 230.
Channing, W. E., 6.
Chantrey's bust of Wordsworth, 44, 71.
"Charge of the Six Hundred" (Tennyson), 250.
Charles I., 155, 187.
Charles V., 211.
Charles X., banishment of, 4.
Charleston, fall of, 282.
Chase, Judge, 8.
Cherwell, the, 202.
China, steamship, 318.
Cholera, in France and England (1849), 108.
Choral music, awakened interest in, 123.
Christ Church College, Oxford, 199, 201, 203.
"Christian Year" (Keble), 156, 212, 215, 216.
"Christie Johnstone" (Reade), 193.
Church establishment in Ireland, debate on, 309-313.
Civil War in America, 11-15.
Clarence and Avondale, Duke of, 175, 176.
Clarendon, Lord, 259.
Clarkson, Thomas, 6.
Clifford, Edward, artist, 272.

Cobden, Richard, death of, 317-318.
Cockburn, Sir Alexander, death of, 168.
Cockermouth, 99, 100, 102.
Coit, Rev. Dr., rector of St. Paul's School, Concord, 136.
Coleridge, Christabel, 124.
Coleridge, Derwent, 55, 61, 63, 64, 114, 119, 120; personal memories of, 123-138.
Coleridge, Derwent (Mrs.), 123, 128, 129, 133.
Coleridge, Edith (daughter of Sara Coleridge), 59, 126, 128, 129; her recollections of S. T. C., 133.
Coleridge, Ernest (son of Derwent Coleridge), 134.
Coleridge, Hartley, his wayward life, 47, 56, 64, 72; his last days, 73, 76; 114, 115, 118-122, 246.
Coleridge, Henry Nelson, 105, 124, 150.
Coleridge, Henry Nelson (Mrs.), see Sara Coleridge.
Coleridge, Herbert, 131.
Coleridge, John Duke, see Lord Coleridge.
Coleridge, John Taylor, 76, 115, 148-165; his "Life of Keble," 168; 169, 170, 174, 219, 220, 246.
Coleridge, Lady, 171.
Coleridge, Lord, 17, 115, 145-150, 154-180.
Coleridge, Mr. Justice, see John Taylor Coleridge.
Coleridge, Samuel Taylor, 87, 105, 114, 116, 117, 124, 125; conversation of, 133-134; 135, 139.
Coleridge, Sara, 25, 59, 64, 96, 105-117; death of, 125, 126, 131, 136, 138, 139.
Collier, Mr., a Queen's Counsel, 307-308.
Confederate schemes, 282-283.
Coniston, 70, 93.
Coniston Water, 83.
"Credibility of Early Roman History" (Lewis), 130, 149.
Creweian Oration, the, 236.
Crimean War, 248, 250.
Crittenden Compromise, 11.
Cropper, Mrs., daughter of Dr. Arnold, 76.

Crummock Water, 85.
Cumberland, scenery of, 83, 114, 126.

Dallas, George M., Minister to England, 296.
Dante, translated by Dr. Carlyle, 63; 207.
Dartmoor, 162.
Davy, John (Dr.), 56, 246.
Davy, Sir Humphry, 56.
Delhi, during the Mutiny, 89.
Demosthenes, 38.
Dennison, Sir William, Governor of Van Diemen's Land, 251.
De Quincey, Thomas, 69.
Derby, Lord, 21, 230, 257, 258, 284-285, 290.
Derwentwater, 63, 67, 68, 85.
De Tocqueville, 165, 186.
De Vere, Aubrey, 107, 116, 118, 276.
Devizes, 309, 310.
Dillwyn, Mr., speech on the Irish Church Establishment, 310.
"Discourses on University Education" (Newman), 153.
Disraeli, Benjamin, 257, 258, 287, 290, 291, 317.
Dissenters object to the Education Bill, 260-263.
Dobrizhoffer, Martin, 115.
Dodsworth, his attack upon Keble, 218.
Douglas, debate with Lincoln, 10, 11, 256.
Drummond, Judge, 173.
Dublin, 86.
Duddon, valley of the, 83.
Dudley, Thomas H., consul at Liverpool, 282, 283, 307, 308.
Dupont, Admiral, 15.
Durham Cathedral, 67.
Dyce, his frescoes in All Saints' Church, 147, 216.
Dyce, Alexander, 119.

Easdale, 69, 70.
Eckermann, conversations with Goethe, 19.
Eden, Charles Page (Rev.), 205.
Edinburgh, literary circle of, 70.
Edinburgh Review, 187.

INDEX

Education Bill, Forster's, 248, 259-263.
Egremont, castle of, 85.
Egypt (in 1856), 165; (in 1884), 270.
Elleray, home of Professor Wilson, 33.
Ely Cathedral, 108.
Emerson, Ralph Waldo, 6, 7, 16, 96; Kingsley's opinion of, 192-193.
Encumbered Estates Bill, 20.
"Enfranchisement of Women" (Mrs. Mill), 24.
"English Traits" (Emerson), 193.
Ennerdale, 85.
Esthwaite Water, 92.
Euripides, 38.
Everett, Edward, 46.
Eversley, home of Kingsley, 183, 184.
Exeter, John Duke Coleridge, member for, 163.

Faber, F. W., 72, 246.
"Fable for Critics" (Lowell), 193.
Fellowships, conditions of holding, 39.
Fenton's Hotel, St. James's Street, London, 250.
Fielding, Copley, 216.
Fish, Hamilton, 265.
Fitzgerald, Mr., his speech in the House of Commons (1865), 287-288.
Fleming, Lady, 50.
Fletcher, Angus, 70.
Fletcher, Mrs., 70, 246.
Foreign Enlistment Act, 308.
Forster, Robert, 241, 242.
Forster, William, 241, 261.
Forster, William Edward, prediction concerning J. S. Mill, 26; a disciple of Maurice, 98; the Alabama claims, 165-167; Kingsley's opinion of, 184, 185, 194; 241-277, 284, 285, 288-290, 296, 308, 309.
Forster, W. E. (Mrs.), 76, 244, 246, 247, 250, 251, 252, 266, 269, 273, 274, 275.
Fountains Abbey, 247.
Fox, Caroline, 246.
Fox, Charles James, lines on the death of, 82.
Fox, George, 191, 242.
Fox Ghyll, home of W. E. Forster, 273.
Fox How, home of Dr. Arnold, 57, 74, 76, 81, 82, 86-89, 91, 96, 246.

Franklin, Sir John, 233.
Fraser, Mr. (Bishop of Manchester), 308-309.
"Friends in Council" (Helps), 193.
Froude, Hurrell, 214, 215.
Froude, J. A., 193.
Fugitive Slave Law, 7.
Funeral, a rural, 188-189, 216-217.

Gambetta, 30.
Garibaldi's descent upon Sicily, 9, 229.
Garrick, David, 127.
Garrison, William Lloyd, 6, 7.
Gaskell, Mrs., 193.
Geneva Arbitration, 166, 228, 264, 265, 294.
"Genevieve" (Coleridge), 63.
George Eliot, 101.
Gerente, H., 108-109, 147.
Gibbon, Edward, 303.
Gibraltar, William Arnold's death at, 275.
Gillies, Margaret, 44.
Gillman, James and Anne, their care of S. T. Coleridge, 134.
Gladstone, W. E., 10; account of the Oxford movement, 147, 148; his scholarship, 151; his appreciation of Lincoln, 162, 315, 316; Lord Coleridge's opinion of, 163; his government, 166; offers a peerage to Sir John Coleridge, 169; Oxford feeling for, 203, 230; the Crimean War, 248; as Prime Minister, 259, 260; his retirement in 1865, 263, 265; succeeds Lord Beaconsfield, 268; his Irish Policy, 269-270; the desertion of Gordon, 270-272; the character of, 273-274, 286; his attitude toward the Civil War, 290; promotes the Geneva Arbitration, 294; appoints the Bishop of Manchester, 309; speech upon Church Establishment in Ireland, 311-313; an interview concerning American affairs, 313-316.
Gladstone, W. E. (Mrs.), 231.
Glenelg, Lord, 128.
Gloucester, 179.
Gloucester Cathedral, musical festival at, 219.

INDEX

Goddard, Wordsworth's lines on the death of, 87–88.
Goethe, 20, 90.
Gordon, Chinese, desertion of, 270–272.
Gordon Cumming trial, the, 177–179.
Gorham Judgment, the, 147.
Goschen, Hon. G. J., 270.
"Grace," at Oriel College, 205.
Grant, Sir Francis, 130.
Grant, U. S., 265.
Grasmere, 57, 59, 60, 70, 75, 86, 99, 119.
Great Seal, charge of, 172.
Greek, the study of, 39.
Greeley, Horace, 8.
Greta, 63, 64, 86, 100.
Greta Hall (home of Southey), 64, 65, 66, 86, 113.
Grey, Earl, 5, 21.
Grey, Sir George, 310.
Griffith, Darby, 309–310.
Grote, Mrs., 23.
Guardian, the, 11, 156, 157, 298.
Guilford, Earl of, 210.
Guizot, Wordsworth's opinion of, 36; Nassau Senior's acquaintance with, 164.

Hallam, Arthur (quoted), 135.
Hanwell, Derwent Coleridge accepts the living of, 135.
Harcourt, Sir William, 259.
Hardy Gathorne, 310–311, 313.
Hare, Augustus, 97.
Hare, Esther, 97.
Hare, Julius, 39, 76, 97, 246.
Hare, Maria, 97.
Hartington, Lord, 263, 270.
Hawkshead, 92, 93.
Hawthorne, N., his description of Macaulay, 132; Lord Coleridge's appreciation of, 146; Kingsley's criticism of, 193; his description of York Minster, 208–209.
Hawtrey, Dr., Provost of Eton, 150.
Heathcote, Sir William, 216.
Heath's Court, home of Mr. Justice Coleridge, 115, 156, 158, 162, 174, 175.
Heights of Abraham, 292.
Helmore, Mr., authority on Plain Song, 123, 131.

Helps, Arthur, 193, 263.
Henry VI., flight after battle of Hexham, 83.
Henry VIII., Wordsworth's opinion of, 37; his entertainment of Charles V., 211.
Herodotus, 38.
Hexham, battle of, 83.
Highgate, home of S. T. Coleridge, 125, 135.
High Street, Oxford, 202.
Holbein, portrait of Henry VIII., 38; portraits by, 226.
Homer, authorship of, 130–131; criticism of, 150.
Home Rule, 269–270, 272–274.
Hope, Beresford, 147.
Hope, James, 147.
Hope-Scott, see James Hope.
Hughes, Thomas, 194.
Hume, David, 303.
Hursley, the home of John Keble, 208, 211, 212, 216, 220, 222.
Hutchinson, Sarah, Mrs. Wordsworth's sister, 77, 118.
Hutton, R. H., 97, 98.

Imperial Federation, 270.
Inaugural address, Lincoln's, 315–317.
Inman, his portrait of Wordsworth, 34.
Interlachen, 242.
International copyright, 47.
Ireland, Carlyle's visit to, 253; Lord Lieutenantship of, 254–255.
Irish Church, bill for disestablishing the, 248.
Irish Land Bill (of 1870), 248.
Irish outrages, 173.
Irish policy, Gladstone's, 270.
Isis, the (river in Oxford), 203.
Isle of Wight, Newman at the, 221.

Jackson, Andrew, 5.
Jeffrey, Francis, 70.
John XXII., 207.
Johnson, Andrew, 319.
Johnson, Samuel, 127.
Jones, William West, Bishop of Cape Town, 225, 227, 228.

Jowett, B., Master of Balliol, 101, 251.
Juxon, William (Dr.), founder of St. John's College, Oxford, 226, 227.

Keble, John, the dedication to Wordsworth of his "Lectures on Poetry," 58; quoted by Emerson, 97; friendship for Sir John Coleridge, 150, 155, 156; friendship for Kingsley, 189, 190; 206, 208, 211–222.
Keble, John (Mrs.), 217.
Keble, Thomas (Rev.), 214, 216, 217, 218, 219.
Keswick, 62, 63, 85, 86, 99, 100, 113, 116.
Khartoum, 272.
Kilmainham Treaty (1882), 269.
Kingsley, Charles, controversy with Sir John Coleridge, 156; interview with, 183–196; his comment on British rule in India, 185, 186; on American affairs, 186; on slavery, 187, 188; on the Oxford Movement, 190; on Quakerism, 191; on American writers, 192, 193; his feeling for Maurice, 194; on Spurgeon's sermons, 195; opinion of Forster, 250.
Kingsley, Charles (Mrs.), 185, 186, 188, 189, 190, 191.
King William's College, Calcutta, 148.
Kirkstone Pass, 59, 61.
Knox, Alexander, 190.
Kossuth, 26.

Ladderbrow, 68.
Lafayette, his reception in Philadelphia in 1824, 3–4.
Laird, Mr., the builder of the Alabama, 301–302.
Lamb, Charles, 87, 116.
Lancashire operatives, their sympathy with the Northern States, 289, 302.
Lancrigg, home of Mrs. Fletcher, 70.
Laud, Dr. William, 226, 227.
Lawford, Mrs., wife of Lord Coleridge, 174.
Lawrence, Sir John, 252.
Lee, General R. E., 318.
Leeds, Forster at, 185.

Leitch, Mr., 63, 64.
Lewis, Sir George Cornewall, 130, 149, 151.
"Liberty" (J. S. Mill), dedication of, 24.
"Life of Dr. Arnold" (Stanley), 246.
"Life of Dr. John Fothergill" (Hartley Coleridge), 122.
"Life of Keble" (Sir John Coleridge), 168, 219.
"Life of Lord Fairfax" (Hartley Coleridge), 121.
"Life of Sterling" (Carlyle), 112.
Lincoln, Abraham, nomination of, 10, 256; debate with Douglas, 10–11; progress to Washington, 12–13; interview with, 13–15; Gladstone's opinion of, 162, 315–316; second inauguration of, 282; feeling toward England, 296; 304.
Lingard, John, 209.
Liverpool, 113, 281, 282, 283, 306, 317.
Lodore, Falls of, 67, 68.
London, 282.
Lord Chancellor, his charge of the Great Seal, 172, 232.
Lot, Captain, commander of the *Persia*, 318.
Loughrigg, 57, 74, 75, 76, 81, 91, 95.
Louis XVI. cited by Kingsley, 187.
Louis-Philippe, 36; government of, 108.
Lovell, Mrs., 66, 67.
Lowe, Robert, 257, 291, 292, 293.
Lowell, James Russell, 49 (note); 193.
Luculentissime, 236.
Lundy, Benjamin, 6.
Luther, Thirlwall's admiration of, 39.
Lyndhurst, Lord, 21.
Lyons, Lord, English Minister at Washington, 305.
Lyulph's Tower, 62.

Macaulay, T. B., 129–133, 191, 242.
"Macbeth," 221.
Macleod, Norman, 263.
Madonna di San Sisto, 34, 213.
Magdalen College, 202, 203.
Maine, Montgomery's march through, 293.
Maine, Sir Henry, 257.

Malle-poste, travelling by, 28–29.
Manchester, 179.
Manning, Cardinal, 40, 107, 147, 218.
Mansel, Professor, 227.
Marriage, an Oriental view of, 149.
Marriott, Charles, Fellow of Oriel and Vicar of St. Mary's, 199, 202, 204, 205, 206.
Marshall's Island, 67, 70.
Martineau, Harriet, 6, 72, 97, 246.
Mason and Slidell, 283–284.
Master in Chancery, Nassau Senior, 164.
" Maud " (Tennyson), 249.
Maurice, Esther, 97.
Maurice, F. D., Hutton and Forster disciples of, 97–98 ; his defence of Kingsley, 156, 190; Thomas Hughes a disciple of, **194**; his estimate of Spurgeon, 196, **266.**
McClintock, Sir Leopold, 233, 235.
McMichael, Morton, 12, 15, 141, 266.
"Memorials **of a Quiet Life**" (Hare), 97.
Merton, chapel of, 202.
Metropolitan of South Africa, 225.
Michael Angelo, 171.
"Middlemarch" (George Eliot), 101.
Middle Temple, banquet at the, 175–177.
Mill, John Stuart, 22–27, 163, 164.
Milman, Dean, 150–151.
Milnes, Monckton, 132.
Milton, John, Tennyson reciting, **71,** 131.
Mitre, the, an Oxford inn, 199, 202.
"Molony's Lament" (Thackeray), **255.**
Montcalm, at Quebec, 292.
Montgomery, General, 292, **293.**
Montreal, 292.
Motley, J. L., 233, **235, 236.**
Mott, Lucretia, 6, 245.
Moultrie, John, 124.
Moxon, **poet** and publisher, 128.
Mozart, **130.**
Müller, engraving of the Dresden Madonna, 213.
Müller, Max, **188.**
Muncaster Castle, 83.
Murat, Lucien, 30.

Napier, Mr., Member for **Dublin** University, 20.
Napoleon, Louis, 30.
Navarino, battle of, 4–5.
Neale, John Mason, 80, 209.
" Nemesis of Faith " (Froude), **193.**
New College, 206.
Newman, John Henry, 107 ; effect of his sermons, 147; his followers, 150; sued by Dr. Achilli, 151–154; influence upon Keble, 155; portrait of, 171; his successor at St. Mary's, 199, 204; his admiration for Pusey, 200; visit to Keble, 220, 221; 205.
New Zealand, 251.
Nollekens, his parsimony, 129.
Nonconformists, their objection to the Education Act of 1870, 260–263.
Notre Dame, rebuilding of the South Transept, 109.

"Oakfield" (W. D. Arnold), 89, 186.
Occam, 207.
"O'Donoghue, The," **310.**
"Ode to the Duke **of Wellington"** (Tennyson), 249, 250.
Oriel College, Hartley Coleridge at, 119.
Orton (the Tichborne claimant), 167.
Ottery St. Mary, Devon, home of Mr. **Justice** Coleridge and Lord Coleridge, 145, 156, 158, 168, 171.
Overend-Gurney failure, 264.
Oxford, 199–222, 288.
Oxford Commemoration, the, 225–237.
Oxford **Movement,** 42, **107,** 147, 190, **206, 214.**
Oxford wine, an, 228.

Paley, William, 131.
Palfrey, John Gorham, 133.
Palmerston, Lord, **10,** 163, **166, 232,** 257, 298, 307, 311, **317.**
Panizzi, A., 150–151.
Paris, first sight of (1849), 29.
Park Crescent, London, home **of Mr.** Justice Coleridge and Lord Coleridge, 148, 150.
Parnell, C. S., Gladstone's surrender to, 269–270.
"Parochial **Sermons**" (Newman), **204.**

328   INDEX

Patterdale, 61, 62.
Patteson, Sir John, 159.
Patteson, John Coleridge, 159.
Peel, Sir Robert, 20, 220.
Penn, William, 242.
Penne, George, 242.
Penningtons, ancient family of the, 83.
Pennsylvania Historical Society, celebration of the fiftieth anniversary of, 267.
Penrose, Mr., a brother of Mrs. Thomas Arnold, 76, 82.
Perry, Dr. (of Bonn), 76.
Persia, steamship, 318.
"Phæthon" (Kingsley), 192.
Phelps, E. J., 16, 17.
Philadelphia, 288, 319; reception of Lafayette, 3.
Philip and Mary, marriage of, 210.
Phillips, Wendell, 6.
Pickersgill, portrait of Wordsworth, 37.
Plain Song, 123, 131.
Plato, 116.
Plotinus, 116.
Point Levi, 292.
Political Dissenters, 262.
"Political Economy" (Mill), Dedication of, 26 (note).
Politician, the meaning of the word in England, 276.
Poonah, college at, 99, 101.
Portinscale, 63.
Portinscale Hotel, 100.
Powis, Earl of, 37.
Praed, W. M., 124.
Prevost, Sir George, 205, 206.
Price, Bonamy, his opinion of Gladstone, 273.
Prince Albert, his German education, 38; his action in the affair of the *Trent*, 301.
Prince of Wales, 177-179; 230, 231; 288.
Punch, quoted, 9.
Punjaub, schools in the, 252, 275.
Pusey, E. B., Mill's opinion of, 26; Sara Coleridge's opinion of, 107; his personal appearance, 199-200; his family, 201-202; 215, 217, 218; meeting with Keble and Newman, 221.

Pusey, Philip, of Pusey, 201.
Pusey, Philip, son of Dr. Pusey, 201-202.
Puseyism, Mill's definition of, 26.

Quakerism, Kingsley on, 191, 261-263.
Quarterly Review, edited by Sir John Taylor Coleridge, 150, 158.
Quebec, fortifications at, 287, 292, 293.
Queen Caroline, trial of, 234.
Queen Victoria, her visit to Ireland, 36; her letter upon hearing the news of Gordon's death, 271; her action in the affair of the *Trent*, 301.
Queenstown, 281.
Quillinan, Dora, death of, 37, 43, 74.
Quillinan, Jemima, 74, 99.
Quillinan, Rotha, 74, 99.

Rabelais, 193.
Rastadt, battle of, 27-28.
Ravenglass, 83.
Rawdon, 253.
Reade, Charles, 193.
Reed, Professor Henry, 34, 47, 48, 51, 55, 56, 88, 105, 109, 123; death of, 138-141.
Reed, William B., letter from Thackeray to, 138, 141.
Reform Bill, 5, 234, 257.
Reid, Wemyss, 249.
Richardson, Lady, 246.
Richmond, Va., 297, 318.
Richmond, portrait of Keble by, 212.
Richmond, James (Rev.), 88.
Rigi, ascent of the, 87.
"Rise and Fall of the Dutch Republic" (Motley), 235.
Robertson, F. W. 196.
Robinson, Henry Crabb, 87, 89, 128, 246.
Rogers, Samuel, 37, 125, 127-129.
Rosthwaite, 68.
Rothay, 57, 59.
Rothay Bank, 71, 75, 85.
Russell, Sir Charles, 178.
Russell, George W., 172.
Russell, Lord John, on the battle of Navarino, 4-5; his oratory, 20; his conferring home rule upon Canada,

21; his retirement from the Aberdeen government, 248; failure of the Reform Bill (1865), 257; as Foreign Secretary, 282-283, 293; C. F. Adams's official relations with, 305, 306, 307.
Rydal, 75, 76, 86, 89, 95.
Rydal, vale of, 57.
Rydal, waterfall of, 45.
Rydal Church, 72, 73, 74.
Rydalmere, 57.
Rydal Mount, the home of Wordsworth, 34, 55, 59, 60, 71, 72, 87, 90, 95, 99, 113, 124.
Rydal Water, 59, 98.

Saddleback, 100.
St. Augustine, 156, 192.
St. Bernard, 156.
St. Cross, hospital of (Winchester), 210-211.
St. Cuthbert, 67.
St. Herbert's Island, 67.
St. James the Less (church in Philadelphia), 108.
St. John's College, Cambridge, 37.
St. John's College, Oxford, 225, 226, 227.
St. John's Vale, 100.
St. Mark's College, Chelsea, Derwent Coleridge principal of, 123, 135-136.
St. Mary's, Oxford, Newman's preaching at, 147, 199, 202, 217, 225.
St. Paul's (London), 227.
St. Paul's School (Concord), 136.
Sainte Chapelle, restoration of, 108-109.
Salisbury, Marquess of, 230, 256, 262, 294.
Salutation Inn (Ambleside), 94.
Scale Hill, 85.
"Scarlet Letter" (Hawthorne), 146.
Schurz, Carl, his escape from Rastadt, 27-28.
Scott, Gilbert, 56.
Scott, Sir Walter, 131.
Seathwaite, 84, 85.
Sebastopol, 248.
Selborne, Lord, appreciation of Lord Coleridge, 168; opposition to Gladstone, 270.

Semmes, Captain, 302.
Senior, Nassau, 164-165.
Sepoy Rebellion, 89, 185, 252.
September massacres, 40.
Seward, William H., 297, 298, 305, 306.
Shairp, Principal, 204.
Shakespeare, 38.
Sharswood, Judge, 266.
"Shooting Niagara" (Carlyle), 258.
Sirius, the first steamship from England, 16.
Skelwith Force, 56, 94.
Skerryvore Rock Lighthouse, 72.
Skiddaw, 64, 66, 68, 90.
Slavery, Garrison's attack upon, 6, 7; Kingsley on, 187-188; freedom of the West Indian slaves, 234; in America, 242, 244, 246, 247, 248, 250.
Smith, Gerrit, 6.
Smith, Sydney, 74.
Smith, W. H., 27.
Sophocles, 38.
South Australia, governor of, 265.
South Shields, cholera in, 110.
Southey, Katherine, 66, 67.
Southey, Robert, 47, 64, 65, 66, 86, 87, 90, 113, 114, 116.
Southey's book-plate, 113.
Spanish Armada, fragment from one of the vessels of, 192.
Speaker of the Commons, respect paid to, 285-286.
Spectator, 98.
Spedding, James, account of Hartley Coleridge, 120.
Spinning-jenny, 257.
Spurgeon, C. H. (Rev.), 195, 196.
Stands, 84.
Stanley, Arthur Penrhyn (Dean), 136, 231, 234, 246, 251.
Stanley Owen (Captain), 251.
Sterling, John, 192.
Stevenson, Alan, builder of the Skerryvore Rock Lighthouse, 72 (note).
Stevenson, R. L., 72 (note).
Story, Judge, 148.
Strafford, Lord, 175.
Sty-head Pass, 68.
Suez Canal, 165.
Suffrage, household, 257.

Suffrage, universal, 257, 258.
Sumner, Charles, assault upon, 7, 186; attitude toward the Civil War, 7-8, 166; his opinion of Douglas, 10; upon the indirect claims, 264, 265; opinion of C. F. Adams, 304.
Sumter, Fort, 13, 296.
Sussex Square (Lord Coleridge's London residence), 171, 174.
Sutherland, Dowager Duchess of, 10.
Sutherland, Duke of, 9.
Swedish Ambassador, honoured at Oxford, 232, 233.
Swift, Augustus M., 136.
Swift, Dean, 84.

Tangar, Mr. and Mrs., 148.
Tasmania, 250, 251.
Taylor, Sir Henry, 23, 46, 116.
Taylor, Herbert, 24.
Taylor, Jeremy, 205, 206.
Taylor, Mrs. John (Mrs. Mill), 23-25.
Tennyson, Lord, 70, 71; opinion of Browning, 127; Life by Hallam Tennyson, 135.
Thackeray, W. M., his letter to William B. Reed, 138-139; "Molony's Lament," 255.
"The Brothers" (Wordsworth), 85.
"The Cathedral" (Isaac Williams), 206.
"The Doctor" (Southey), 64.
The George, inn at Winchester, 210.
The Month, 162.
"The Warden" (Trollope), 210.
Thiers, 164.
Thirlmere, 99.
Thirlwall, Bishop of St. David's, 39.
Thompson, George, 6.
Tichborne Case, the, 167.
Tichborne, Sir Roger, 167.
Ticknor, George, 35, 133.
Times, 12, 285, 289, 299.
Tipperary, disturbances in, 269.
Tipperary Nationalists, 269.
"To the Pennsylvanians" (Wordsworth), 140.
"Tom Brown's School Days" (Hughes), 194, 228.
"Tom Quadrangle," the, 200, 201.
Tottenham, Robert Forster, of, 241.

Town End, home of Wordsworth, 78.
Townshend, Chauncey Hare, 124.
Trench, Archbishop, 9.
Trent, affair of the, 283, 284, 297, 298, 299, 300, 301.
Trinity College, Cambridge, foundation of, 37.
Tritton, Mr., his liberal gift to All Saints' Church, 147.
Trollope, Anthony, 210.
Twining, Mrs., daughter of Dr. Arnold, 76, 81.
Twiss, Dr., Regius Professor of Civil Law, 233.
"Two Years Ago" (Kingsley), 187.

Ullswater, 61, 62.
"Uncle Tom's Cabin" (Stowe), 244.
Union League of New York, 267.
Unitarians of New England, 148, 196.

Van Diemen's Land, 251.
Vice-Chancellor of Oxford, 230, 231, 232, 233, 234, 235, 236.
Viollet-le-Duc, 109.
"Vision of Judgment" (Southey), 65.

Wadham, Warden of, 229.
Walton, Izaak, 210.
Ward, Artemus, 255.
Ward, Mrs. Humphry, 251.
Washington, drinking the health of, 70.
Washington, funeral of Lincoln at, 319.
Watendlath, 68.
Waterhead Inn, Coniston, 94.
Welles, Gideon, Secretary of the Navy, 301.
Wellington, Duke of, 4, 11, 17-20, 230, 250.
Welsh, John, entertains W. E. Forster, 266.
Welsh, William, 266.
Wemyss, Earl of, 272.
Westbury, Lord, 232.
Westminster Abbey, funeral service for Hon. W. E. Forster held in, 275.
Westminster Review, 247.
Wharfe, the, 243, 244.
Wharfeside, home of W. E. Forster, 76, 244, 249, 250.

Whately, Archbishop, 76, 164, 246.
White, Mr., member for Brighton, 293.
"White Doe of Rylstone" (Wordsworth), 126.
Whiteside, Mr., reply to Gladstone, 312–313.
Whitman, Walt, 193.
Wicklif, 207.
Wilberforce, Samuel, 229.
Wilkes, Captain, 293, 301.
William of Wykeham, 209.
William Rufus, 209.
Williams, Isaac, 206.
Wilson, Professor John, 33.
Winchester, 208, 209, 210, 211.
Winchfield, station for Eversley, 183, 196.
Windermere, Lake, 33, 59, 61, 75, 92, 98.
Wishing Gate, 78, 99.
Wolfe, General, 292.
Wolseley, Lord, 271, 272.
Woolwich Band, 227.
Worcester College, 227.
Wordsworth, Christopher, master of Trinity, 39, 93.
Wordsworth, Dora, 74, 113.
Wordsworth, Dorothy, 73, 90, 118.
Wordsworth, John (vicar of Cockermouth), 100.

Wordsworth, William, a visit to (1849), 33–51; portraits of, 37; university honours, 37; his thought of the classics, 38; reflections upon university life, 39; recollections of the French Revolution, 40; attitude toward the Oxford movement, 42; opinion on international copyright, 47; memorial tablet to, 58, 62, 70; his grammar school, 93; 71, 72, 73, 76, 77, 78, 82, 85, 87, 88, 98, 99; death of, 81–82; 105, 106, 113, 118; estimate of Hartley Coleridge, 120; opinion of S. T. Coleridge, 125; on Pennsylvania, 140; 203, 243, 246.
Wordsworth, William (Mrs.), 35, 40, 41, 42, 55, 60, 71, 73, 75, 77, 79, 80, 89, 90, 91, 95, 118.
Wordsworth, William (grandson of the poet), 59, 71, 73, 75, 86, 89, 90, 99, 100–102.

"Yeast" (Kingsley), 156.
Yewdale, 94.
York Cathedral, compared with Winchester, 208–209.

Zug, Lake of, 87.

Alfred Lord Tennyson

A MEMOIR, BY HIS SON

Two Vols. 8vo. Cloth. In Box. Price, $10.00, *net*

These volumes of over 500 pages each contain many letters written or received by Lord Tennyson, to which no other biographer could have had access, and in addition a large number of *Poems hitherto unpublished.*

Several chapters are contributed by such of his friends as Dr. Jowett, the Duke of Argyll, the late Earl of Selborne, Mr. Lecky, Professor Francis T. Palgrave, Professor Tyndall, Mr. Aubrey de Vere, and others, who thus expressed their Personal Recollections.

There are many illustrations, engraved after pictures by Richard Doyle, Samuel Lawrence, G. F. Watts, R.A., etc., in all about twenty full-page Portraits and other Illustrations.

"The biography is easily the biography not only of the year, but of the decade, and the story of the development of Tennyson's intellect and of his growth — whatever may be the varying opinions of his exact rank among the greatest poets — into one of the few masters of English verse, will be found full of thrilling interest not only by the critic and student of literature, but by the average reader." — *The New York Times.*

"Hallam Lord Tennyson has done wisely. His very self-effacement has enabled him to present a biography that deserves to have applied to it his father's line — 'in its simplicity sublime.' In the most unostentatious manner it reveals the grandeur of its subject." — *The New York Herald.*

"The poet's son has done his duty in a way which should be an example; and many choice spirits among Tennyson's closest friends have added their recollections and impressions with generous and loving hands. Such a book is a new and priceless gift from the spirit of one of the loveliest and purest poets who have set human speech to immortal music." — *The Century Magazine.*

"It is no exaggeration to say that it is the most important literary biography since Lockhart's 'Scott' and Moore's 'Byron.' Two reasons combine to give this memoir its great value: First, the unique position of Lord Tennyson among nineteenth-century poets; and, second, the skill, tact, and taste with which it is written." — *Hartford Daily Times.*

"This Memoir is a witness to the genius, gravity, dignity, and essential sincerity of its central figure." — *London Academy.*

THE MACMILLAN COMPANY,
66 FIFTH AVENUE, NEW YORK.

THE LETTERS OF

Elizabeth Barrett Browning

EDITED WITH BIOGRAPHICAL ADDITIONS

BY

FREDERIC G. KENYON

WITH PORTRAITS

Two Volumes. Crown 8vo. Price, $4.00

The earliest correspondence quoted took place when the writer was a young girl, and every period of her life is represented in these frank and simple letters. She knew many interesting people, was in Paris during the *Coup d'état* in 1851, and lived in Florence during years of great excitement in Italy. Among other pen pictures she gives one of the few English sketches we have of George Sand, whom she met several times.

INTER-OCEAN, Chicago.

"Mr. Kenyon has edited this large collection of Mrs. Browning's letters in the most perfect way. They tell a chronological story and form almost an autobiography. . . . Books and humanity, great deeds, and, above all, politics, which include all the grand questions of the day, were foremost in her thoughts, and, therefore, oftenest on her lips."

THE MACMILLAN COMPANY,
66 FIFTH AVENUE, NEW YORK.

www.ingramcontent.com/pod-product-compliance
Lightning Source LLC
Chambersburg PA
CBHW031854220426
43663CB00006B/621